GUIDE TO OLD RADIOS

POINTERS, PICTURES AND PRICES

GUIDE TO OLD RADIOS

POINTERS, PICTURES AND PRICES

David and Betty Johnson

Wallace-Homestead Book Company
Radnor, Pennsylvania

Copyright © 1989 by David and Betty Johnson
All Rights Reserved
Published in Radnor, Pennsylvania 19089, by
Wallace-Homestead Book Company

Designed by Anthony Jacobson
Manufactured in the United States of America

Library of Congress Cataloging in Publications Data

Johnson, David, 1933-
    A guide to old radios/David and Betty Johnson.
        p.   cm.
    Bibliography: p. 221
    Includes index.
    ISBN 0-87069-518-5 :
    1. Radio—Receivers and reception—Collectors and collecting.
    2. Radio—Receivers and reception—Conservation and restoration.
    I. Johnson, Betty.   II. Title.
    TK 6563.J573   1989
    621.3841'36'075—dc19
                                                    88-51499
                                                        CIP

1 2 3 4 5 6 7 8 9 0 8 7 6 5 4 3 2 1 0 9

Cover photo
Clockwise, from top left: RCA model 103 cone speaker with tapestry front; RCA Superheterodyne radio scarf used in showroom; Fada model 1000 Catalin table radio; Sentinel model 195ULT Catalin table radio; St. Regis small cathedral.

We dedicate
this book to
Hugo Gernsback . . .

. . . who made the
impossible
seem possible
even before
it *was* possible.

"Here is the 'Radiotrola,' which will take the place of the phonograph in our homes soon. It could be so designed that only one adjustment would be necessary to tune in music, news, etc., which could be sent at the same time on different wave-lengths." Hugo Gernsback felt that radios would have to be easy to use to make them popular. Looking at the 1921 sets, it's easy to see why he felt this way (Radio News, December 1921).

Contents

Acknowledgments

WE want to say "thank you" to many people who helped us with this book. Some of these people are radio dealers, while others are radio collectors. Some are primarily antique dealers. There are corporations, as well as individuals, who permitted us to photograph radios at radio swap meets. Also, our thanks to those people who wanted to remain anonymous. All were necessary; without them, this book would not have been possible.

Ed and Irene Ripley
John Wilson
Shirley Olson
Delayne Rand
Charles Auenson, "The Studio"
The Antique Center of LaCrosse Ltd.
Gene Harris Auction Center of
    Marshalltown, Iowa
General Electric Company
Radio Corporation of America
McGraw-Hill Book Company
Zenith Radio Corporation

And to the women and men who helped develop personal computers and their software, a special thanks. Without the speed and flexibility of modern computers, word processing programs, and data bases, this project would have been an ordeal rather than a challenge.

Part One

Background for the Collector

Radio,
the Voice
from the Sky

BACK in 1872, a man by the name of Joshua Coppersmith was arrested in New York City. The charge: that he was attempting to extort money from gullible people by convincing them to invest in an instrument he said would transmit voices over wires. He called it a *telephone*. Coppersmith may or may not have been a con man. Within four years, however, Alexander Bell did send a voice over wires and did call it a "telephone." What is interesting is the reaction of the Boston paper that reported the case: "Well informed people know that it is impossible to transmit the human voice over wires...[and] were it possible to do so, the thing would be of no practical value." What would that writer have said about something that seemed even more impossible — transmitting voices without wires!

Let us define terms. Transmission of Morse code through the air was common in 1920. This transmission without wires was called *wireless*. Transmission of code had an excitement of its own with an aura of mystery surrounding its operators, and it enabled people even in smaller towns and cities to keep in regular touch with the world. It required someone to interpret those dots and dashes and convert them back into something that anyone could understand.

Typical 1922 crystal detector.

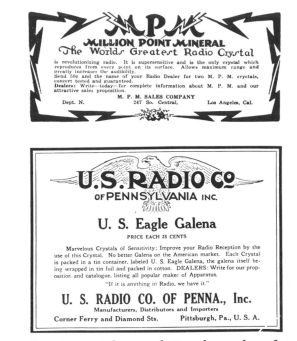

Certain crystals were better than others for bringing in stations. The Million Point Mineral here claims to be the "world's greatest" but doesn't mention what type of crystal it is. Generally, the galena crystal was preferred.

Radio, on the other hand, is the transmission of *voice* without wires. Anyone who could get a radio working could actually listen to voices from Pittsburgh or New York City, even though they were thousands of miles away.

In 1920, the very idea of plucking a voice or music out of the air from hundreds or thousands of miles away still had a magical quality that is very hard for us to imagine today. At this time, newspapers in cities could keep their readers up-to-date because they received the news in code by "wireless," but for the person living in a small town or on a farm, current news might be a week or more old. Trips to town, often by horse, were a weekly rather than a daily event for many people. There was no daily mail delivery for farmers, so the only time to catch up on the news was on those weekly trips. Entertainment at home was a wind-up phonograph or a piano in the parlor. No wonder people took to radio with enthusiasm.

In spite of the difficulties of early radio, people gathered around tinny-sounding horn speakers or sat with earphones clamped to their heads, with rapt looks on their faces as they listened to those voices from the sky. Houses and apartments sprouted huge antenna systems. Thousands of kids put together crystal sets and simple one-tube sets to the amazement of their parents and relations. Never had anything caught the imagination of the science-oriented young person the way radio did. A few years ago, we saw this same kind of enthusiasm in the way kids took to computers. Radio was as far out to most people in the 1920s as the computer is today—and just as fascinating to the young!

Yes, radio was the miracle of the age. Now we simply consider it another appliance and give it as little thought as we give a toaster, washer, or electric razor. Part of the joy of collecting old-time radios is the discovery of some of that earlier excitement and awe. Old radio magazines and advertisements from the 1920s make fascinating reading as you discover their enthusiasm about things we now take for granted.

An example of a fairly sophisticated crystal set. This Radio Phone was available as a pattern only (Radio News, October 1922).

The first decade of radio (1920-1929) was one of radio's most fascinating times. Things were happening with great rapidity. Something considered impossible at the start of the decade (non–battery–operated radio, for instance) was common by the end of it. Beginning the decade as a home-built concoction, radio ended the decade in a place of honor in the living room. Instead of broadcast studios operating out of the men's room or women's cloakroom, radio now had network broadcasting that covered the entire United States.

It was a time of impressive growth. As we look in greater depth at the components of radio during the 1920s — most importantly, technical improvements, cabinetry, and broadcasting — we will gain a better understanding of early radio.

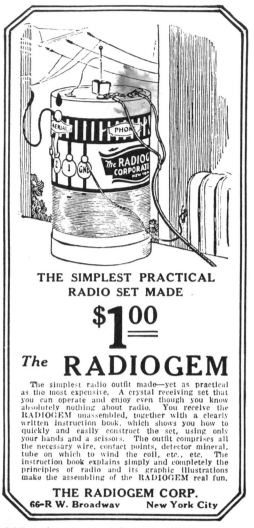

THE SIMPLEST PRACTICAL RADIO SET MADE

$1.00

The RADIOGEM

The simplest radio outfit made—yet as practical as the most expensive. A crystal receiving set that you can operate and enjoy even though you know absolutely nothing about radio. You receive the RADIOGEM unassembled, together with a clearly written instruction book, which shows you how to quickly and easily construct the set, using only your hands and a scissors. The outfit comprises all the necessary wire, contact points, detector mineral, tube on which to wind the coil, etc., etc. The instruction book explains simply and completely the principles of radio and its graphic illustrations make the assembling of the RADIOGEM real fun.

THE RADIOGEM CORP.
66-R W. Broadway   New York City

1925 Radiogem crystal set; available only as a kit and designed for the youthful builder, it is a simpler set than the Radio Phone.

This Philmore crystal set was highly popular.

Sometimes the radios were free if the child wrote for the Free Radio Plan.

1922 Frost-Fones; the romance and enchantment of radio in the early 1920s is revealed in this ad (Radio News, June 1922).

A selection of Philmore crystal sets from the World War II era (John Wilson).

BAKELITE MODEL

Novel midget crystal radio with self-contained earphone. Very neat and compact. Complete set is housed in polished mahogany-color bakelite cabinet of modernistic streamlined design. Earphone fits conveniently into compartment in case. Average range is about 25 miles. Has extremely sensitive fixed crystal; one tuning knob controls reception. Weighs only 5 ounces; measures but 4x2½x 1⅝". Supplied complete with earphone, aerial wire, and full instructions. Wt., 2 lbs. $**1.62**
B9314. NET......

This set from 1941 is designed to look like a modern small plastic radio. It comes from a 1941 Allied Radio catalog.

Heathkit crystal set; model CR1; the styling is the same as many of the other Heathkit products of the early 1950s (John Wilson).

A 1921 Brandes headset made a perfect Christmas present.

Some Radio Basics

TO collect, enjoy, and appreciate old radios, those "miracles from the past," you do not have to understand everything about their workings. It is helpful, though, to have some idea of what happens in the broadcasting and receiving processes. Let's look at a drawing.

With all the technical jargon removed, we'll try to break down a complex task into a few simple ideas. Broadcasting starts at the sending end, the *radio station*. A sound (voice or music) is converted by a microphone into an electrical signal, which in turn is converted by the transmitter to a radio signal and sent into space through the antenna. That radio signal, or radio wave, will travel thousands of miles through space at the speed of light (which is almost inconceivably fast: 186,000 miles per second).

When we get to the other end of that radio signal, we see that the *radio receiver* works in a way exactly opposite of the way the transmitter works. The radio receiver's antenna captures a portion of that radio signal, its internal electronics convert this back into an electrical signal, and the loudspeaker produces the sound we hear.

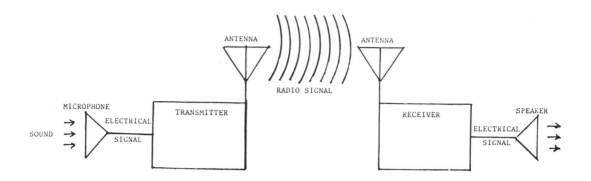

This is the simplest picture we have of what happens. Unfortunately, the receiving end isn't really quite that simple. To judge the radio receiver we're examining or buying, it is good to know a little more about radio reception. Let's take a closer look at that radio receiver.

Again, we will ignore electronic theory and stick to what happens, in plain language. There are six basic parts in the receiver.

1. The *antenna* gathers the weak radio signals. There are dozens of different signals from as many stations, all crowding into the radio through the doorway of this antenna. The antenna is a wire of some sort. It may be a wire outside the house, carefully insulated from everything but the receiver. It may be a short wire that you attach to your receiver. It may be hidden inside the radio as a "loop" wound on a flat cardboard frame. In one form or another, your radio has an antenna.

2. You must select the particular signal you want through a process that is called *tuning in* the radio. To understand why tuning is necessary, you need to know that each radio signal has a frequency and a wavelength. The *frequency* is the rate at which a signal changes its character, measured in cycles per second, kilocycles (1000 cycles) per second, or megacycles (1000 kilocycles) per second. Every station on the air has an assigned frequency. The usual broadcast band of frequencies is 550 kilocycles to 1600 kilocycles per second. Originally this was called the broadcast band (shortened to BC); now it is known as the AM

(amplitude modulation) band. Making things more confusing, the word cycle has now been replaced by *hertz*. This means that what was once called "kilocycle" (kc) is now called "kilohertz" (kHz). Most old radio literature talks of kilocycles.

Since each of these radio signals travels out at a rate of 186,000 miles per second, you can also measure a signal in terms of its wavelength. The *wavelength* is the length in meters of one cycle (or one complete change in character and back) that the signal travels in a second. If you want to move between the two ways of measuring, you can do a little algebra. The formula is frequency (in kilocycles) times wavelength (in meters) equals 300 (F x W = 300).

You will find stations identified by either their frequency of transmission or the

1926 loop antenna made by Eclipse Radio Laboratories; a basketweave antenna could be rotated easily on its pivot.

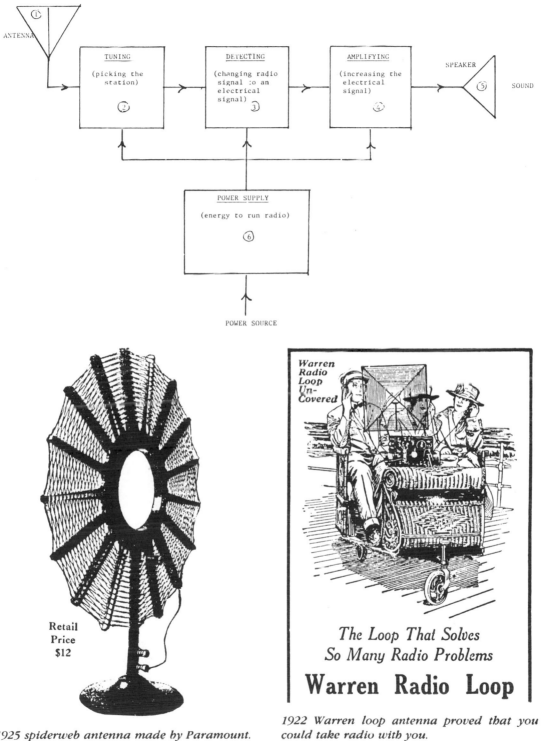

1925 spiderweb antenna made by Paramount.

1922 Warren loop antenna proved that you could take radio with you.

wavelength they use. Again, the tuning section of your receiver does the selecting of the station you wish to receive when you turn the tuning knob or knobs on the outside of the set.

3. The sound you want is encoded in the radio signal. Your radio must *detect* this sound signal, extracting an electrical image of the sound from the radio signal.

4. This weak electrical image must now be *amplified* (increased) to the point where it is strong enough to operate the loud speaker.

5. The *speaker* converts the electrical signal into sound waves that resemble the original sound at the radio station. Your ears do the rest.

6. Electrical energy needed to operate the radio is provided by the *power supply*. A power supply can be a group of batteries, or it can be an electrical circuit that provides the correct energy levels from an outside power source (usually the plug in the wall).

That's all there is to it. The complex and differing ways that various radios have of accomplishing their mission can provide you with many hours of study. Some people find it fascinating work to understand and fix old sets.

If you want to service old radios, you will need to learn radio theory. Trying to skip this important step is futile and unsafe. Learning the theory of tube sets becomes a do-it-yourself project, since there aren't schools teaching it any longer. There are books that will help you to understand radio circuitry and teach you how to repair tube-type radios. Some of these books are listed in the section titled "Further Helps" at the end of the book.

Radio schools were a great boon for the ambitious.

The manufacturer bragged about the marble, but it was only for looks; a capacitor actually coupled the antenna to the power lines.

Radio News for December, 1922

A tower's height made a tremendous difference in the number of stations that could be received.

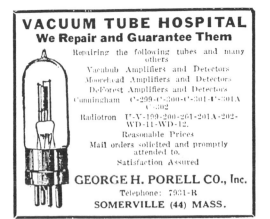
Another way of rebuilding burned-out tubes was to put a new filament in them.

Tube rejuvenator; brings back tubes to "full efficiency," especially in the summer when tubes are working at higher voltage.

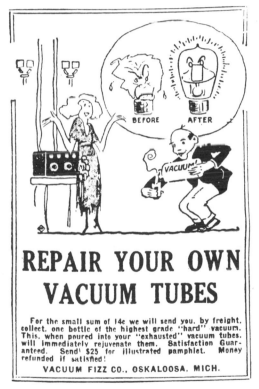
There were spoofs in those days, too.

Distortion Kills Music
The Curves Show Why

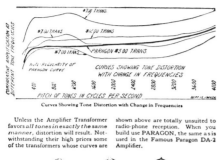

Curves Showing Tone Distortion with Change in Frequencies

Unless the Amplifier Transformer favors *all tones in exactly the same manner*, distortion will result. Notwithstanding their high prices some of the transformers whose curves are shown above are totally unsuited to radio-phone reception. When you build use PARAGON, the same as is used in the Famous Paragon DA-2 Amplifier.

A Home-Built Paragon Amplifier

Response curves have been around since 1922; from a Paragon ad.

It All Began with Batteries

RADIO in the early 1920s was a new field, and, as such, it had major limitations. Radios were unwieldy, especially since most of them required both external batteries and an external speaker. It was at this time (1922) that Hugo Gernsback made a strong argument that radio would never become successful if it couldn't be used easily and attractively in the living room, by anybody. "The telephone would never have become as popular as it is to-day if you had tried to sell each man an instrument he had to connect himself, and in order to do so learn all the 'how and why' of telephony." The easier it was to use, he felt, the more necessary it would be in everybody's lives[1].

To better understand radios, their workings, and some of the peripheral problems arising from the use of batteries, it's good to have a little background about radio in the 1920s.

1. Hugo Gernsback was one of the major forces in making radio popular. Not an inventor, more a futurist, he could see practical applications of scientific knowledge. He wrote and edited books and magazines about radio, science, and science fiction. Practical as always, he ran the earliest radio supply company. See his article, "The Radiotrola," in *Radio News*, December 1921.

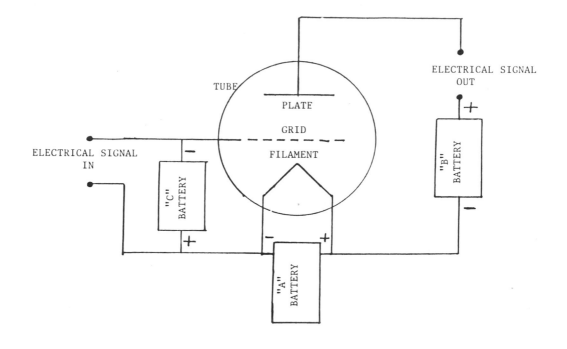

TUBE

PLATE

GRID

FILAMENT

ELECTRICAL SIGNAL IN

"C" BATTERY

"A" BATTERY

ELECTRICAL SIGNAL OUT

"B" BATTERY

Crystal Sets

Admittedly, the earliest radios didn't require batteries and certainly couldn't supply enough power for a loudspeaker. These crystal sets did require a great deal of fiddling to get the station to come in properly, and anyone listening was forced to use headphones.

Oddly enough, a crystal set would be thought of, today, as a "solid-state" set. What else is more solid-state than an electrical reaction taking place in a mineral? And the crystal was, of course, a mineral that was receptive to radio waves. It took all of its energy from the radio frequency signal of the transmitter. Since the crystal could not amplify or increase the energy (loudness) of the received signal, it required a large antenna and a good ground to get the most out of it. Even with this help, you could only get a station a few miles away. Signals from exceptional distances were occasionally received—advertisements sometimes claimed 1000 miles—and were certainly bragged about.

Early Tubes

The development of the vacuum tube triode (Lee DeForest's Audion) made it possible to amplify the intensity of any electrical signal fed into its control grid. This characteristic was used to build a practical radio receiver.

Vacuum tubes, though, need power (energy) to work. There has to be a supply of electrons made available by a heated *filament*. The A battery is used to heat the filaments. To pick up the electrons sent by the filament, the tube has a *plate* which attracts the electron stream because it has a strong, positive (+) charge. Since the charge of electrons is negative (−), the electrons are attracted by the positive plate. The intensity of the flow is controlled by the *grid*, which is the third part of the tube. The positive charge for the plate of the tube is supplied by the B battery, which has the higher voltage (22 to 135 volts) needed to do this job.

Some amplifying circuits need to put a certain negative voltage on the grid in order to operate well. When this is necessary, the battery providing the voltage is called the C battery.

The voltages a tube needs may come from either batteries or another power supply. The tube doesn't care, so long as the right amount of power at the right polarity (+ or −) reaches it. All batteries supply direct current (DC), which flows in one direction only, from the − to the + connections. (Later, when alternating current (AC) became the power source, radio design took care of this problem.)

Batteries

Zinc-carbon batteries. The basic cell, called the zinc-carbon cell, is still commonly found in ordinary flashlight batteries. (The currently popular and better-quality alkaline battery has a different composition.) A zinc-carbon cell obtains its electricity by a chemical process that gradually destroys the zinc metal casing. Once the zinc casing develops enough holes, the chemicals inside the battery dry out and the cell dies.

Batteries are made up of a group of dry cells, usually connected in series to provide a voltage that is some multiple of the dry cell's 1.5 volts. Thus B and C batteries are simply groups of cells and provide voltages such as 3, 4.5, 6, 7.5, and so on.

The earliest radio sets using batteries were one-tube designs. The tube is an amplifying detector which changes the radio frequency signal from the transmitter into an increased audible signal for the listener. Sometimes a crystal detector was even used with a tube, and the tube simply amplified the signal.

The early sets generally had tube filaments, designed to run on about 1.1 volts so the common and cheaply available "No. 6 Cell" zinc-carbon cells could be used. The 6 in the number means the battery is 6 inches tall. These big single cells were used for doorbells, local telephones, and even auto-

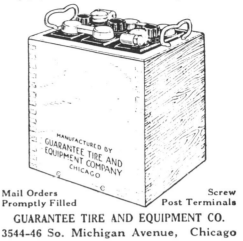

A typical early 6-volt A battery in a wood container.

mobile ignitions. They were relatively long-lasting and readily available. The cell supplied 1.5 volts, which was reduced to 1.1 volts by an adjustable resistor which could be changed as the A cell got older and its voltage dropped. This resistor could be adjusted from the front of the set using one of the knobs. In some cases, there was an adjustment for each tube.

Since these early sets were something of a novelty, they weren't used a great deal. For this reason, the simple A cell was satisfactory, and the B battery lasted a long time in such use. However, as multi-tube sets, and particularly loudspeaker sets, became popular, the use of nonrechargeable A batteries became too expensive, and a cheaper source of filament power was sought.

A better nonrechargeable A battery was developed by Eveready during the early 1930s, a miracle battery called the "Air Cell." Basically, the Air Cell was a zinc-carbon cell, but an imaginative method was used to prevent hydrogen buildup on the carbon center electrode, which had been a problem with zinc-carbon cells.

The Air Cell promised longer life at a more steady voltage than the regular cell, but it had one major fault. If it was overloaded, that is, if more current was drawn from it than it was designed to supply at one time, it was quickly ruined. It also was more expensive than its simpler competitor, and it didn't succeed.

Lead-acid batteries. Again designers looked to readily available sources of power. The 6-volt lead-acid battery was just coming into use in automobiles. It was used for starting the car as well as the rest of the electrical system. The battery had many faults. It was heavy. It could be smelly. It could bubble over or spill corrosive sulphuric acid. Looking at the shelves of many old radio tables, you will see acid burns that are the results of spilled batteries. The lead-acid battery was also rather expensive. However, it did have two excellent qualities: it was rechargeable, and it could supply a great deal of power.

Because of its chemical composition, a lead-acid cell puts out about 2.2 volts. In the normal auto battery, 3 cells were packaged in a wood box lined with tar to protect the wood or, later, in a hard rubber container.

Nickel-iron batteries. Another rechargeable cell was designed by Thomas Edison. Used in Edison's electric trucks, it was able to supply about 1.2 volts per cell. It had several advantages. It supplied an even output voltage as it discharged. It was not touchy about overcharging or storage. It had a steel case that was indestructible. It used a liquid alkaline electrolyte which was far less corrosive than the acid in the lead-acid battery. And it could be recharged more often than a regular battery. So why didn't it succeed? Because of its cost. It was much more expensive than the already high-priced lead-acid rechargeable battery.

Tubes. Tubes were designed to use the new filament power source. Now they had 5-volt filaments. Again it was decided to use adjustable resistors to cut down the voltage from 6.6 volts. As the battery discharged, its voltage dropped slowly, and

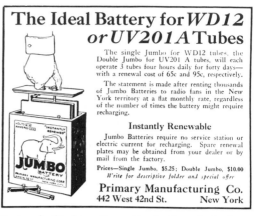
Instead of taking the entire battery in to be recharged, the owner of a Jumbo could remove just the plates from the case and replace them with fresh ones.

the adjustable resistance was reset to keep the voltage on the tube filaments at the correct level.

The adjustable resistance knob could be used as a crude volume control to reduce the loudness of the radio when receiving closer stations. This use meant that it was possible to run the filaments at too high a voltage in order to get just a little more power on weak stations, which shortened the life of the tubes.

Among the new tube-types created by RCA, the preeminent tube design and manufacturing company, were the 201A, the 200A, and the 212A. Together, these three types made more powerful radios possible.

Battery Charging and Chargers

Battery charging. That big 6-volt A battery eventually had to be charged. There were "Charging Stations" in many towns and cities. A battery had to be taken to one of these stations and recharged at a cost. There were a number of problems with this procedure. The heavy battery had to be taken physically to the station. Recharging cost money. If the battery were

HOMCHARGE *your* *Radio Battery for a nickel!*

A battery charger allowed recharging in the home. The ad also shows the problems of hiding the battery and battery charger.

kept overnight, that meant another charged battery would have to be available in order not to miss favorite radio programs. (There was no way to tape the broadcasts at your neighbor's back then.)

If you had electricity (110 volts AC) coming into your home, you could purchase a battery charger for your A battery. There were chargers for rechargeable lead-acid B batteries, but they never became very popular. Recharging a B battery was not cost effective. Rechargeable C batteries were not used, since C batteries lasted for years anyway.

The battery chargers of the time were not sophisticated in design. If you were not cautious, you could overcharge your battery, making it give off fumes, heat up, and sometimes bubble over. Overcharging also shortened the life of the battery.

Battery eliminators. For those with "wired" homes (those on 110-volt AC lines), battery eliminators came in all sizes

$20
Wessco Battery Charger
De Luxe

$12.95

Special
Introductory
Price

A typical 6-volt A battery charger.

and types. These were top-selling accessories in the late 1920s. You could do away with A batteries or with batteries altogether; however, getting rid of the A battery was the most important, since the B lasted for several months of normal use and the C lasted for years.

OH! WHAT A DIFFERENCE
Here is the New NIAGARA "SWITCH LEVER" "B" BATTERY
The *modern* "B" Battery you have been wishing for

STOP FUSSING WITH BATTERY CLIPS OR CONNECTOR LEADS.
SELECT AND CHANGE VOLTAGE INSTANTLY. JUST MOVE THE special patented SWITCH LEVER to proper contact point—and there you are!

Twice the Life of the Ordinary "B" Battery. Large Cells Scientifically Proportioned Ingredients for Radio Service.

Refillable of course like ALL NIAGARA Batteries and Noiseless too. The Most Handsome and Efficient "B" Battery Manufactured.

LIST PRICE ONLY $3.50 EACH
15 cells—22½ volts.   Size 7″x 4¼″ x 3″

ASK YOUR DEALER or WRITE TO US DIRECT

TO DEALERS—This will be the fastest selling "B" Battery. Immediate deliveries. Get behind this wonderful new item. Write for our liberal proposition now.

NIAGARA SALES CORPORATION
Mfgrs of "SUPER QUALITY" RADIO ESSENTIALS
No. 5 Waverly Place, New York City

A built-in switch allowed voltage adjustment for best results.

WESTINGHOUSE UNION BATTERY COMPANY
Swissvale, Pa.

"B" Battery
22-M-2

Built by Westinghouse —you know it's right

Rechargeable B batteries were never very popular; they required a special charger.

TEST YOUR BATTERY IN 15 SECONDS

Your "A" Battery was costly, yet you run a chance of ruining it every time you allow it to go dead or whenever the acid fails to cover the plates.

The success of an evening's entertainment depends upon the condition of your battery: test it every day, and see that it is fully charged and plates fully covered,

CHASLYN "Sink - or - Swim" Ball Battery Tester

Green-Lean
White-Right
Red-Dead

makes this the work of a moment.

The *Depth-Guage* tells you how much acid you have; the *Ball Hydrometer* tells its condition, and the *Air Controlled* Stopper makes it easy to add just enough distilled water.

Hydrometer contains three Balls of different specific gravities:
"Float all three—Charged fully
Sinks the *white*—Charge still *right*
Sinks the *green*—Charge is *lean*
Sinks the *red*—Charge is *dead*."

More accurate than the graduated scale hydrometer, and ten times as easy to read.   Also saves your carpets and rugs from acid burns.

Order from your dealer.   If he doesn't have it, send ONE DOLLAR and his name, and set of three parts, illustrated will be sent you postpaid.

CHASLYN COMPANY
4311 Kenmore Ave.   Chicago, Ill.

Radio batteries, like car batteries, had to be tested.

A typical replaceable B battery.

St. Regis miniature cathedral. No model identification. Early 1930s.

1931 RCA; model R5, the "Radiolette." Cathedral style (Ed and Irene Ripley).

ATWATER KENT RADIO

"Radio's Truest Voice." Atwater Kent Radio Speakers are offered in three sizes. Your choice is a matter of personal preference. Tone quality is uniform. Satin finished in brown and gold or bronze and gold. Models E, E-2, and E-3, each $20.

"IN the elder days of Art
Builders wrought with greatest care
Each minute and unseen part;
For the gods see everywhere."

So Atwater Kent all-electric radio is built today. Accurate to a fraction of a thousandth of an inch! 222 tests or inspections of every set. No skimping or "cutting corners." So —"it works and keeps on working."

Prices slightly higher west of the Rockies

ATWATER KENT RADIO

Model 40 electric. America's favorite radio. Tone, selectivity, power, compactness and good looks at a moderate price. FULL-VISION Dial. Satin finish. Uses six A. C. tubes and one rectifying tube. Without tubes, $77. Also, Model 41 D. C. set, $87.

PRUDENT purchasers of radio ask, "How many people have bought it, and what do they think of it?" Atwater Kent Radio is already in nearly 2,000,000 homes and is first in sales everywhere. There are owners all around you. They'll tell you that the 1929 all-electric set is even better than they expected. And house-current that supplies all the power costs considerably less than a cent an hour.

*Write for illustrated booklet of
Atwater Kent Radio*

Atwater ads, 1928; speaker model E, model 40 electric.

1939 Sentinel; model 195ULT. This is a butter-scotch Catalin radio with burgundy trim. Notice pushbuttons on the top right side. Highly collectible.

1956 Dumont clock-radio; model RA-346. The label on the bottom of the set identifies this model as a clock-radio but shows the tube layout for another, similar radio without clock but the same model number.

RADIOLA 62

SUPER-HETERODYNE

106

THE magic of the incomparable RCA Super-Heterodyne—finest achievement in radio—with all the refinements that have come from ten years of research. The new simplified electric operation. The new RCA Electro-Dynamic speaker. The most popular cabinet model in high quality radio instruments ever designed by RCA and its associates—General Electric and Westinghouse. And the great manufacturing resources of these companies make possible the attractive price of $375 (less Radiotrons).

RCA ELECTRO-DYNAMIC SPEAKER 106
— A new power-operated reproducer of remarkable range and tone. Ideal to use with Radiola 60. $88

Buy with confidence where you see this sign

60

RCA RADIOLA 60—Table model of the new RCA Super-Heterodyne. Finest instrument of its kind ever built. Simplified house-current operation. $175 (less Radiotrons)

RADIO CORPORATION OF AMERICA
NEW YORK   CHICAGO   SAN FRANCISCO

Radiola 62 ad in a nice Deco style; 1929. Reproduced with permission.

Star-Lite. A small, colorful radio from Japan. Dates to the mid-1950s.

1934 Atwater Kent; model 318K; console, AM/ SW. This picture shows how beautifully veneers were mixed and matched in the better consoles of the 1930s.

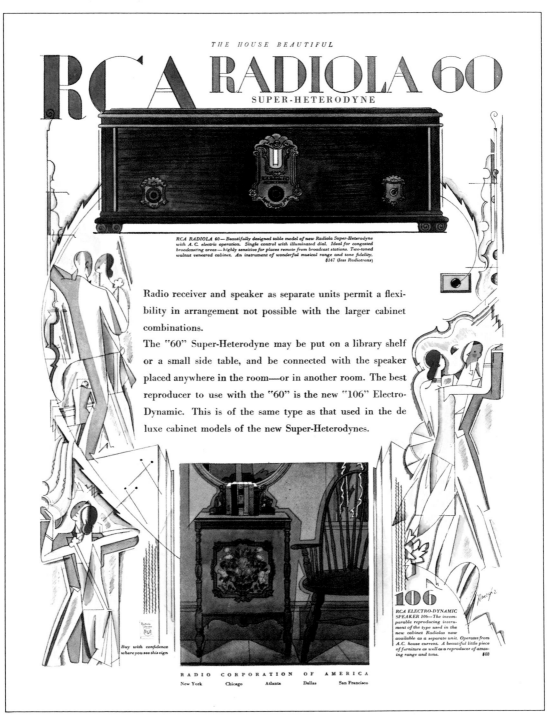

Radiola 60 ad; 1929. Reproduced with permission.

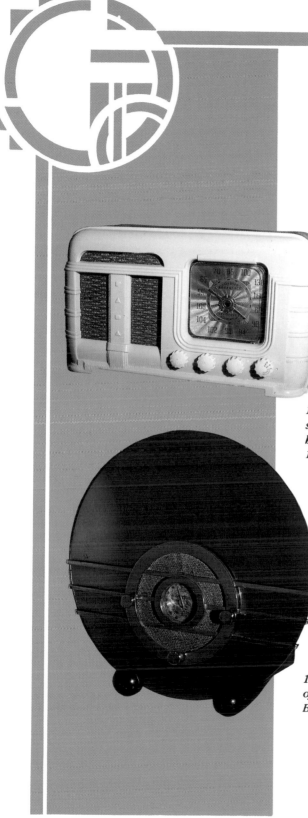

1948 Fada; model 790; white urea. The Deco style of this radio is misleading. It appears to have been made in the late 1930s instead of 1948, when it was built.

1935 Sparton; model 506 "Bluebird." The first of Sparton's highly collectible mirror radios. Beautiful blue color.

Globe Navigator. Globe turns on its north–south axis to tune station (John Wilson).

Pathé Magnetic Pickup in original box. This unit would allow a windup phonograph to play electrically through a radio. Made about 1929 (Gene Harris Auctions).

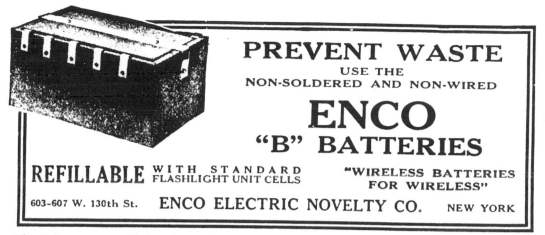
This B battery was filled with standard flashlight batteries.

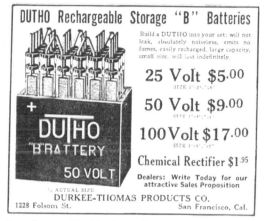
A rechargeable Dutho B battery; this is one of the more unusual-looking ones.

Battery eliminators were not perfect. They often added some "hum" (buzz) to the sound heard from the receiver, because the DC produced was not as smooth as that from a battery. They were expensive, too, but for heavy radio users they made sense.

Experimenters who had a 110-volt AC line into their houses tried to do without the A battery eliminator altogether. Using a simple voltage-changing transformer, such as a doorbell transformer, they reduced the 110 volts to the 5 volts AC that would operate a tube safely. It would operate a tube safely, that is, but not successfully. The light weight of the filaments in tubes designed for battery use (needed to conserve batter-

ies) coupled with the audible rate of change in the AC current direction (60 times a second) produced a buzz that made the system, unless very carefully balanced, virtually impossible to listen to.

Alternating Current Tubes

What was needed now was a tube designed for AC on the filament. The theory said that a tube shouldn't care what kind of current (AC or DC) is used to heat the filament, so the designers set to work.

Any vacuum tube requires DC on the plate in order to amplify, since a steady positive voltage must be present to attract the electrons from the filament. By necessity, the grid voltage (C) had to be DC as well. The AC coming into the grid was the signal that had to be amplified. So a radio still had to contain a B eliminator or power supply to provide the necessary DC voltages. The C voltage was usually produced in the radio itself, directly from the B supply.

It was much cheaper to heat the filament wire with AC. It did mean that the wire would have to be heavier than for DC tubes. This was done successfully in tubes like the 26 and the 45.

"Sorry, but we won't be able to listen in tonight.
My "B" batteries are dead".
This embarrassment need never happen to you again.

This battery eliminator removed the problems of B batteries.

In another design, the *cathode* (electron emitter) was insulated from the filament (now called a *heater*). The cathode was heated enough to provide the needed electrons. Common early types of this sort of tube were the 24A and the 27.

The AC-operated radio soon replaced the battery set in homes where AC was available. The radios were heavy and, in their early years, expensive. However they performed well and were cheap to run.

Later Battery Sets

Battery sets are still being manufactured today; these are our portable radios. There are few places, however, still using them as home radios.

Technology kept improving the battery systems available for homes without an AC line, which were primarily rural homes. Until the Rural Electrification Agency came along in the 1930s, most farmers did not expect to ever be on an AC line. Because electricity was important not only to their comfort, but more importantly to their farming operations, many farms had some sort of power plant. The Delco system that is often referred to was a 32-volt DC system that charged its batteries with a gasoline engine. Radios that ran on 32 volts were available for this system.

With some radios it was possible to avoid the B battery completely. Using a 6-volt car battery and a *vibrator* power supply, these radios could be used in nonelectrified areas. A number of Zenith radios during the 1930s were 6-volt radios.

Here's the *Simplest* Way

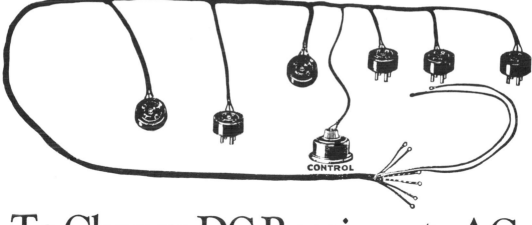

CONTROL

To Change DC Receivers to AC

Absolutely no Rewiring Necessary on Standard Sets

The Eby AC Adaptor Harness can be used in practically any standard five or six tube set equipped with separate B battery and C bias feeders for the last AF stage *without changing the wiring in any way.*

An AC adapter harness; this wiring harness allowed the use of the new AC tubes in earlier battery sets.

There was never any doubt that farmers would bring in AC power when it was available. Allied Radio catalogs in 1938 advertised not only AC radios and battery radios of various voltages, but also AC/battery radios. The assumption was that AC power would reach farms during the lifetime of these radios, and the farmer could easily switch over his radio without having to go out and buy another one. Crosley also made radios designed to operate as either battery or AC radios.

It is impossible to know when battery radios stopped being used in homes. They were produced until sometime in the early 1950s; Philco was advertising "Farm Radios" into the late 1940s in farm magazines. Many rural areas didn't get electricity until after World War II was over; the plans to bring light to the farms of America had been shelved for the duration of the war. It was almost 1950 before some parts of hilly, southwestern Wisconsin were hooked up to

electric lines, for example, and it was probably still later in other parts of the country. So "Farm Radios" remained around for a long time.

The Change from Batteries to AC

Assuming that line power was available in a city in the 1920s, the change in that city from battery radios to AC ones was rapid. As has been seen, batteries were pesky, expensive, short-lived, messy, and altogether a thing people were eager to get rid of.

There were, for instance, those dratted holes in the carpet. If one were unfortunate enough to slosh over the battery acid while moving the battery around, it would leave a large burn hole. If the battery charger were unsupervised and the liquid started to bubble, small acid burns would be found in the rug. Because of this, many housewives tried to limit the radio to the attic where the spots wouldn't show. Inevitably, there would be an important broadcast that many of the family would want to hear. If the set were brought down to the dining room table, "just once, mind you," it generally remained downstairs. Clustering around the speaker or sharing the headphones, it brought a bit of the outside world to the family. Once people had sampled radio, they didn't want to give it up.

Trying to hide the batteries was another problem, for they were big and cumbersome. It would be like hiding today's car battery in the corner and hoping that no one would see it. Radio tables developed, tables long enough and narrow enough to hold one of the mid-1920s sets, with a shelf underneath to hold the batteries. Some of them had oak or wicker fronts to hide the batteries and make them more attractive. This meant getting behind the table to remove the battery for recharging, which increased the chance of spilling the battery acid.

Batteries had a bad habit of dying at important times. Numerous cartoons and advertisements from the late 1920s showed men coming home from work and telling their wives that they had invited the Smiths in that night to listen to the radio, only to have the wife or child lament, "But the batteries are dead! I listened to the radio this afternoon." It must have happened often enough to make a point to the readers.

Then there was the constant cost of keeping up those batteries, particularly as radio became more important to the family and the family started planning its life around certain programs. The radio was used more and more often, and for more and more hours.

Manufacturers and dealers were not at all reluctant to encourage this high regard for radio. The ads from the late 1920s implied, if not stated, that modern families used modern radios. There were many ways to get people to turn in their old, "obsolete" battery sets and get one of the new, modern AC sets. Just in case the point was missed, National Radio Week in 1929 used a number of gimmicks. In Milwaukee there was a parade, complete with decorated floats and trucks, that led to a giant bonfire where old trade-in sets were destroyed. In St. Louis, nearly 3000 old sets were burned in a similar event. The mayor himself lighted the fire in Buffalo. "The agreement on the trade-in allowances, the special window displays, the generous use of newspaper space, and propaganda of obsolescence — by these many means the dealers, acting together, gave these campaigns a cumulative force to which the fire itself was a fitting climax."[2]

The AC set had won.

2. Collectors of old battery sets flinch at the thought of this mayhem, but *Radio Retailing* proudly boasted of this coup. "Clearing the Way with Fire!" was the title of its article, which goes on to say that National Radio Week "inspires many dealer associations to 'burn the bloopers.'" For further information, see of *Radio Retailing*, November 1928, page 72.

General Electric Tungar charger (reprinted with permission).

Broadcasting:
An Important Part of Radio

RADIO history doesn't only include the history of radio technology and radio manufacturers, but it also includes the field of broadcasting—what was broadcast and how. Broadcasting is an increasingly popular field of radio history. Museums grow, and clubs meet to listen to old programs and read aloud original scripts. When the fates are kind, the clubs may even get a member of the original cast to join in one of these readings.

While the 1930s is considered the golden age of broadcasting in terms of programming, by then the mechanics of broadcasting itself had become settled. It was during the 1920s that almost anything could happen, and sometimes did. There were no established standards, so each station tried to define broadcasting in the best way possible for its own particular audience. Trial and error played a large part as the stations learned on the air.

1921 Westinghouse; model RC; includes both the RA and DA in the same box; battery set sold by RCA; original price $125.00 (Gene Harris Auctions).

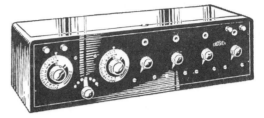

1922 Crosley; model X; one of the larger Crosley models. Crosleys were famous for their low prices; even so, this model comes in a mahogany cabinet; original price $55.00.

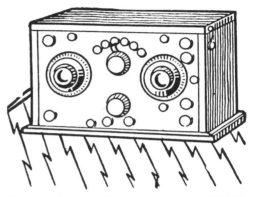

1922 Tuska; type 224; original price $35.00.

1922 RCA Aeriola Sr. made by Westinghouse; popular one-tube set (John Wilson).

1923 Telmaco; one-tube receiver; original price $25.00.

28

When Marconi heard the AERIOLA GRAND

© UNDERWOOD & UNDERWOOD

RCA

Look for this
trademark at
your dealer

"IT comes closest to the dream I had when I first caught the vision of radio's vast possibilities. It brings the world of music, news and education into the home, fresh from the human voice. It solves the problem of loneliness and isolation.

"The Aeriola Grand is at present the supreme achievement in designing and constructing receiving sets for the home—a product of the research systematically conducted by scientists in the laboratories that constitute part of the R C A organization."

C. Marconi

1922 RCA Aeriola Grand; testimonials were just as important then as now.

First Stations and Station Firsts

Probably the first question people ask about broadcasting is: What was the first station? The answer to that depends on exactly what we mean by the question. The first station to broadcast voices? The first to broadcast a regularly scheduled program? The first to be licensed?

KDKA (Pittsburgh) has the honor of being the first station in the United States licensed not for experimental or amateur use, but for broadcasting under the 1920 federal regulations. Frank Conrad, Westinghouse's chief engineer, had been making experimental broadcasts since 1916 from his garage. They were to the Westinghouse plant in East Pittsburgh, where the Radio Engineering Section was working on developing radios that would be better than the

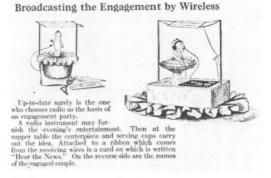

Broadcasting the Engagement by Wireless

Up-to-date surely is the one who chooses radio as the basis of an engagement party.

A radio instrument may furnish the evening's entertainment. Then at the supper table the centerpiece and serving cups carry out the idea. Attached to a ribbon which comes from the receiving wires is a card on which is written "Hear the News." On the reverse side are the names of the engaged couple.

Radio was a cute idea for a party.

crystal sets of the day. Although the Department of Commerce suspended all amateur broadcasting licenses as a security measure once the United States became involved in World War I, Conrad's test station was exempted. He continued to use it during the war, with government approval, to test military equipment for Westinghouse.

When the ban was lifted after the war, Conrad resumed his amateur broadcasting.

"Above them all"

TRESCO

TRESCO

Seven Years in Radio
—Think What That Means!
TRESCO
SECTIONAL UNIVERSAL
Licensed Under Armstrong U. S. Patent No. 1,113,149

The Tresco Tuners were among the first ever made under the Armstrong Patent. They are found in all parts of the world, giving satisfactory service. The sectional idea is original with us.

The instruments are identically the same as those we have been manufacturing for seven years—but we have made their casings on the plan of the sectional bookcase—each a separate unit which, when put together with a top and base, forms one complete section.

The set consists of three units:

1. **Tuner and Detector.**
2. **Two-Stage Amplifier.**
3. **Case for "A" Storage Battery.**

The sections are of oak, finished in French gray, making an extremely attractive piece of furniture—something you will be proud to have in your home, beside your phonograph or piano. No wires or battery on the floor.

PRICES

Tuner and Detector Unit without vacuum tube, head set or "B" Battery . . . .\$ 50.00

Two-Step Amplifier Unit without vacuum tubes or "B" Battery . 35.00

"A" Battery Unit for holding "A" Battery 9.50

Top and Bottom, which, when added to the three other units, make a complete section all in one. Each, $5.00; both . . . 10.00

Complete set of five units—Total $104.50

The units when assembled make a cabinet 40 inches wide, 15 inches high and 10 inches deep.

We do not furnish vacuum tubes, batteries or head sets.

TRESCO SECTIONAL UNIVERSALS are being supplied to dealers and jobbers just as fast as possible. Order from your local dealer. If he cannot supply you, we will fill your order upon receipt of prices as given.

Dealers and jobbers are rapidly finding out that TRESCO is one of the very few manufacturers who are actually in position to take care of large volume orders for immediate shipment. Liberal discounts are given to jobbers and dealers for quantity orders. We do not furnish vacuum tubes, batteries or loud speakers.

TRESCO RADIO
Used All Over The World
J. Matheson Bell, Sales Mgr.
Davenport, Iowa, U.S.A.

1922 Tresco Super-Universal tuner; original price $100.00.

Tresco; model W receiver and amplifier; not listed in Tresco literature.

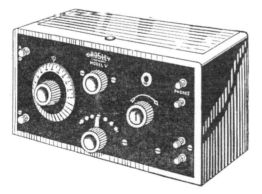

1923 National Airphone; one-tube set on a base; no cabinet; original price $10.00.

1923 Crosley; model VC. This is a model V with an engraved front panel. One month later, in June 1923, it was being advertised as the Ace Model V, "formerly known as the Crosley VC"; original price $20.00.

World War I had pushed the whole field of radio into rapid development. The advancement of vacuum tubes during the war was remarkable, giving radio greater sensitivity and volume. Along with the tests he was conducting, Conrad occasionally played phonograph records. Letters arrived from listeners, delighted with this type of programming. The Hamilton Music Store saw that there were advantages to radio broadcasting and provided the records in return for a mention on the air. The record concerts became a regularly scheduled event, once a week at first, but soon on a daily basis. Until this point, people who listened to radios were primarily experimenters and amateurs. But public attention was drawn to Conrad's broadcasts when the Joseph Horne Department Store ran an ad mentioning the broadcasts as a way of promoting their new wireless department.

Harry Davis, a Westinghouse vice president (and the reason for the *D* and the *A* in KDKA), saw the public relations value of a radio station. If you could broadcast interesting programs, people would buy your radios. With new federal guidelines in effect for licensing broadcasting stations, Westinghouse applied for a license and received it in only eleven days, on 27 October 1920.

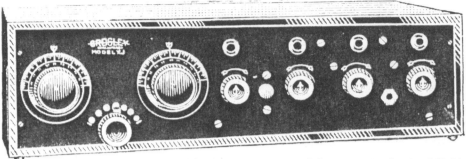

1923 Crosley; model X-J; original price $65.00.

KDKA went on the air with the results of the Harding-Cox presidential election on 2 November 1920, less than a month after it had applied for a license.

What about the first voice broadcast? Certainly it was earlier than 1920? On Christmas Eve 1906, Reginald Fessenden broadcast a program from Brant Rock, Massachusetts, that started with the "CQ,CQ" of Morse code, and then switched to a human voice. There are no words that can adequately describe the surprise, shock, and amazement of shipboard radio operators who suddenly, at sea, heard a woman singing in their radio rooms. At this time, remember, wireless was all in code. And they didn't hear just an isolated song, either. Besides hearing the woman singing (taken from a phonograph record), they heard a poem, a violin solo (played by Fessenden himself), and a speech. It was a complete Christmas program. Fessenden then asked people listening to write him and let him know how far the broadcast had carried. The following New Year's Eve program was heard as far away as the West Indies.

Many other stations claim various firsts, but the first regularly broadcasting station (Fessenden didn't broadcast on a regular schedule) has to be KQW (San Jose, California). It was started by Charles Herrold in 1909. It wasn't known as KQW then—this was before there were call letters. In fact, this was before there were any regulations regarding broadcasting stations. The station announcement was "This is San Jose," followed by the address of the College of Engi-

1923 Kennedy; model 311 Portable; radio in wood case; storage for headphones; one-tube set; original price $75.00.

neering that Herrold had started. Herrold, a self-trained engineering genius, at once made radio the focus of the college. Voice transmission was his immediate goal.

At first Herrold made only occasional experiments, but soon voice broadcasts were a regular feature. Every Wednesday night the station was on the air with news bulletins and phonograph records (provided by a local store). Anyone with a crystal set in the area planned on listening to these programs. Unfortunately, they didn't always hear the end of them. Herrold carefully planned the entire program, but pushed so much power (15 watts) through his carbon microphone that the program sounded more and more mushy as the evening went

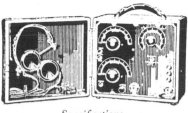

Specifications
Regenerative Tuner.
Vernier Control of wave length adjustment.
Detector and 1 stage Amplifier.
Two telephone jacks.
1 Pair Brandes Head Telephones.
3 Flash Light batteries.
2 B Batteries.

Price $97.50

1925 RCA Radiola II.

on. Often he had to simply stop and shut down. The next week he would apologize for the incident, but often the same thing would happen again. On New Year's Eve 1915, he decided to welcome in the New Year with a blank shot from an old Army pistol. There was a sharp sound, and he was off the air again.

Herrold shut down the station during World War 1. When he restarted it after the war, he was unable to make it a success again. Eventually he sold it to a Baptist church, and it finally got call letters and became KQW. After several other sales, it ended up as KCBS, the Columbia Broadcasting System station in San Francisco. Lee DeForest, in 1940, said that KQW could "rightfully claim to be the oldest broadcasting station in the entire world."

There were others—lots of others— who had various claims to being first. Canada considers that the first scheduled broadcast in North America occurred over station XWA (Montreal) on 20 May 1920, over five months earlier than KDKA's. Europe was also developing its own broadcasting. The question we asked originally has to be carefully phrased because there are so many answers. Everyone wants to be first, and the words "radio broadcast" or "regularly scheduled" can have many interpretations.

The firsts that took place the first year after KDKA began are awesome. Everything

1923 Radiola RS; manufactured by Westinghouse; sold by RCA; original price $87.00.

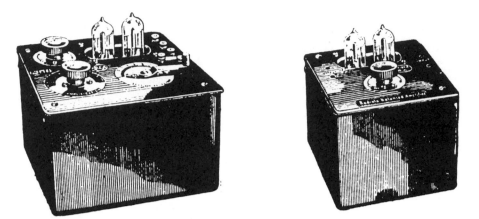

1924 RCA Radiola III and Radiola III Balanced Amplifier; each housed in boxes. The combined model is the Radiola IIIA. Original prices: III, $35.00; amplifier, $30.00.

1923 Radak; model C23; made by Clapp-Eastham; original price $125.00.

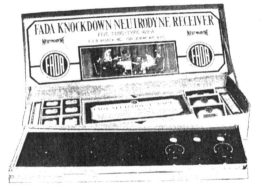

1924 Fada; kit; original price $25.00.

Price $**18**.50

without tube, batteries or phones.

1924 Radiotrola Baby Grand; made by National Airphone; one-tube set, with space for headphones; original price $18.50.

was a first, and the stations were willing to try just about anything. This list is selective and incomplete. There are certain to be other stations claiming some of the following records:

31 August 1920	First election returns, Detroit primary (WWJ: Detroit)
October 1920	First World Series (WWJ)
2 November 1920	First national election returns (WWJ, KDKA)
31 December 1920	First New Year's Eve celebration (WWJ)
2 January 1921	First church service (KDKA)
	First remote broadcast was of this same church service.
3 January 1921	First weather forecasts given by voice (WHA: Madison, Wisconsin)
11 April 1921	First boxing match, Johnny Dundee and Johnny Ray (KDKA)

1924 Adler-Royal Neutrodyne; original price $160.00.

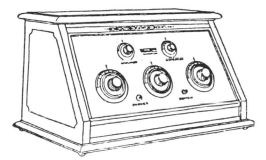

1924 Work Rite; Air Master model; original price $160.00.

9 May 1921	First live broadcast from theater stage (KDKA)
4–6 August 1921	First Davis Cup matches (KDKA)
5 August 1921	First play-by-play baseball (KDKA)
16 October 1921	First radio section started by a newspaper *(Newark Sunday Call)*. Although not a broadcast first, these newspaper departments were important in making people familiar with radio.
11 November 1921	First live opera performance (KYW: Chicago)

These first years of broadcasting were exciting. No one really knew where radio was going, nor how it would get there. But everyone was convinced that radio was a great benefit for mankind. In this vein, an article in *Radio News* in December 1922 said:

> There will be concerts such as we really want to hear, college courses for the boy who could not go as far as the university, business information in condensed form so that dad will not have to ruin his eyes and fill all his home time with reading. All will be systematized and on time like the visits of the postman. Probably we shall have individual receiving sets for the different members of the family, so each can hear what he wishes. They will be cheaper and more efficient than they are now, and simpler to operate. Radio will not take the place of the telegraph or the telephone, the newspaper or the magazine, the theatre or the moving picture show. It is just one more marvel of modern science that enriches our lives and fills [them] with pleasant, useful entertainment.

Radio Studios

In the beginning, radio studios weren't even primitive, they were nonexistent. They provide a perfect example of learning through trial and error, since there was no real information about what was necessary to produce a clear, understandable radio program. Accounts of early

1924 Zenith portable; model Super Portable; first portable radio with built-in speaker; original price $240.00 (courtesy Zenith Radio Corp.).

stations leave one wondering how the programs ever got on the air.

Take, for instance, the way KDKA developed its studio. Broadcasting the election returns was easy with one man sitting in front of a microphone. When KDKA experimenters tried to broadcast the Westinghouse band from a hall, they ran into acoustical problems they had never foreseen. Placing so many instruments inside a large room led to such reverberation that the broadcast sounded like bedlam. Up onto the roof of the building they went, and the broadcast went just fine. When rainy weather came, a tent was erected to protect the musicians. Finally a strong wind blew the tent down, and they went back inside again—but this time they erected the tent inside the building. The tent softened the room acoustics and allowed the broadcasts to sound fine. As time went on, the tent was replaced by hangings to do the same job.

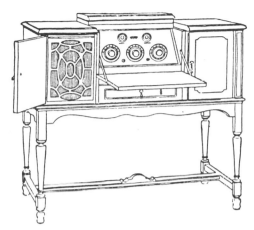

1925 Work Rite; Aristocrat model; designed to look like a buffet when the radio and speaker compartments are closed; original price $350.00.

MU-RAD ⭐ RECEIVER
MA-15

1924 Mu-Rad; model MA-15. This ad reflects the excitement and mystery of radio.

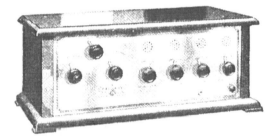

1924 Faraway; model F. According to Radio Collector's Guide, Faraway made only four models. The light-colored front panel is different from most other sets of that date; original price $59.50.

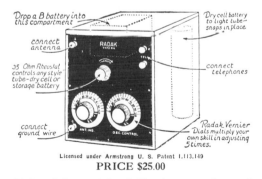

Licensed under Armstrong U. S. Patent 1,113,149
PRICE $25.00

1924 Radak; model R-4. The diagram shows that this is a self-contained small radio, including even the batteries; original price $25.00.

1924 Ultradyne; available in kit form; made by Phenix Radio Corp.; original price $24.50.

MU-RAD ⭐ RECEIVER
MA-18

1924 Mu-Rad; model MA-18. Notice the Radio Map on the wall—apparently the listener has been marking the stations he has picked up; original price $110.00.

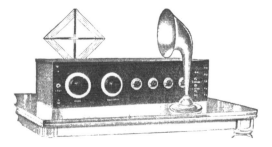

1924 Magnavox; model TRF-50. Elaborate doors cover the workings of this table set; original price $150.00.

1924 A&P. "The most beautiful and efficient neutrodyne set in the world," it claimed; original price $97.50.

HALLDORSON

1924 Halldorson. The company made three models in 1924. Originally it was a transformer manufacturing company.

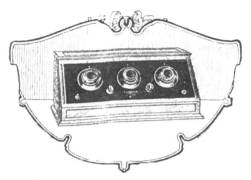

1924 Thompson; model Parlor Grand; original price $145.00.

1924 Kennedy; model V; also available in 1923; original price $86.50.

1924 Colin Kennedy; model XV-430; TRF, battery set; original price $142.50 (Gene Harris Auctions).

The WJZ studio in Newark, New Jersey, was also on the roof of a Westinghouse building. It put its new transmitter in a shack on the roof, reachable only by an iron ladder and through a hatchway. An Edison phonograph, which they were planning on using to play records, was too big to go through the hatchway to the roof and instead had to be hoisted up the outside of the building. After several weeks of testing and of receiving letters of praise from people who were excited about this new entertainment, WJZ began regular programming. A few performers made it up the ladder to the shack, but it soon became very evident that the studio should be easily accessible. Draping part of the ladies' cloakroom with flannel was the solution to the problem.

Another example of how primitive early broadcasting could be was seen at what later became the Columbia flagship station,

1924 Zenith; model Super-Zenith VII; original price $240.00 (courtesy Zenith Radio Corp.).

1924 Day-Fan. This cabinet can be either the OEM-7 (4-tube, original price $98.00) or the OEM-11 (3-tube, original price $90.00).

WOR (Newark). Its first programs were broadcast before there was a completed studio. With no studio, WOR broadcasters needed a soundproof room to monitor the first day's programs. They ended up using the men's room.

There were some ambitious opening shows for stations. KYW (Chicago), another Westinghouse station, took advantage of the expertise Westinghouse was developing in radio to begin its broadcasting with the most ambitious project one could think of: a live production of the Chicago Opera

Company. This opening show was immensely successful, and nightly broadcasts of the opera continued to the end of its season.

In an attempt to look elegant (and, incidentally, to hide the dirt), WJZ dyed its flannel red. Studios in the early 1920s tried hard to look like living rooms or front parlors. Since most of the performers were used to a live audience in an unamplified room, they were intimidated by the microphone. With no audience present for whom they could perform, many of them suffered

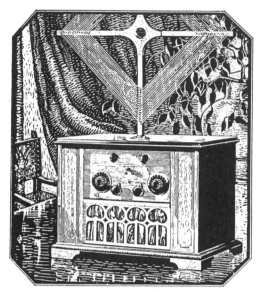

1924 De Forest; model D-12. The loop antenna fits into a hole in the top of the cabinet. This particular model was available for either dry batteries or storage batteries. The case was gray-and-black Fabrikoid or two-tone mahogany. Original prices were from $161.20 to $195.00.

1924 Pfanstiehl; model 7 Overtone. A bit of a radio table shows at the bottom. Not much wider than the radio itself, this table gave a shelf on which to place the batteries; original price $150.00 (radio only).

1924 Day-Fan; model 5107 Dayradia; slant-front radio with enclosed speaker; original price, $225.00.

1924 Federal; model 59 ("Fifty-Nine" was the way Federal ads referred to it); available in both this wood table set and in a metal table cabinet; original price $177.00. The Model 61 was identical except that it was designed for a loop antenna and cost $223.00.

1925 RCA Radiola; model 26; portable, loop antenna; battery-operated; beautiful wood case, with gold-colored dials; original cost $225.00 (Gene Harris Auctions).

1924 Ozarka; no model number; original price $39.50.

1924 Crosley; model 3R3 Trirdyn Special; original price $75.00; with tubes and earphones $90.75.

1925 Jones; Model J-75. This set was made by Joseph W. Jones (New York City), rather than the Jones Radio Co.; original price $75.00.

DE FOREST F-5 AW

1925 De Forest F-5 AW; original price $90.00.

"mike fright." To overcome this, studios went to great extremes to hide what they were. Photographs of early studios show many popular decorative ideas for studios of the period. There were those elegant-looking flannel or burlap draperies, a great way to disguise a plain room as well as to deaden the reverberations. Reproduction Oriental carpets covered the floor, not only giving a comfortable feel to the room, but also muffling footsteps. A piano was a necessity, of course, to accompany the many soloists who appeared; like the piano at home, it was covered with a paisley scarf. Potted plants gave the room a nice homey feel. Amplifiers could hide in innocent-looking commonplace phonograph cabinets, but there was still the microphone to handle. It had to be hidden to keep performers from becoming nervous. Suddenly the studios had ornate, floor-standing "lamps," with fringed lampshades carefully disguising microphones. An old picture of an early studio usually gives the impression of an over-elaborately decorated, tasteless, middle-class parlor.

Glorious 1922! Radio was booming, stations were starting, and performers were delighted to be on the air. No one thought about wage scales and hours. WJZ, a Westinghouse station located across the river from New York City, had early access to a large number of performers. There was a problem in getting them to agree to come to the studio because the station was located in a factory district on the wrong side of the river. Undaunted, WJZ had limousines to meet the artists at the ferry, a doorman to greet them at the studio, and an announcer who appeared in a tuxedo or, occasionally, white-tie-and-tails. Artists wanted to come, to appear on this new medium. It was modern and it was exciting.

This euphoria didn't last long, however. Soon other stations in New York City itself were broadcasting. Without the need to bribe performers to come, the amenities soon declined. The performers also learned that there was money to be made from radio and that performing for the thrill or the publicity was no longer necessary.

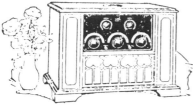

DE FOREST F-5 M

1925 De Forest F-5 M; enclosed speaker; original price $110.00.

1925 Gilfillan; model GN-2; introduced in 1924; original price $140.00 (without the horn).

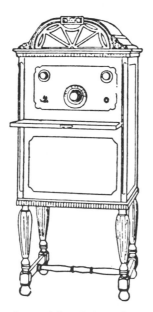

1925 Mohawk; model 115 Console; same as the 110, but with a floor cabinet instead; original price $225.00.

1925 Mohawk; model 110, consolette version. With its curved top, this table-top radio is highly styled; original price $175.00.

Advertising on the Air

Early broadcasting had certain ethical problems. One was the matter of advertising or not advertising on the air. Nowadays it seems impossible to believe that radio seriously considered being advertising-free. There was a possibility—remote to be sure—that it would be limited to the kinds of announcements public radio uses today: "This program has been brought to you by the XYZ Corporation, a leading manufacturer of widgets, located at 123 State Street." This approach wasn't likely to last long, businessmen being businessmen who already knew the value of the printed ad.

Back in 1916, the chief engineer of Western Electric had said, "We [do] not think it seemly to advertise on radio." Even at the first Washington Radio Conference in 1922, Herbert Hoover, then Secretary of Commerce, said, "It is inconceivable that we should allow so great a possibility for service to be drowned in advertising chatter." An attempt was made in 1925 to pass a law to prohibit advertising, but the attempt failed. As time went on, the talk wasn't about banning all advertising, only "direct advertising," and the lines became increasingly less distinct.

Even before radio advertising was acceptable, corporations found that they could gain early recognition of their products by naming a show after the company.

1925 Gilfillan; model GN-1; introduced in 1924; original price $175.00.

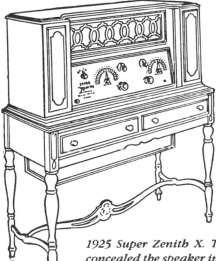

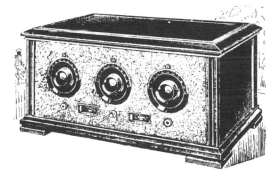

1925 Eisemann; model 6-D; introduced in 1924; original price $125.00.

1925 Super Zenith X. This horizontal highboy concealed the speaker in the top of the compartment; available as either an AC set or a battery set; original price $550.00.

1925 Standardyne; model B5; original price $60.00.

Wolper; model RS5; slant-front radio in very deep case, with stepped-back enclosed speaker; mid-1920s. The radio is sitting on a separate table (Paul Johnson).

1925 Mohawk; model A5. Some applied wood trim decorates this rather conventional slant-front cabinet; original price $115.00.

1925 Hammarlund Roberts.

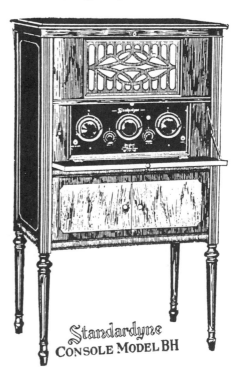

1925 Standardyne; model BH; original price $135.00.

FADA ON THE AIR

Hear the Fada Orchestra with David Mendoza conducting, broadcast every Tuesday night at 10 o'clock, Eastern Standard Time, over the Columbia network.

Atwater Kent was sponsoring "The Atwater Kent Hour" as early as 1925. Kent felt that the extra cost of radio advertising was well worth the money, although it cost almost twice as much each week to put on the program as it cost for the entire year's printed advertising. The Stromberg-Carlson Sextette, on weekly over the Blue Network, was "definitely designed to aid the dealer in selling Stromberg-Carlson receivers," according to an ad the company ran in *Radio Retailing* in May 1928. Fada turned its initials (F-A-D-A) into a musical signature.

Not everyone questioned the merits of advertising. American Telephone and Telegraph began station WEAF (New York City) in 1922. Since they had no radio equipment to sell, unlike most of the other parent companies, they weren't particularly interested in broadcasting. They were used to handling toll charges for telephones and telegraphs, however. It wasn't a big jump for them to conceive of the idea of "toll broadcasting," an opportunity for anyone who was willing to pay the time rate to basically own that period of time to do with it what he or she wanted. An indication of where this all was going came in WEAF's first paid program. On 28 August 1922, Mr. Blackwell, of the Queensboro Corporation, gave a ten-minute talk. The announcer who introduced him mentioned Nathaniel Hawthorne and his ideals about a healthful home life. Then Mr. Blackwell began. After a token mention of Hawthorne and his ideals, Mr. Blackwell got right to the point. The Queensboro Corporation was selling a group of apartments (in "Hawthorne Court," naturally). The apartments proposedly exemplified Hawthorne's dreams about healthful living, and for the

1925 Operadio; portable; very early Deco style.

rest of the ten minutes Mr. Blackwell gave unarguable reasons for buying into this great opportunity.

The battle against advertising was really lost almost as soon as it began. With the exception of educational and public radio, there was no way that broadcasting could remain unsullied by commercialism. Today there's a feeling that this is happening even to public radio, as sponsors not only give their names and locations, but also include some sort of slogan or short spiel.

Early Regulations

Radio grew. What had begun in 1920 almost as an experiment was by the end of the decade a vast, established business. David Sarnoff, of RCA, gained a reputation as a prophet for accurately predicting the growth of radio. His prediction was

The WorkRite
CHUM
$75

1925 Work Rite; model Chum; introduced in 1924.

1925 Music Master; model 215; spinet desk style; original price $215.00.

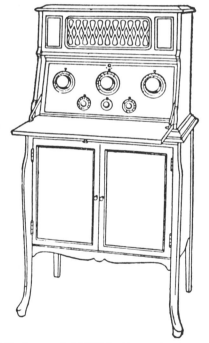

1925 Fada; model 185/90A Neutrola Grand. The slant-front radio sits on a base with doors; enclosed speaker; original price $295.00.

1925 Brunswick; kit; no model information; sold by Radio Shack; original price $39.49 (kit without the fancy illustrated dial).

1925 Kodel; model C-11; original price $10.00.

1925 Kodel; model C-13; original price $28.00.

1925 Kodel; model C-14; original price $32.50. The battery storage cabinet and horn speaker were extra.

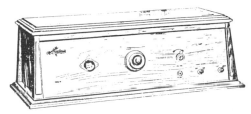

1925 Pfanstiehl; model 10 Overtone; original price $155.00.

made early in 1920, before there were any licensed stations on the air. He visualized that the "Radio Music Box" could be made for $75 per set, and that in the first year there would be sales of $7,500,000, in the second year $22,500,000, and in the third year $45,000,000. RCA didn't believe these figures and was caught unprepared when KDKA went on the air and radio began booming. A shake-up the next year made Sarnoff the general manager, while RCA rushed to make up lost time. The first year that RCA sold radios, gross sales were $11,000,000. The second year they matched the prediction, while in the third year they were $50,000,000. This success consolidated RCA's position in the field and Sarnoff's reputation as a visionary.

KDKA began in 1920. By the end of that year, there were three stations licensed. Nine months later, there were 451 stations, in all states except Wyoming. Almost immediately a major problem arose. All of the stations (except those broadcasting governmental reports such as weather or crop news) were licensed at 360 meters. Crop reports and weather were to be found at 485 meters. A station would use 360 meters for entertainment and news, then switch to 485 meters for its weather reports. As soon as two stations in the same area were broadcasting, some sort of compromise was necessary. The government had not allotted any time periods, so it was up to the stations to make their own arrangements. With no supervision, a station could exceed its time

1925 Miraco Ultra 5.

1926 Showers; console model; gold-painted front; original cost $60.00 (Gene Harris Auctions).

1926 Westingale. Single-dial set with interesting design painted on the front panel; original price $57.00.

and make life difficult for its companion station. Some sort of allocation of the radio band was going to be necessary.

Meanwhile, every group wanted to be in on radio. Newspapers started their own stations, stores developed them to help sell radios, colleges and universities wanted them to help educate people in the remote parts of their states, and churches saw them as a method of expanding their ministries.

As the decade progressed, reassignment of radio frequencies was common, as was sharing a frequency with one or more other stations. The smaller stations were limited to certain hours of certain days, making it difficult for them to develop their own listening audiences. Since new listeners wanted to be able to brag about hearing

1926 Masterphone; made by the Boston Radio Manufacturing Co. (John Wilson).

one of the large stations (KDKA, WJZ, or WWJ, for instance), it was necessary to do something about the local stations that were broadcasting on the same wave length. At first there was "Silent Night," one night a week when the local station would stay off the air and its listeners could try to catch one of the major stations. Different nights were chosen in different parts of the country. For a while it worked, but the local stations eventually became tired of losing revenue for that night, and the idea slowly died.

Stations were still starting up haphazardly, and something was going to have to be done about the chaos. When several stations were all sharing the same frequency, it became a major undertaking to tune in to any one of them clearly. The government attempted to solve the problem in 1922 when the Commerce Department added a 400-meter band for broadcasting, with strict limitations. The band was for Class B stations, who would operate on 500 to 1000 watts and were prohibited from playing phonograph records. Stations that couldn't meet these terms (the Class A stations) were fated to stay at the 360-meter band. Listeners liked this arrangement, as did all those who favored a few powerful stations rather than a plethora of smaller ones. The 400-meter stations were relatively safe from overcrowding, at least for a while.

But the Class A stations saw no improvement in their situation. In fact, since there was still virtually no regulation of the airwaves, the plight of the smaller stations was becoming worse than ever. This predicament encouraged them to wander off their given frequency in the hope that somehow or other they could be picked up more easily by the listener. Voluntary time sharing wasn't working out. The Commerce Department was forced to assign frequencies and to allocate time in an effort to bring some order to the situation, even though there was no certainty that the law specifically permitted these actions.

Although regional stations were located over more of the broadcast band, there

were still 86 stations operating at 360 meters in 1924. To spread these out, the Commerce Department made an arbitrary decision: stations operating at 500 watts or more were assigned to the regional sections of the band, while those of a lesser power were lumped together in still more time-sharing plans.

An example of this time-sharing involved station KMA of Shenandoah, Iowa. This was the station of the Earl May Seed Company. Earl May purchased a 500-watt Class B transmitter and went on the air in the fall of 1925. Although the station had a large enough transmitter to qualify as a Class B station, it was assigned Class A status and ordered to share its frequency (252 meters) with Western Union College, Le Mars, Iowa. Western Union would be broadcasting only once a week, while KMA was permitted to be on the air an hour at noon, an hour in the evenings, and two hours on Tuesday and Thursday evenings. Like so many other stations, KMA didn't stick to the letter of the law about these hours.

Shenandoah was a town with two major (although Class A) radio stations. The Henry Field Seed Company had beaten KMA to the punch and gotten on the air earlier with KFNF. Now the two friendly competitors were next assigned the same channel (461 meters). Each station would broadcast for an hour or two, then go off the air to let the other one broadcast. To get around this sharing, the two stations looked around, found different little-used spots on

1927 Zenith; model 11; walnut veneer; original price $110.00 (courtesy Zenith Radio Corp.).

1926
MODEL

$60.00

1926 Somerset; model 5.

1928 Grebe; model Synchrophase A-C Six; mahogany cabinet with burled walnut panel; original price $197.50.

A radio-clock to straighten out the confusion of time zones. It could be taken out of its cabinet and installed in the panel of the receiver.

50

1928 Grebe Synchrophase Five; mahogany cabinet with mahogany Bakelite panel; original price $105.00 (less tubes).

1929 A.C. Dayton Navigator; model AC-98; walnut table with inlaid veneer top; original price $98.00.

1929 A.C. Dayton Navigator; model AC-9960; walnut lowboy; matte, not gloss, finish; original price $148.50.

1929 A.C. Dayton Navigator; model AC-9970; wood lowboy with sliding doors; original price $165.00.

the dial, and each began broadcasting at nonassigned frequencies.

It was inevitable that Congress would have to vote power to some organization to regulate radio stations; it finally established the Federal Radio Commission (FRC) in 1927. Herbert Hoover, then Secretary of Commerce, warned against channel-jumping, citing, among others, KMA and KFNF of Shenandoah. The two stations decided that it was too risky to play around now and stayed at their newly assigned, weak frequency of 270 meters.

With the situation in Washington, KMA's new assignment didn't remain unchanged for long. In August 1927, KMA was offered a new frequency (740 kc) if they would share it with a Shreveport, Louisiana, station. So KMA had four different frequency assignments in three years and had shared time with a college station, a competing seed company station, and finally with a rabidly anti-FRC station in Louisiana. Unlike many others, KMA's story ended happily. They are still broadcasting today.

Networks

Network broadcasting started seriously in 1923. AT&T, owning as it did the telephone lines, began developing "chain broadcasting." Through experiments, AT&T found that the normal telephone lines were not good enough for radio broadcasting. Special circuits would be needed, as would cable developed for this purpose. On 31 July 1923, the first transcontinental hookup took place between San Francisco and New York, broadcasting Warren Harding's speech on his return from Alaska. At this point, chain broadcasting was a monopoly of AT&T, which had a rate card (ranging from $150 per hour for Davenport, Iowa, to $500 per hour for their flagship station, WEAF) that let the sponsor choose which cities it wished to cover with its advertising.

As chain broadcasting developed for AT&T, other companies became interested. RCA, General Electric, and Westinghouse formed a new company, the National Broadcasting Company, in 1926. This company bought out AT&T's stations, and network broadcasting, as we think of it, began on 15 November 1926. This network, anchored by WEAF (New York), became NBC's "Red" Network. By the first of the year, station WJZ (Newark) led the "Blue" network, which was the second NBC network.

A question always arises about how NBC named its networks. "Red" and "Blue" aren't the sort of names we might expect. There are two different stories about how the naming took place, both of them plausible. According to one, radio engineers knew it wouldn't be good to send out a "Blue" network program on the

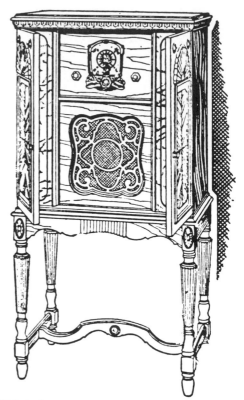

1929 A.C. Dayton Navigator; model AC-9990; wood highboy with cabinet doors; original price $188.00.

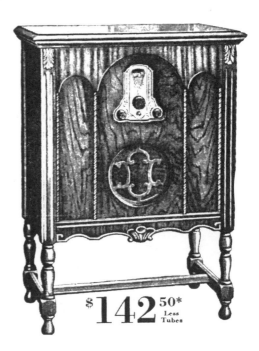

$142 50 Less Tubes*

1929 Stewart-Warner; model 900; "Approved Jacobean cabinet No. 35." Cabinet was made by Louis Hanson Co. (Chicago) or Burnham Phonograph Corp. (Los Angeles); original price $142.50 with cabinet.

1929 Fada; model 35-B; original price $255.00.

1929 Sparton; model Equasonne 301; ornate highboy; elaborate applied decoration on both the doors and the back panel; original price $274.00.

"Red" network, so there had to be some way to keep them straight in the control room. The plugs on the patch cords were accordingly colored red or blue to aid in keeping things straight.

The other story says that the names were decided on even before the network was on the air. A group of NBC personnel, sitting on a train and trying to figure out what stations were being linked with either of the anchor stations, used a red pencil line for the one and a blue line for the other.

The Columbia Broadcasting System didn't start with the resources of three major communications companies behind it. Its original name was the Columbia Phonograph Broadcasting System, since the Columbia Phonograph Record Company was the parent company. In the late 1920s, phonograph companies had lots of money but, due to radio, faltering sales. It was logical for them to consider getting into the new action. The first program of the Columbia Phonograph Broadcasting System was broadcast on 18 September 1927, but financial disaster soon loomed. The company owed AT&T $40,000 for rental of telephone lines, and the Columbia Phonograph Record Company declined to put any more money into the network. Some fast footwork found enough money to keep the network afloat until it was refinanced in 1929. At that time William S. Paley became its president. For the next five decades, CBS did not have financial problems.

It wasn't until World War II that someone realized that NBC was actually two networks and was thus subject to antimonopoly laws. Either the "Red" or the "Blue would have to be sold. The "Red" network was NBC's most important one, with the best shows and the strongest stations. Obviously, the "Blue" would be the one to go. As the time for the sale came, the two networks divided up stations, equipment, and personnel. The Blue Network, its legal name by this time, was sold in 1943 and became the American Broadcasting Company.

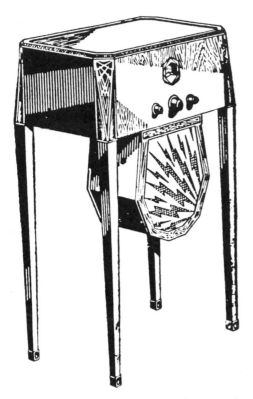

1929 Crosley; model 82-S; original price $160.00 (less tubes).

1929 Crosley; model 31-S; original price $56.50–$65.85. Legs were an additional $5.00.

1929 Crosley; model 34-S; original price $116.00–$126.00.

1929 Crosley; model 33-S; walnut veneer; original price $112.00 (less tubes).

1929 Colonial; model 32 Cavalier AC; original price $268.00.

1929 Caswell PowerTone; a phonograph designed to be placed on top of a radio and blend in with it; original price $49.50.

Fitting In and Looking Good

A radio is not only a technical gadget, it's something the owner has to live with every day. One of the problems that early battery sets had was their looks. There was no very satisfactory way to decorate around a long, narrow box which required a table, another box, or some floor space to stash the necessary batteries. Adding to the decorating worries was a good-sized horn speaker that stood on top of the radio or next to it.

Making the radio fit in with the rest of the living room was important. In a room already crowded with things, the cumbersome radio was a lot to cope with. As late as the 1920s, most people were still influenced by the Victorian front parlor, wherein every square inch of table and wall space was occupied. This crowding left rooms with a feeling of clutter.

57

1922 Magnavox horn speaker; type R-3.

TRADE MARK

Complete
$25

Atlas Radio-Reproduction Loud Speaker.

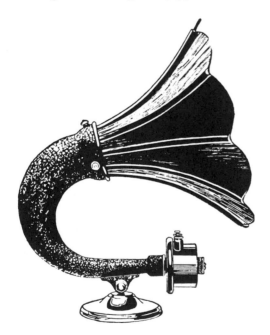

Amplion Dragon horn speaker; model AR-19. A classic of speaker design, the horn is made of wooden sections; original price $42.50.

Speakers

Very early on, attempts were made to improve the radio's looks. Speakers were the most noticeable part of the radio. Early speakers were horn speakers, using the technology that had gone into phonograph horns. (By the way, the same problems of decorating applied to phonographs; people were delighted when they could finally get enclosed horns and not have to cope with an external one.) The first magnetic cone speakers were produced around 1923, but it wasn't until 1927 that more cone speakers were sold than horn speakers.[3] It was hard to get around the fact that most horn speakers looked exactly like a horn — curved, perhaps, but still with a narrow neck and a large bell. Ordinary cone speakers resembled a bowl-shaped piece of heavy paper standing on edge and held in a metal ring. Sometimes the cone speaker was enclosed in some sort of a metal box that, round or square, looked remarkably like everyone else's metal box.

An attractive horn speaker was harder to design than an attractive cone speaker. Attempts were made to either glamorize the horn or to hide it. Probably the easiest way of hiding it was to build it into a speaker table. Now the horn was hidden in a long, narrow table, and there was enough space on the top of the table to place the radio itself. However, the speaker table was never as popular as the radio table. They look similar, but the difference is that a speaker table incorporates the speaker into the table, while a radio table holds the batteries on a shelf under the table. Until batteries disappeared, it was more important to find a place for them than to hide the speaker. The physical design of a horn speaker (long neck and large bell) also created problems for anyone trying to design a table around it. Probably this is why there are few speaker tables shown for horn speakers.

Another design possibility was to stop trying to hide the shape and, instead, to turn it into an asset. Take the horn, straighten its neck, cover the bell with a grille and grille cloth, and place it on the floor. Immediately it becomes a decorative column, 40 inch high or so, which might fit into the decor of a room better than a plain horn would.

Victorians had always been in love with seashells. In England, where trips to the sea were a recognized holiday even for working people, the overcrowded parlor often housed a seashell as a souvenir from the beach. (This wasn't as true in the United

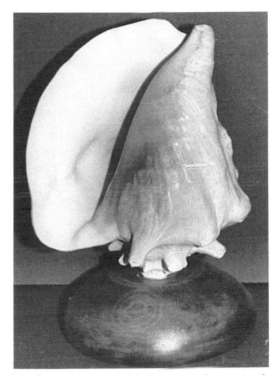

Shell speaker; possibly homemade. A single Brandes headphone is glued in the bottom.

States, where the distance to the beach from much of the country made trips there impractical.) Now thanks to innovation, it was possible to display a decorative seashell that also housed a speaker. Some of these speakers were installed in real conch shells. Because nature doesn't create shells to measure, the advertisements indicated size ranges (12 to 13 inches, for instance). There certainly would have been something striking about a mounted shell that stood 16 inch tall.

Perhaps the family wanted a more modern, less naturalistic shell and didn't want to spend money on a loudspeaker. Sheltone (the name certainly explained its product) made a smooth synthetic shell out of Pyralin (a DuPont celluloid) that saved the purchaser money, because he or she never had to buy a speaker at all. The Sheltone simply amplified the sound that

3. The best authority on horn and cone speakers is Floyd Paul. Much of the information in this section came from ads he has accumulated, as well as from articles he has written. His book is listed in "Further Helps."

1922 Madera horn speaker; made from papier-mâché by the American Art Mache Co.; original price $25.00.

Mellow Light
Beautiful Music
Amazing Radialamp
a Perfect Loud Speaker

Radialamp speaker. It used the "lamp base" and the shade to create a horn speaker. This strategy neatly hid an eyesore, since horn speakers tended to dominate a room.

1928 Sterling Vari-tone speaker; model R-2; original price $25.00.

came through the headphones of a set. Put the headphones in the correct location, and the shell shape did the rest.

If natural shells weren't formal enough, and plastic shells appeared a little cheap, Florentine Art Productions made a fantastic, artistic shell out of Italian gesso. Gesso is something like papier-mâché, only it is made with plaster instead of ground paper. It molds beautifully, and its properties allowed Florentine to come up with the "Voice from the Sky"—a Grecian figure with flowing robes standing in front of a shell-shaped horn. Available in walnut, mahogany, or ebony, this figure would certainly have been the focal point of any room—after all, it stood 24 inches high.

Another great way to hide a horn speaker was in a speaker lamp. Designed to look like a normal table lamp, many could actually be used as lamps, while others were simply speakers. These speaker lamps came in different styles to fit in with many different decorating styles. Most commonly, they seem to have had heavy fringe around the edge of the shade, making them suitable for the Victorian-style front parlor. At least one company (Bel-Canto) made a speaker lamp that would have fit well into a mission-style room. Others were typical 1920s lamps. A floor model version was the Speak-O-Lamp. It had an 11-inch deep shade, either hand-painted or silk-covered. Still another model, known as the "DeLuxe," had a pleated silk shade over a double silk-lined shade, trimmed with lace to match. But hiding your speaker did cost money; the DeLuxe model was $65.00.

Cone speakers were not as difficult to place in an average living room. Although they took up space, they were relatively shallow. Because of that, companies didn't seem to spend as much time trying to hide the cone speaker. They spent more effort using the cone shape for decorative purposes.

There were still speaker tables. A cone speaker could be easily attached with screws to a hole in the front of a speaker table. The grille and grille cloth made the speaker less noticeable. It also gave a place on which to put the radio, and, since tables could be found to harmonize with most living room styles, it kept the radio from overpowering the room.

Otherwise, most of the decoration involved the cone itself or the metal framework surrounding the cone. At its simplest, it meant painting some sort of design (a Greek key, for instance, or a fleur-de-lys) around the edge of the convex cone. Sometimes the decorations were more elaborate, such as the silhouette of a young woman with a branch or a painting of a full-rigged ship.

Ships seem to have gradually replaced shells as a major decorating theme. The full-rigged ship was more often seen cast with the metal frame of the speaker than painted on the cone. Tower, Vitalitone, and Timmons all decorated cones with sailing ships. The ships sail across space with the speaker cone as background.

1928 Sterling cone speaker; original price $75.00.

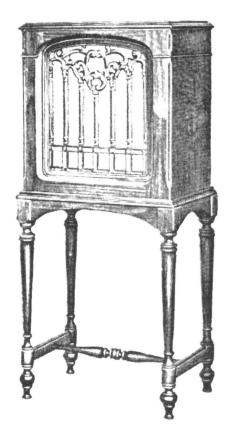

1928 Sterling speaker; floor model; original price $90.00.

Because a cone speaker is relatively flat, it was possible to hang a cone speaker on the wall, which was something that could never be done with a horn speaker. It also meant that a very large cone could be used.

The eventual solution to the decorating problem was to enclose the speaker in

Red Seal Map-Loop antenna. Wires are concealed between two maps. The maps give station locations. A creative attempt to hide an indoor antenna; original price $20.00.

Tatro. Cabinet model is CR-557, which may or may not be the radio model. An extremely plain lowboy. c. 1930.

1930 Gloritone; model 27. Gloritone took a totally different approach to building cathedral radios. Strong angles were used instead of pointed arches. There is another version of this model with rope-like trim (John Wilson).

1930 Philco; model 20B; one of the traditional Philco cathedrals (Ed and Irene Ripley).

1930 General Electric. The model is actually called "Lowboy." Because it's wider than the normal lowboy, it looks quite impressive.

1930 Crosley New Buddy. The front is repwood, a type of molded wood (Ed and Irene Ripley).

the same cabinet as the radio. When this happened, visible speakers disappeared until the advent of high fidelity in the late 1940s.

Radios

The earliest radios were table models. They were utilitarian-looking sets, with lots of knobs and dials, housed in a long wood box. Nothing too terrible, but nothing very glamorous, either. Sets became more simple, one-dial tuning came in, and tube voltages didn't need to be reset, but the cabinet remained the same. It was inevitable that someone would step into the gap and design a set to appeal to the women in the family.

In 1928 *Radio Retailing* was pointing out the advantages of having the customer buy a good cabinet. For one thing, everything could now fit inside the cabinet. The cabinets were being made of good wood (walnut, mahogany, oak, and gumwood) and were well constructed. The workmanship could be as good as that of conventional furniture, and hand-carving was possible. Radio cabinets could now harmonize with whatever decorating style the homemaker had. And, last but not least, customers could put $200 to $500 into a cabinet, knowing that a replacement radio could always go inside the same cabinet. (This view changed rapidly. In 1930, after the stock market crash, manufacturers were predicting that separate cabinets and speakers were no longer going to be strong sellers.)

Cabinets were generally being made by companies other than the radio manufacturer. For example, Atwater Kent made its first console set, the model 52, in 1928. Before that they had manufactured wood or metal table models only. If an earlier Atwater Kent shows up at an auction in a fancy wood cabinet, the first thought may be that someone is trying to pull a fast deal, but this isn't necessarily true. Even though

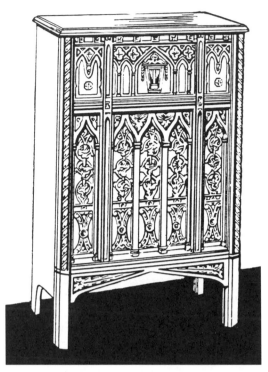

1930 Sentinel; model 15. "Gothic design, superbly ornamented"; original price $137.50 (less tubes).

THE ST. JAMES MODEL

1930 Stewart-Warner; St. James model; solid walnut front "with artistic genuine carving"; original price $197.50 (less tubes).

MODEL 11

1930 Sentinel; model 11; deco style; original price $130.00 (less tubes).

the company itself wasn't producing furniture, other companies were. They were even designing their cabinets to fit particular models of the Atwater Kent. In 1928 there were a number of ads in *Radio Retailing* in which Red Lion, Pooley, Bay View, and others advertised that their cabinets were designed to house the Atwater Kent. In fact, Red Lion advertised itself as "the authorized furniture for all Atwater Kent radios." Other cabinets were produced for sets of other manufacturers who were still making only table radios. Certain cabinet manufacturers created cabinets that still, today, aid in selling a radio. A Pooley cabinet, for instance, is often mentioned in ads.

Left to right: 1936 Zenith chairside, model Portola, manufactured by United Air Cleaners for Zenith. 1931 model 64, original price $370.00. 1930 model 40A; original price $850.00. (Notice push-button tuning to right of dial on these two models.) 1929 model 60, original price $145.00 (courtesy Zenith Radio Corp.).

1932 General Motors; model 252. A sliding door pulls up to cover the dials when not in use. It's an unusual radio because the speaker faces out the bottom of the set.

The cabinet most prominently mentioned nowadays is the Kiel table. The Kiel table is six-legged and six-sided. It usually housed an Atwater Kent (either model 55 or 60) in the front skirt of the table, although it could handle other brands as well. The radio was hidden behind a door; when the door dropped down, the radio controls were within easy reach. The speaker was inside the table, pointed down towards the floor, giving a smooth, nondirectional sound. The left rear leg housed the antenna and the ground wires, while the right rear leg housed the power cord. The ads truthfully said, "No unsightly wires." With a marquetry design in the hexagonal top, these tables are still attractive pieces of furniture.

Many companies had decided by this time to sell their radios in their own cabinets. Various elaborate cabinets were designed. Splitdorf had marketed one of their radios in 1928 in a model called "The Winthrop," which is a corner secretary including a desk, radio, and bookcase that retailed for $600. Sparton had highboys that not only had applied pressed-wood trim on the doors covering the cabinet, but also had a panel down the back to the floor, also with pressed-wood trim.

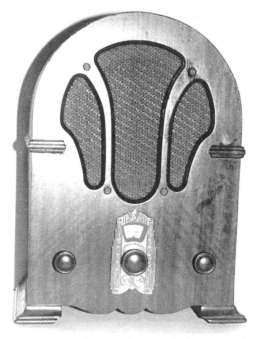

1931 RCA; model R5, the "Radiolette"; cathedral style (Ed and Irene Ripley).

1933 Philco; model 81; a simple cathedral (Ed and Irene Ripley).

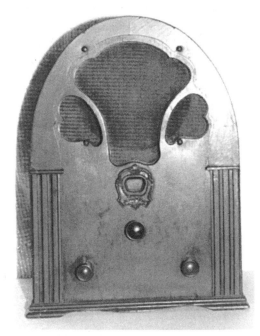

1932 Crosley; model 125; cathedral radio (Ed and Irene Ripley).

Radio as furniture was disappearing in late 1929. The first of the midget sets (midget by the standards of the day) were arriving. Cathedrals were coming into style. Now that everyone had a radio, there wasn't the desire to have the set as a showpiece. The neighbors weren't being invited in any more — they had their own sets. The Depression meant that radio became a workhorse and was no longer a stylish thoroughbred. Utility was more important than looks.

The fine cabinets from the 1920s didn't disappear, however. People didn't throw good cabinets like those away. A radio was used until it broke, and then the cabinet was saved. Sometimes it was saved in a barn, where the moisture and mice didn't do it any good. With luck it stayed in the house. Often it was converted into a bookcase or a bar or a desk. So often one of these radio cabinets shows up at auctions now, but minus a radio.

Radio table. Note the batteries in a drawer that opens from the front.

1933 Philco; model 16B. The cathedral arch has disappeared, leaving only a slightly pointed top. This set is almost a console, with 11 tubes and a 10" speaker.

1928 Grebe power amplifier table; shown with the Grebe Synchrophase A-C Six; original price $227.00 (without tubes or radio set).

1928; model 820. Grebe sold this impressive cabinet to fit any of their radios; original price $97.00 (console only).

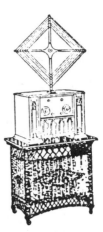

Wicker radio table. The batteries were hidden behind the solid wicker panel.

1928 Grebe speaker table; model 2250; shown with the Grebe Synchrophase Seven A-C; original price $24.50 (table only, no speaker or radio).

When Was That Radio Made?

THE best way to date a radio is, of course, to know the model number of the particular set. With this information, it is moderately easy to come up with an approximate date. Through the use of service manuals, instruction books, and advertisements in magazines, a given radio can usually be dated to within one year. The qualification "usually" covers those exceptions that inevitably occur. Some companies reused the same model number for totally unrelated radios two or three times over a period of years. In this case, a general idea of the age of the set helps immensely. Some brands or models never seem to have made it into the service manuals, eliminating one of the best dating sources and leaving rough dating as the only possibility. Advertisements were built around specific, highly salable radios and ignored the vast majority of run-of-the-mill sets. But, all things being equal, manuals, instructions, and advertisements should permit dating of the vast majority of radios.

1934 Powertone; sold by Reliable Radio Co., New York; original price $9.95 (4-tube); $12.95 (5-tube). (Both prices without tubes).

1934 Reliable; Treasure Chest model; sold by Reliable Radio Co., New York; original price $9.50 (less tubes).

1934 General Electric auto radio; model B-52; operates at both 6 volts and 110 volts; brown crackle finish metal. This radio could be placed on the front seat; the dial would face the driver.

1934 Grunow; model 750.

1934 Philco; model 84B. The later cathedrals tended to modify the pointed arch (Ed and Irene Ripley).

1935 American Bosch; model 604. Note that the center knob is not original.

Trying to make a rough guess is more difficult. Like anything else for the house, designs came and went, overlapping each other and always trying to be new and different. In spite of this, it is possible to come up with some general guidelines. Why is this important? Well, in the case of a model showing up several times during a company's production, it makes it easier for anyone fixing the radio to find the service information. Or someone may come up to you and describe a radio available for sale. Knowing how to roughly date a radio from a verbal description saves unnecessary trips to see unsuitable radios. At an auction, a clever buyer can sometimes pick up a good buy simply by having a better understanding of how old, and possibly how valuable, in general, a certain radio may be. In none of these cases is an exact figure essential — a good ballpark figure gives a solid place to start.

The following rough dates for various styles are exactly that — rough. They make no claims to accuracy. All rough dating must take into account that eras overlapped. Battery sets were finished by the 1940s, but — . That's right, there were some made into the 1950s. Highboys went out around 1932, but someone didn't tell RCA, who made one as late as 1934. Nothing is cut-and-dried. Practically every style started before there was a demand for it and lasted until after most people had switched to something different. No matter what a style is, or how popular, people become tired with it. Change is different and exciting and has always been a part of the radio industry.

1935 Crosley; model 555; AM/SW.

St. Regis miniature cathedral; no model identification; no year known.

Garod; model 769; AM/SW; push-button; mid-1930s.

1935 American Bosch; paper label is missing. This unique set was sold by the German American Bund to raise money for the 1936 Berlin Olympics.

GEC; model 8336; made by General Electric Co. (England): c. 1936.

1935 Coronado; model 686; 3-band.

Dials

Multi-dial sets. Multi-dial sets were common from the beginning of radio up until 1927. In all but the one-tube sets, two or more dials were necessary to adequately tune in the radio. Generally, there were three dials for tuning in the station, and two knobs, one that controlled the detector filament and one that controlled the filaments of other tubes. The tuning scale wasn't marked with the 550 to 1600 kc we use today. Instead, there was a linear scale (0 to 100) on each dial. All of the dials would be set at approximately the same place, but not exactly. For instance, one dial might be at 20, the second at 22, and the third at 18. To avoid the nuisance of fiddling with all the dials each time the station was tuned in, and trying to remember exactly where each was set, a logbook was kept with the radio. In it the listener noted the numbers where the station had come in and started with those numbers the next

time. It still might require a little more tinkering to come up with a clear station, but at least it gave the listener a close place to start from. (By the way, some early radios still have their logbooks. Whether used or unused, these books are a plus when buying a set.)

One-dial tuning. One-dial tuning began to come in around 1925. As can be seen, there was an overlap of several years from the first use of this feature to the time when multi-dial tuning was out. One-dial tuning simplified radio. It made it possible to tune in a station by ear. Remembering the station location using one number was much easier than keeping three numbers straight.

Airplane dial. The airplane dial appeared around 1934. This feature was reminiscent of airplane instruments, with a round dial housing a pointer that went around in a circle. The design was still around after World War II. Zenith made a design statement out of the airplane dial by

1936 Zenith; model 6B129; a 6-volt farm radio.

1936 RCA; model 13K; 4-band console.

1936 Crosley; model 167; cathedral radio (Ed and Irene Ripley).

1936 Grunow; model 1291, chassis 12B; teledial; 12-tube, 4-band (Gene Harris Auctions)

1936 Airline; model 62-425; wood table model with decorative grille (Ed and Irene Ripley).

1936 Silvertone; model 4500; black Bakelite; first plastic radio offered by Sears (Ed and Irene Ripley).

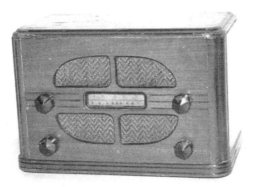

1936 General Electric; model E-52.

1937 Wells-Gardner; model 108A1-704; wood table with telephone dial.

1937 Clarion; model 691; wood table with telephone dial; original price $49.95.

making theirs very large (dominating the entire front of the set) and coloring it black. Big Zeniths are easily recognized by this feature. If big and round was stylish, then the new style would have to be very different. And it was.

Slide-rule dial. The slide-rule dial became popular about 1938. This dial is a long rectangle, with the pointer moving straight across the scale to mark the stations. The slide-rule dial is still found on stereo systems today.

Telephone dial tuning. Telephone dial tuning appeared in 1936. Put a finger in the hole, just like a telephone dial, and turn the dial until it stopped; the station would then be tuned in. It seemed much more up-to-date than turning a knob and watching a pointer move. It was soon replaced with easier to use push buttons.

1937 Clarion; model 770; AM/SW; wood table; original price $19.99.

1937 Troy; model 100; wood table with telephone dial; original price $32.50.

Floor Models

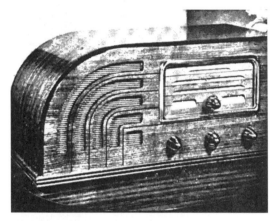

1937 General Electric; model F-63; wood table with strong Deco lines; louvered dial.

Floor models have gone through several styles. There was the highboy of the 1920s, the lowboy of the 1920s and 1930s, and the to-the-floor console of the 1930s and 1940s. Another striking style was the long, horizontal console of the 1940s. There were variations to each of these major styles.

Highboy. The height of the highboy's popularity was 1927 to 1932. The highboy is, by definition, a radio on legs that are approximately one-half the height of the radio. (This is not what the term means in the antique furniture field. As with many terms, manufacturers took highboy to mean what they wanted it to mean. There was no industry standard defining a highboy.) A highboy usually had four legs. It wasn't until it looked like radio was here to stay, and particularly after AC radios became common and found a place in the living room, that people began putting money into an important-looking cabinet, rather than into the radio itself.

Lowboy. The lowboy style began at approximately the same time as the highboy style. These two styles are the first of the

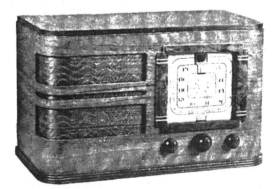

1937 RCA; model 87-T; AM/SW; wood table; original price $49.95.

non-table, floor model styles to become popular. The lowboy continued in popularity longer than the highboy, lasting until about 1934, although sets were built like this until the end of the 1930s. The lowboy is defined as having legs that are anywhere from 6 inches high to half the height of the cabinet. A lowboy has four or more legs. Many had six legs, and there is at least one model (Stewart-Warner, model 51) that had five. The vast majority of early floor model radios were lowboys. They don't all look alike, since the proportions of the cabinet to the leg height can be very different.

Highboy or lowboy with doors. Highboys and lowboys with doors were popular between 1927 and 1931. Doors to hide the radio were popular at the beginning of the radio era, just as they were with early television, when many sets came with doors to close the screen off from the room. Later on, when television sets became commonplace, no one felt the need to hide them, and the same appears to be true of radios.

Console. The console, or what we consider as the floor model, became popular around 1932. The console has sides that go to the floor or feet less than 4 inches high. It continued to be popular through the 1940s. The word *console* in the 1920s could refer to all floor radios in general, but, by the end of the 1930s, it had come to mean this style. Because of World War II, when all radio-building for the home ended, these radios stayed around until close to 1950.

Console radio-phonograph. Console radio-phonographs were popular from just before World War II, approximately 1938, to 1942. The phonograph was built into a console radio, either rolling out to play or, more usually, tipping out. Remember that for this era the phonograph would

1937 Arvin Phantom Prince; model 1237; wood console; original price $99.50

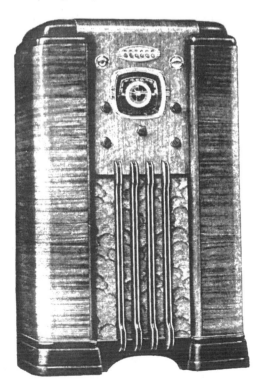

1937 Sparton; model 1068; wood console with push-button tuning.

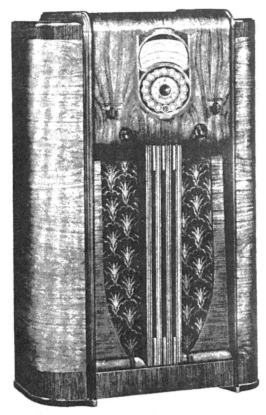

1937 Fairbanks-Morse; model 9AC-4; wood console with automatic tuning; original price $105.00.

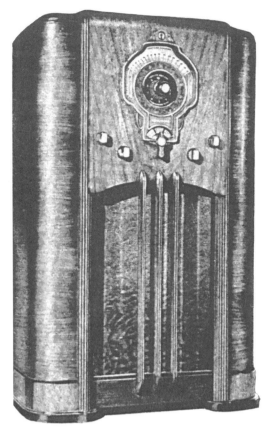

1937 Motorola; model 10Y; wood console; original price $99.95.

1937 Belmont; model 602; Bakelite table. An interesting grill is carried down the back, making this a radio that could show from either side.

1937 RCA-Victor; model 811K; wood console with automatic tuning; original price $150.00.

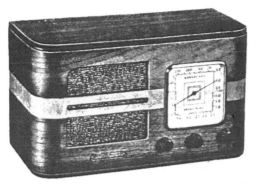

1937 Freed-Eisemann; model FE-28; wood table; AM/SW; original price $29.95.

1939 Firestone Air Chief; model S-7403-4; small wood radio with angled wood grille.

1937 Zenith; model 6S229; AM/2SW.

General Motors portable; late 1930s; called a "Plug in portable." The middle control switches from AC to battery operation.

1937 Trav-Ler; no model information; AM/SW (Ed and Irene Ripley).

be a 78-rpm record changer only. If it's a three-speed changer, either the changer has been replaced or the radio was made from 1948 on.

Phonographs had been built into radios since the 1920s. They appeared in highboys, lowboys, and some massive affairs that seem to defy mere words to describe them. However, unlike the radio-phonograph consoles of the late 1930s, they never were a dominant style. If one of them shows up, date it by its cabinet style.

Horizontal radio-phonograph console. Although the horizontal style was around from before World War II, it became important after the war. These radio-phonographs had the phonograph side-by-side with the radio, making them as wide as

1937 Zenith; model 5-R-236; chairside; original price $29.95.

1937 Philco cathedral; model 37-93. By this time, cathedrals had become much simpler. The peak was gone, and so was much of the wood trim (Arie Breed).

1937 General Electric; model G-50; wood table radio with teledial tuning.

1937 Crosley; model 566; farm set. The impressive grille and the very small dial make this an interesting set.

1937 Stewart Warner; model R-180A; side speakers.

or wider than they were high. They came in all sorts of styles to harmonize with the living room. Virtually the same arrangement could fit into a blond modern living room or a Chippendale room. All it took was a change of wood color and trim.

Chairside. The chairside which was popular from 1936 to 1941, just prior to World War II, started with Philco in 1933 and gained popularity quickly. By the middle of the 1930s it was an important style. The chairside put the dial right in the table, making changing a program exceptionally easy to do. This style is defined by its function (chairside) rather than the way it looks. Chairside models came in rectangular shapes, as well as oval and semicircular ones. Bookshelves or magazine storage was often built into the chairside cabinet.

Table Radios

1937 Crosley. A logical step for a company producing both refrigerators and radios was this — a refrigerator with a radio built in.

It all began with table radios, and, long after television has become dominant, it is table radios that we still use today. They have lasted this long because of their immense practicality.

Slant-front wood table radios. The slant-front table radio, popular from 1924 to 1926, was an attempt to dress up the original plain wooden table radio. Looking at pictures of the early sets, it isn't surprising that there was an attempt to glamorize them. There was nothing exciting about the cabinets of most of the early sets. They were sensible wood boxes designed to hold the necessary apparatus to permit radio listening. In a slant-front set, the panel (of Bakelite, Formica, or the like) was angled back from the front of the set instead of being set in vertically. The angling made the set look dressier. (Philco revived this style for both large table and console models in the

1937 Stromberg-Carlson; model 249-R; fancy, unusual, semicircular Deco design; original price $197.50.

1940s. Again, the general style of the radio itself will clearly show whether it is from the 1940s or the 1920s.)

Metal table radios. Metal table radios appeared for two different eras: 1926 to 1928 and 1940 to 1948. The earliest ones were the bright idea of Atwater Kent. He was fascinated by the new technology of forming steel, and he couldn't see why it shouldn't be adapted for radios. Decidedly it made a statement that radio was modern, a technology come of age. It had a real benefit, as well, in that it provided shielding which allowed better performance and less interference. The cabinet was simply a metal box in which the radio chassis was placed, fitted with a metal cover. The finish was often brown crinkled paint. Crosley, RCA, and Philco all produced metal sets. The style only lasted for three or four years.

In 1928, for one year only, Philco decorated its plain metal sets with hand-painted floral designs to appeal to women. Their ad states that they "are offered in a variety of hand-decorated, softly modulated, two-tone effects... which [are] enhanced with color effects by Mlle. Messaros, one of the foremost colorists in the decorative arts. The colors are applied *by hand* under her personal direction."

The later metal table radios (from the 1930s and 1940s) were midget sets, usually cheap and always small, that looked like normal radios. They are very similar to the small plastic sets of the same period. Where the earlier metal sets had removable tops to permit servicing the radio chassis, the later ones slid the chassis in through an open back.

Wood midget sets. Wood midget sets were available from 1930 on. These sets were shaped like a normal horizontal table radio. They became popular because their timing was right. The first ones were manufactured just before the depression. When money became tight, the midget sets continued to sell well, while sales of the large, impressive sets sagged. In 1931, midgets were still considered stopgaps by the larger

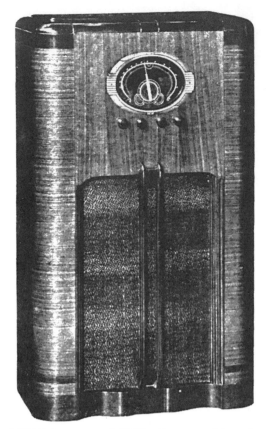

1937 Belmont; model 840; all wave, with tuning eye included in dial design; wood console.

manufacturers. Predictions were made that "midget radios will never replace the console receiver as the major radio installation." As time went on, midgets became smaller and smaller. Midget sets from 1930 would seem to be very large table radios to people in the late 1950s. Usually the sets were varnished or lacquered, although some of them were painted. (These are the radios considered as traditional, inexpensive radios by people over age fifty. Under fifty, the set considered traditional would probably be a plastic table radio.)

Cathedral. Cathedral sets came on the popular scene around 1930 to 1934. The cathedral style arrived in the nick of time, just before the Depression wiped out the market for more prestigious sets. Cathedral sets weren't expensive at the time, and

1937 Grunow; model 1183; wood console with telephone dial; original price $149.95.

1938 Philco; model 38-7.

so could substitute for the more expensive lowboy. They were certainly more impressive than the plain wood table radios. Because they stayed popular for many years, there were modifications in the style. Some versions had very pointed, Gothic arches; others had rounded arches for which the basic proportions (height to width) remained the same as the pointed-arch models; and there were models for which the curve of the top was completely removed and straight lines were substituted. The almost square (height equals width), rounded-top beehive (1933) is usually included in this category. In all cases, there was a lot of overlapping of these substyles. The manufacturers, by the way, never referred to them as "Cathedrals." Instead they called them "Gothic."

Cathedrals not only looked impressive, but they could also sound that way. Some of the large cathedrals, such as the Philco 90B, had the same radio chassis as was used in the large consoles.

Upright wood table. Upright wood tables appeared between 1933 and 1940. Taller than they are wide, these, too, include many substyles. Rounded corner tombstones, stacked-top Deco sets, even cathedrals would fit into this classification. The emphasis was on the "modern" look of an upright table radio as contrasted with the "Gothic" look of the cathedral. By World War II, the upright wood table had been replaced in turn by the conventional horizontal wood and plastic table radios. Once money was freer than during the Depression, anybody who wanted to buy an impressive radio bought a console instead.

Table radio-phonograph. Introduced in about 1938 and lasting in popularity until 1950, table radio-phonographs were large square boxes that held both a 78-rpm phonograph and a radio. After 1948, they might have a two- or three-speed changer instead of a single speed 78-rpm one. Occasionally Bakelite, they usually had wood cabinets. They were designed to go into a living room or a recreation room and look nice, while not taking up valuable floor

1938 Emerson; model BA-199; brown Bakelite.

1938 Setchell-Carlson; cloth-covered portable case; AC/battery operation.

1938 Howard; model 368; 3-band.

1938 RCA; model 86T; 3-band; curved wood.

1938 Philco; model 38-8.

space. High-fidelity systems eventually replaced these sets.

Plastic table radios. Plastic table radios have been around since 1933. Plastic was still a novelty when it began to be used in radios. Plastic radios were first introduced in 1931. Although at this time plastics had been around for fifty years, they hadn't been usable for radio sets. The earliest plastics (celluloid, for instance) would soften and melt when they got hot, which wouldn't do for a radio, in which the tubes produced much heat. The advent of thermoset plastics was a boon for radios. Included in this group of plastics are Bakelite, Catalin, and urea. These plastics, unlike some others, won't soften or melt in heat. Even leaving them on the back shelf of a car on a 100-degree day won't faze them. Once set, the plastic retains its shape until it is hot enough to simply burn, and it takes a bonfire to get that much heat. Plastics became the set of choice for a number of reasons. First, molding a cabinet of plastic is cheaper than the manual work of gluing a cabinet together and putting a finish on it. Second, the particular properties of thermoset plastics meant that the heat buildup inside a tube set was no longer a problem. Third, because various plastics could be used in making radios, there were a lot of colors that could actually be molded into the radio. These colors may alter with age, but they won't chip off the way paint does. (Bakelite radios in light colors are painted, though, and have all the same problems with chipping that painted wood cabinets have.)

Styling Details

Sometimes it is the little things that help to date a set. So often a cabinet style lasted over most of a decade or more, but many of the styling details were around for only a year or so. This frequent change in detailing makes dating a set relatively easy.

Pressed-wood fronts. Pressed-wood fronts were available in 1933 and 1934. Crosley loved using pressed-wood fronts on its table radios, giving a lot of detail and interest to an otherwise plain set. This type of

1939 Sentinel; model 195ULT. This is a butterscotch catalin radio with burgundy trim. Pushbuttons are on the top on the right side.

1939 General Electric; model HJ-624; push-button.

1939 Stewart Warner; model 03-5C1-WT.

1939 Majestic; model 1A-59.

1938 Zenith chairside; model 7-S-240; walnut finish, large black dial; 3-band (courtesy Zenith Radio Corp.).

1939 Zenith; model 8S463. Here is one of the reasons Zenith has a reputation for making big, impressive console radios. It's a large radio that becomes the focal point of the room.

1939 Zenith portable; chassis no. 5416; battery only.

detailing had been used earlier, in the 1920s, when additions of carved or pressed-wood moldings had made highboys and lowboys more expensive-looking. But rarely had the pressed-wood design dominated the set as it did with Crosley's.

Deco. The Deco style was popular from 1933 to World War II. This style was inspired by the Chicago World's Fair (1933–1934), with reinforcement of the style found at the New York World's Fair (1939–1940). The style had started in Europe with an exhibition in 1925, but the Chicago World's Fair popularized it in the United States. While the style didn't dominate radio design of this period, it did make an impressive statement. Deco radios reflected the spirit of the Deco movement. They could be angular cathedrals, or stacked-top upright radios, or radios with wrap-around modern grilles. They were made in both plastic and wood. Radio design relied much on fronts curved boldly into one or both sides, emphatic straight lines, either vertical or horizontal, and strong contrasts of color (such as chrome against dark wood, two-tone plastic, or two-tone wood). For a short period, strongly designed chrome grilles were used. Probably the best adjective to describe the Deco style is *bold*.

Chrome-plated grille. Chrome-plated grilles, available in 1934, primarily had one year of popularity. Extremely Deco-styled, this detail seems to have been inspired by the Chicago World's Fair.

Mirror radios. Another short-lived Deco fad (1935–1936), mirror radios ranged from mirrors screwed on to flat panels to the highly collectible Sparton "Bluebird" and "Nocturne," in which the radio was of secondary importance to a large

1939 Arvin; model 502. This radio is in a metal cabinet that looks very much like the plastic cabinets of 1939.

1939 Zenith; model 6D414; brown Bakelite; inverted Bakelite chassis.

1939 Setchell Carlson; model 588.

1939 Belmont; model 636; brown Bakelite.

1939 Firestone; model S-7403-8; AM/2SW.

round mirror. In the 1930s colored mirrors were popular, and many of these radios came with blue or peach mirrors. Although Sparton is the best-known company that produced mirrored radios, there were many other companies producing them as well.

Green tuning eyes. Green tuning eyes were a characteristic feature of many radios from 1935 until World War II. The round, green tuning eye became popular shortly after its invention in 1935. It was found on middle- and higher-priced radios; in fact, it was almost standard. The more exactly a station was tuned in, the closer the green lights came to touching each other. For many people, the green eye is the single feature they remember from the sets they grew up with.

1939 Airline; model 62-376; AM/SW; 6-volt battery.

1939 Firestone Air Chief; model R-3051; 2-band (David Tuttle).

1940 Philco; model 40-120. The handle is for convenience only. This is not a battery radio.

1940 RCA Victor; model 45X11; brown Bakelite (Ed and Irene Ripley).

1940 Stewart-Warner; model 0751H (Ed and Irene Ripley).

1940 RCA Radiola 520; maple finish (Ed and Irene Ripley).

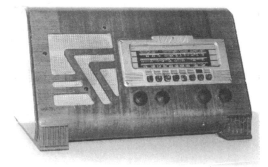

1940 Philco; model 40-155; 3-band table radio.

Continental; model 1000; striking lines; c. World War II (Ed and Irene Ripley)

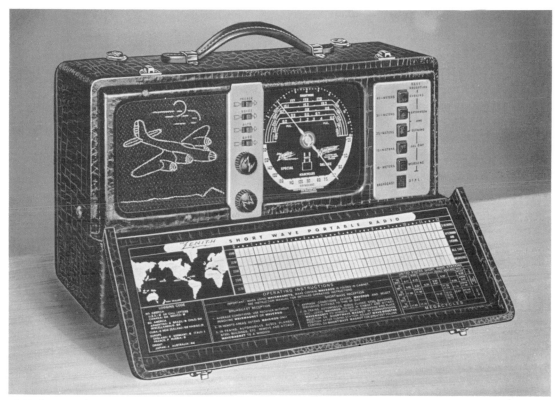

1940-41 Zenith Trans-Oceanic portable; model 7-G-605; black leatherette (courtesy Zenith Radio Corp.).

1941 General Electric; model L-916; large console with push-buttons; AM/2SW.

1941 Zenith; model 5F134; farm (6-volt) set; AM/3SW bands.

1940 Philco Transitone; model PT33; brown Bakelite (Ed and Irene Ripley).

Airline; c. 1940; made by Belmont (Ed and Irene
Ripley).

1941 Knight; model B10517; sold by Allied Radio. This radio had no identification, since the
decal under the push-buttons had disappeared
sometime in the past. It was only by chance that
it was identified.

1941 Airline; model 62-476; available in both
white and brown Bakelite; complete with both a
tuning eye and a telephone dial. There are
leaves embossed on the top, and pillars on the
sides (Ed and Irene Ripley).

Airline. There is no model identification on this
radio; the paper label generally found has disappeared. c. 1940 (John Wilson).

1940 Motorola; model 41A; brown Bakelite.
Grill looks like an auto's; 1½ and 90 volts. This
particular radio was given a battery eliminator
sometime in its past.

1941 Crosley; probably model 52-TG (label is partially gone); (John Wilson).

1941 Admiral; model 4204-B6; interesting lyre-shape grille.

1941 Zenith portable; model 6G-601-M; cloth-covered.

1941 RCA Radiola; model 512; wood table.

1941 Airline; model 14WG-806A. Curving the grille out from the front of the radio adds design interest.

1941 Zenith; model 6R631; tone controls on left, station push-buttons on right.

1941 Airline; model 14BR-522A; white plastic radio with simple lines.

1942 General Electric; model JCP-562. Cabinet has been refinished.

1942 Philco; model 42-KR3; white painted wood radio.

1942 General Electric; model L-641; AM/SW (John Wilson).

1942 Philco; model 42-321 (John Wilson).

1941 Emerson portable; model FU-427.

1942 Philco; model 42-350. The large curves give it a heavy modern look.

1942 Musicaire; model 942T; wood table; Coast-to-Coast Stores brand.

1946 Airline; model 54BR-1506A. The dramatic dial makes this ivory Bakelite radio stand out (Ed and Irene Ripley).

1946 Zenith; model 6D029; one of the most unusual shapes found for a dial (John Wilson).

1946 Farnsworth; model ET-067. The only distinction this wood radio has are the grooves on the top of the case. The log scale on the dial gives the impression that this set has more than just the broadcast band.

Musicaire; model unknown; straightforward wood table radio with interesting grille; probably made around World War II (pre- or postwar).

Buying That Special Radio:
Where to Look and What to Look For

ANYONE hunting for a radio wants two things—the perfect radio and the lowest possible price. Fortunately for collectors, not everyone considers the same radio to be "perfect." One person wants a breadboard, whose price is already high, while another wants a console, which is still relatively low-priced. Sometimes, however, everyone wants the same set. At present, Catalin radios are the radios everyone wants, and their prices have skyrocketed. Several years ago, you could get one for $5 to $10; they were considered cheap plastic radios. Now they are hard to find at any price.

Everyone does want to find that special radio cheaply. Here are some hints about where to look for radios and what sort of prices you may have to pay. (Remember, the prices in the price guide are based on radios that are in working condition and are being sold in the retail market.)

1946 RCA; model 65X1.

1946 Philco radio-phonograph; model 46-1201. Record is placed in drawer in bottom.

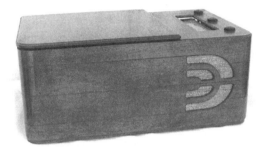

1946 Puritan radio-phonograph; model 503.

1946 Fada; model 1000. This Catalin radio has become highly collectible in the last few years.

1946 Den Chum; made by Wilmak; model W-446. Although it would appear that the top radio is the earlier model, this isn't true. The knobs on the bottom radio have detents and only tune the stations that are preset on the bottom of the radio.

1946 Westinghouse; model H-130.

Where to Look

Friends, neighbors, and relatives. Most often radios from this source will have come out of the attic or basement, and the owner considers them surplus. Because you know the owner, there is a good chance that the price will be low. The condition of the cabinet may be only fair, but if it doesn't cost much it may be a good deal anyway. Up to a point, the same goes for the electronics, but if the insides look really terrible (extensive mouse nests or wires that don't go anywhere), the radio may not be a good buy at any price.

Garage sales/yard sales. The biggest problem with trying to find things cheaply at garage sales and yard sales is that there is a wide variety of sellers. They range from people who are trying to clean out things they don't want and just hoping to pick up some extra cash to people who are professional dealers in everything but name. There are garage sales where the prices are as high as those found in antique shops.

It may take visiting a lot of garage sales to find the right radio. Many sellers won't have any radios, while others will consider theirs almost priceless. Some people swear by shopping at these sales, while others swear at the time they've spent with too few results.

One smart idea is to plan your garage sale trip in a logical route, through older neighborhoods. Most young couples won't have moved radios into an already-crowded starter home. Read the local newspaper ads to find out who's having garage sales and where. Spotting the most common days for sales saves time and gas. Near a city, driving around and watching for those cardboard signs nailed to light posts will lead you to many sales, even some you might have missed in the paper.

Auctions. There is no way to predict prices realized at an auction. The prices depend on so many things: how many people

1946 Arvin; model 544 (Ed and Irene Ripley).

1946 Silvertone; model 07025; brown Bakelite; Deco.

1946 Musicaire; model 576. Some people claim it looks like a miniature console; others think it resembles a jukebox. Sold by Coast-to-Coast Stores; same model as the Detrola model 576-1-6A.

come, whether there is another auction that is draining off many of the bidders, what the weather is like, and how long it looks like it will take to get to the things you want.

At an auction, find out what guarantees are given by the auctioneer. If you can't talk to the auctioneer, ask the clerk. Some auctions guarantee an electrical item to be working. If you plug it in and it doesn't work, you can immediately bring it back to be resold. Before you test the radio, however, check the line cord. *If the line cord is in bad condition, do not plug it in.* Assume that you're going to have to replace the cord before you do anything else. Auctioneers often say that the radio was working before the sale. "Working," in their parlance, means that there was sound coming from the set. Sound from the set does not mean that the radio actually picks up stations. It may still be that the radio doesn't receive any stations, or the sound may mean that the radio picks up only the strongest local station. Don't count on more than that.

Radio swap meets. If you live near a medium-size city, there is a good chance that it has a local radio club, that runs swap meets/parking lot sales periodically. Because the members of the club are often tinkerers, you may find the radios are not working. The sellers will tell you this, and often give you hints for repairing the radio. Many times the radios are duplicate sets, so the seller has little ego tied up in them and therefore the prices are often reasonable.

The question is how to find a radio club. There are two practical methods. One is to contact the public library in your city. Libraries usually have a list of local organizations. With luck, there will be a radio club listed. The other method is to write to the Antique Wireless Association, Inc. (Holcomb, NY 14469) to get a list of clubs nearby and their current addresses.

Flea markets. Flea markets can be a good source for radios. If there are lots of dealers, there's a good chance that someone will have brought along several old sets.

1946 General Electric; model 321.

1946 Sparton; model 7-46.

1946 Trav-Ler; model 5066; brown plastic (Ed and Irene Ripley).

100

1946 Artone; model R-1046-U; white painted Bakelite with aqua dial; identical to an Olympic model.

National Radio Institute; model 7AN2. Kit was probably built as part of a home radio course. Cabinet is homemade (John Wilson).

1946 Crosley; cabinet marked 63TJWC; label missing—probably model 66TC; "Victory" model.

Prices will generally be higher than at garage sales because the dealer has an idea of what his merchandise is worth. There is some leeway on prices. Trying to get a better price from a dealer is well worth the effort. If the dealer says no, you're no worse off then if you hadn't tried. If the price can be substantially lowered, you'll be happy. Flea market dealers like bargaining. A good idea is to make a fair offer. It may be accepted, or you may agree to some compromise price.

Mail order. You'll have to get one of the radio magazines to find out about mail order radios. It seems that more and more radio collectors are advertising their sets this way. It can be difficult to tell the real condition of a set by reading a classified ad though. Some dealers print a list that tells what you'll find—scratches, repairs, tubes missing, and so on. Others use one of the various grading systems.

Numerous attempts have been made to standardize grading of radios, but no grading system has been universally accepted. The Antique Wireless Association tried on two different occasions. "Excellent" continued to mean perfect from 1979 to 1983, and "Very Good" meant that the finish could have some scratches. But when it came to the poorer radios, the grading moved upwards during those four years. What had been "Poor" now became "Fair" (extensive repairs needed), and "Fair" became "Good" (refinished cabinet). A controversy developed in 1984 when another system was suggested in which "Mint" meant perfect, "Excellent" meant a scratched finish, "Very Good" included refinished cabinets, and "Good" meant extensive repairs would be necessary. Of course this suggested system led to still more suggestions. One system would have coded in virtually all electrical and cabinet flaws; it had the problem of being too complicated. This confusion is why one mail order dealer prefers to describe a radio in

1946 Motorola portable; model HS7; cloth-covered.

1946 Temple; model F616; wood table.

1946 Emerson; model 520; swirled brown plastic, white front; aqua dial; not original knobs.

plain English. Here's an example from one of the dealer's sales lists: "PHILCO 1949 #49-602 hand-bag–shaped 3-way portable, chocolate brown styrene with black leather carrying handle, horiz. louvered grill, slide rule dial, cracks bottom & back, clean." You have a good idea of what this radio looks like just from reading the description, which is the same information you want from any seller.

Beware of sellers' claims. "Mint" should be exactly that: never used, absolutely perfect original finish, all parts original. Very few items fifty years old are in mint condition. "Near Mint" is a better description. If you put two identically manufactured radios together, both described as "Mint," most likely one would look more "mint" than the other. Since it's virtually impossible to make this comparison, be cautious and believe that the radio is NM ("Near Mint").

If you've come across a set you want, the first thing to do is to call the dealer and find out what, precisely, is its condition. Is it original? refinished? restored? Does it have the correct knobs? Does it work? Can you return it (at your expense) if it isn't as you expect? Before you send a check, understand what you're getting. Ask lots of questions. Don't worry about sounding foolish; it's more foolish to send off money trustingly. If a picture would make you feel better about buying the set, ask the seller to send one. Even if there's a charge for this extra service, it's still a good investment. Certainly it's cheaper than sending a radio back.

Be sure to find out how long it is before you can expect to receive the radio. Since the seller may want to have your check clear before shipping the set, a three-week wait is not unreasonable. If it's going to be much longer than that, find out how long. Everyone has at sometime ordered something and then waited and waited for it to come through, all the time becoming angrier and angrier. Avoid the problem: know in advance.

If you're planning on spending a lot of money for a radio and you don't know the

1946 Air King; model 4604-D; AM/SW. Reverse painting on dial is flaking off. Watch out for this when buying a set.

1947 Smokerette; made by Porto Products; radio built into smoker's stand; includes ashtray, humidors, and pipe stand (John Wilson).

1946 Electromatic radio-phonograph; model 512; wood cabinet; one of two models the company made.

1946 Monitor; no model number; almost a "generic" radio—no identifying characteristics; date approximate.

1947 RCA; model X551.

seller, consider having the order sent COD. This strategy avoids the problem of someone taking the money and disappearing.

Antique shops/antique malls. At an antique shop or antique mall you will find the highest prices because the dealer has regular costs of business (rent, utilities, salaries) that are not major expenses for any of the other sellers listed in this chapter. The dealer is also concerned about his reputation and will not want to sell an unsafe item (unless it's clearly marked "not working" or "as is"). Many dealers have refinished poor cabinets so the radio looks fresh; they are working at the retail level, which is the price level reflected in this price guide.

As with flea marketers, shop or mall dealers may allow some flexibility in their prices. Some antique dealers do not believe in dickering. They consider themselves professional retailers and believe that since local department stores don't make deals, they shouldn't either. There are some dealers who love to wheel and deal and who consider a sale more enjoyable if bargaining has gone on. Making an offer, instead of asking for the "best price," will allow any dealer to state his or her policy without anyone being insulted.

There was an article several years ago that said dealers were buying items for 25 to 30 percent of the selling price, which would have allowed a good deal of dicker room. Unfortunately, most dealers buying from individuals or at auctions today are paying closer to 50 percent of the selling price. Be reasonable when you make an offer.

Examining the Radio Chasis

Condition. Condition is very important, and this price guide assumes that the radio listed is in working order. "Working order" means the knobs should all be in place and be matching. (It doesn't guarantee that the knobs are the

1947 National Union; model G619.

1947 Firestone; model 4A27; black plastic (Ed and Irene Ripley).

1947 Delco; model R-1229; two-tone wood radio (John Wilson).

correct ones, but that's an assumption you'll have to make. If they don't match, there's obviously something wrong.) All the tubes should be in place, and the cord should be in good condition. (If it isn't, do not, repeat, *do not* plug it in. Get it replaced first thing. The dial should move and the knobs should work. If not, lower the price accordingly. When looking at the chassis from the back of the set, don't worry about dust. You may also find a little rust or some oily looking spots, but these are not problems.

1947 Howard; model 906; wood table radio.

Those are the simple, first steps in checking out a radio. Sometimes that's all you can do, so you really won't have an idea of whether or not the set will be good, or how expensive it will be to fix. If possible, check further.

Problems. Be on the lookout for problems. If you see a lot of greasy wax or black tar on the chassis, something is wrong. There has likely been some overheating of the radio. It will take an evaluation by a repair person to know how serious the problem is. Unless you know about radio repairs, don't pay too much! And don't tinker with a radio yourself unless you know what you are doing. If you have a chance, try the radio before you buy it. (Of course, if you're only buying it for the cabinet, this is not necessary; go on to the section about cabinet condition instead.)

Important! This safety measure cannot be repeated too many times: Before you plug a radio in, make sure the power cord is in safe condition. If you can see any copper wire or the insulation is badly broken, *do not plug it in!*

Look in the back at the chassis. If any tubes are missing from their sockets, don't bother to plug it in. It won't work anyway. Is the loudspeaker in there? The loudspeaker is a separate circular metal frame with a paper cone. If it's missing, don't bother to try the set. If there are many wires that are not attached to anything, don't turn the set on. There may be, however, two wires coming

1947 Zenith; model 6R886; blond wood table model radio-phonograph.

Matching stand for 1947 Zenith radio-phonograph.

1947 Airline; model 64BR-1808; push-button; 3-band.

1947 Gilfillan portable; model 66B, "The Overland"; leatherette covered with unusual copper grille.

through a hole in the back of the chassis. These are the antenna and ground wires. Normally, there will be nothing attached to their ends. These are no problem. You may have to add a little wire to one of these two to get many stations, though.

If nothing seems amiss, you can turn on the radio. Turn the volume control up about halfway. Now watch the back of the radio. If there is a loud sputtering sound, any sparking, or any smoke, do not turn the set off. Instead, pull the plug! You've got problems.

1947 Emerson; model 547A (Ed and Irene Ripley).

If all is still going well, continue to watch the back. The tubes should light up. Any black-painted metal tubes should get warm after a few minutes. Any small bulbs used to light up the dial most likely will be burned out. They aren't hard to replace.

After a couple of minutes, you should hear something. Is there a soft humming sound from the speaker? That's fine. If it is dead silent there is something wrong. If all is well, you will hear some soft crackling sounds and hiss, showing that most of the circuits are functioning.

1947 Emerson; model 578A; wood, European styling (Ed and Irene Ripley).

Now try the switches on the front of the set. Band switches (AM/SW/PHONO) produce a noticeable pop in the speaker when they are moved. If they produce any other strange sounds, it shows that they are in need of cleaning, which is not a difficult task. If there is a band switch, make sure it is set to the regular broadcast band. Turn the volume control almost all the way up. If there is a loud scratching sound in the

1947 Pilot FM tuner; model T-601; played through the phonograph input on a conventional AM radio.

1947 General Electric; model 202.

1947 Regal portable; model 747; metal case with plastic front and back; flip-up cover; AC/battery operation.

you hear any station at all, the set is not in bad condition.

By now you have had the set operating for several minutes. It's time to check it again. Does it smell hot? Waxy? Is there any burning smell, even if there is no smoke? If there is any strong smell from the set, some component is going bad and will need to be fixed.

If you do receive a local station you may still have one or two problems that need attention. There may be a loud hum that makes it hard to hear the station. If so, the filter capacitors will need to be replaced. The sound may be very disagreeable, distorted, and hard to listen to. If this is the case, you may have problems with your speaker or need replacement coupling capacitors.

These old radios are not high-fidelity, but they do sound good. A properly operating old tube-type radio will have a mellow, pleasant sound on local stations, with a just barely noticeable background hum and a little hiss and crackle. Anything other than this means the radio is not as good as it could be. It still may be good enough for you—you are the judge.

speaker when you move the knob, this control will need to be cleaned as well. Try tuning the dial from one end to the other. It should, of course, move. There should be some sort of sound from a local station. If

Coradio coin-op radio; grey metal; from a hotel in Black River Falls, Wisconsin.

The very small (and cheap) old radios, by the way, will not sound very mellow. They will sound very much like the cheap transistor sets which followed them.

WARNING! If the label on the bottom or on the inside of the radio says anything about AC-DC operation, use extreme caution when plugging it in. Some — not all — of these radios have a dangerous design fault which places 110 volts on the metal parts of the radio. If you touch a metal part and are standing on damp ground or touching a sink, *it could be fatal*!

1947 Fada; wooden table, similar to series 652 catalin radios.

If you want to test an AC-DC set before you decide to buy it, you can do all of the above checks, but be careful that you are not on anything damp or touching any metal on or off of the radio. You might prefer to test nothing at all until you know conditions are safe.

For further information on testing, evaluating and repairing old radios, see our other book, *Antique Radios: Restoration and Price Guide* (Wallace-Homestead Books).

1947 Sentinel; model 309-I; ivory Bakelite (Ed and Irene Ripley).

110

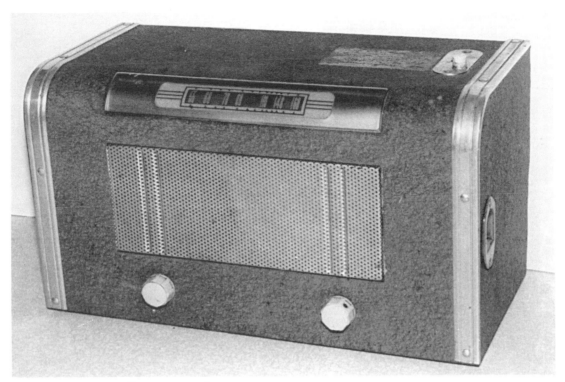

Unknown coin op radio; grey metal.

1948 Fada; model 790; white urea. The Deco style of this radio is misleading in that the radio appears to have been made in the late 1930s instead of 1948, when it actually was manufactured.

Repairs. How do you decide how much to lower your offer if the radio requires repairs? Try this. Find a local radio repair person and ask what the average radio repair is. Your radio won't be average, but it gives you a place to start. Once you have a figure in mind, subtract it from the suggested price to come up with what you can spend.

How do you find someone who repairs radios and can give you that information? This can take some looking. Start with the local television service shops. They are unlikely to work on old radios, but they may know someone who does. Ask at the local antique shops. Many dealers have a list of repair places that they use themselves. If there's a local radio amateurs' organization, someone in it may do the work. The best place to find people to work on old tube-type radios is a local radio club. Contacting one of its members is bound to turn up someone who works on old radios. Information about finding such a club is given in the section on buying at radio swap meets.

If you're seriously interested in collecting old radios, figure out how to handle the repairs before you get a garage full of non-workers.

Examining the Radio Cabinet

Condition. Condition is the single most important item to consider when looking at a radio cabinet. If the condition is good, you won't have any further expense in getting the set into your house. If it's not very good, then you have to lower the price you're willing to pay. After all, you're the one who's going to have to pay for repairs.

If you're going to pay price guide prices, wood cabinets should be good enough to place in your living room without work. This requirement doesn't mean that the finish must be great, but it certainly

1948 Philco; model 48-250.

1948 Motorola portable; model 67L11; simulated alligator. Note square knobs.

1948 General Electric; model X-415. This multiband set has both of the FM bands.

112

1948 Emerson; model 541.

1948 Arvin; model 358T; beige plastic (Ed and Irene Ripley).

shouldn't need a complete facelift. If cabinet repairs or refinishing will be necessary, lower the price you will pay.

Problems. Before buying a radio, make sure you are aware of any problems it has. If you see that gluing will be necessary, or that major cabinet repairs are essential, the cost of the repairs is probably going to make the set worth very little—unless you have the skills to do the job yourself and like doing it, or the radio is one you desperately need for your collection.

Veneer repair is costly. It's possible to get a piece of veneer that is the right thickness and the right grain to go into a place where the original is missing, but it takes patience and careful work to do the job right. If the missing piece is on the side of the cabinet, it won't be too noticeable, even if the repair is not perfect. On the top or the front of the radio, on the other hand, the repair needs to be extremely well done. Think carefully about buying a cabinet with a piece of veneer missing.

Beware of painted grain. When it is new, it looks great, almost as good as the expensive veneer that it copies. Unfortunately, when it becomes badly scratched the temptation is to have it stripped and refinished as any other wood. If you try this, you will find that the stripper removes the underlying paint (used to get the correct base color) and you have a sludgy mess on your hands and nothing resembling fancy wood on your radio. If painted grain is in bad condition, avoid the radio.

Paper veneer is even worse than painted grain when it gets in bad condition. Stripping paper veneer leaves you with a mess of stripper-soaked soggy paper and a cabinet usually constructed of cheap, unmatched woods.

Missing trim can be more difficult to solve than poor cabinet finishes. If it's wood trim, you have to find someone to duplicate it, a time-consuming, expensive project. Then you have to get it stained and finished to match the cabinet. If it's simply a matter

1948 RCA; model 75X16. The frame around the radio is brass.

1948 RCA portable; model 8 BX 6; operates on both AC and batteries; aluminum and plastic.

1948 Philco radio-phonograph; model 48-1401; slide-in record player; black plastic top, wood bottom (David Tuttle).

1949 Stewart Warner; model C51T1; ivory Bakelite with blue dial (Ed and Irene Ripley).

1949 RCA; model 8-X-71; brown Bakelite.

1949 Philco Transitone; model 49-506; wood cabinet.

of hardware missing from the cabinet itself, you may be able to replace it with something similar.

If the plastic or glass dial cover is cracked or broken, do not buy the set unless you like it the way it is. If the plastic or metal dial surround is gone, do not buy the radio. You're unlikely to find replacements for either of these.

At this time, plastic cabinets are not repairable; there is no way to repair a cracked or broken Bakelite or Catalin set. It seems that you should be able to melt some scrap Bakelite to fill the crack. It won't work! Bakelite is a thermoset plastic. Instead of softening and melting, it burns like wood when the temperature gets hot enough. Currently there is no glue that works, either. If the crack isn't going to bother you (if its on the bottom of the cabinet, for instance), you may want the radio anyway. But know that your chances of selling it for near-book are very low.

Repairs. Getting a rough idea of the cost of repairing or refinishing the cabinet is easier to do than finding the cost of fixing

115

1949 Coronado; model 43-8360A; brown plastic with aqua front.

1949 Sentinel; model 332.

1949 RCA; model 9X571; brown plastic case with brown fake wood front.

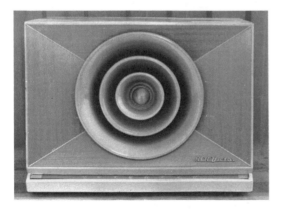

1949 RCA Victor; model 9X572; blond plastic.

1949 Silvertone; model 7054; chassis number 101.808. Postwar styling with rounded cabinet corners.

1949 Silvertone; model 132.857; brown Bakelite (Ed and Irene Ripley).

1949 Bendix; model 75P6U; AM/FM; brown plastic.

the chassis. Lots of firms do stripping and refinishing. You still have to find one who can handle old radios, however.

Most old radio cabinets are veneered. The glues holding the veneers together are forty or fifty years old and are dried out and crumbling. Many of the cabinets are made of mixed woods. When the manufacturer finished them with colored varnish or lacquer, the woods used looked like a single species. When the finish comes off, they may be completely unmatched and look nothing like the radio you bought.

Search for a good refinisher as carefully as you searched for a good radio shop. If you know someone who has had lots of luck with having old furniture refinished, start there. Do you like what you see? Find out if any of the furniture that person had had done was veneer. How long ago was it done? How well is it holding up?

Another option is to check with local refinishers. No matter what stripping technique they use, find out if they have handled any old veneer. If they're not careful, the veneer can loosen, and the job becomes a major repair.

Subtract the price of all estimated repairs from the figures in the price guide. If you can do either the chassis or cabinet repairs yourself, you have more flexibility. Remember, however, that your time is valuable too. When repairing either a radio cabinet or chassis, remember this rule of thumb: Don't do anything that can't be undone later if it's wrong.

Deciding How Much to Pay

Condition. Condition is the single most unpredictable factor in deciding what to pay. The prices given in the price guide are for working radios in good condition. Subtract from the given price for the things that need to be repaired. There are some fine-quality radios out in the world, but most of them aren't that good.

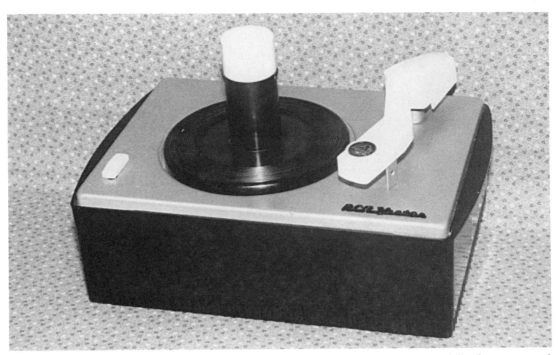

45-rpm phonograph attachment for radios. Usually these are found with the top of the changer in red, rather than white. They were designed to plug into the phono jack on the back of many table radios; original price $12.95; c. 1948–49.

1950 Zenith; model H-725.

1948 Setchell-Carlson portable; model 447; AC/battery (Ed and Irene Ripley).

1949 Philco portable; model 49-602; purse-shaped, brown plastic; slide-rule dial (Ed and Irene Ripley).

Styles and fads. Styles and fads can cause a radio's price to change rapidly and unpredictably, as has happened with some (certainly not all) plastic radios in the last few years. Ten years ago, collectors turned up their noses at these cheap sets. The popular area then was cathedral radios. Today, certain plastic sets have been "discovered." Catalin, urea, and some Bakelite sets are immensely collectible; their prices have increased anywhere from tenfold to 100-fold. Presumably these prices will settle down again, but no one knows when, or even if, that will happen. Who knows what other style will become the next "in" radio. No price guide can predict these fads, and the prices can soon be badly out of date.

Regional preferences. Price guides reflect averages not regional preferences. If a particular style of radio is popular in one part of the country, the prices there will be higher than those listed. People from that area look at the guide and wonder why in the world they're paying so much. If local premium prices were included in the guide, people in the rest of the country would wonder how the authors could be so far off in their figures.

1950 Capehart; model 3T55E; brown plastic.

1950 Jewel clock-radio; model 920; telechron clock; brown Bakelite (Ed and Irene Ripley).

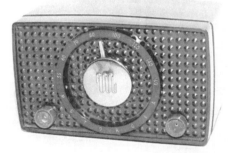

1950 Motorola; model 5H11; brown plastic with red knobs.

1950 Stromberg-Carlson; model 1500; red plastic.

If something is popular where you are and not elsewhere, you'll just have to expect to pay more for it than we suggested. It's the law of supply and demand.

Crossover buyers. Crossover buyers are the ones who turn the whole pricing structure into a shambles. There is the Coca-Cola collector, for instance, who is bidding against you for that Coke cooler radio. Not because it's a radio, but because it's Coke. Or the Disney collector who wants a Mickey Mouse radio because it's Mickey. When two fields like this collide, prices usually become very high.

At an antique shop, the price that goes on the radio depends on what customers the dealer expects. If there are few Disney collectors around, Mickey's price may remain comparatively low. The dealer will think of it as a "cute" radio, price it for a quick sale, and you'll have a chance of getting it at a moderate price. If there are a number of Disney collectors, the price will reflect that group of buyers and may be higher than what you are willing to pay.

Our general feelings about prices. Personally, we feel that there are certain guidelines concerning radio prices. If you're looking at radios as an investment,

1950 Policalarm; model PR8; a police-band radio, made by Regency Electronics (Ed and Irene Ripley).

1950 Packard Bell; model 5R1 (Ed and Irene Ripley).

1950 Silvertone; model 2001; metal cabinet.

1950 Coronado; model 05RA22-43-8515; AM/FM.

our guidelines might be useful as of 1989; however, we consider buying radios (or any collectible, for that matter) as an investment particularly risky. No one can predict what people will want in ten years. If we could, we'd all be wealthy. So buy a radio because you like it. If the price goes up, that's great. If the price falls it doesn't matter, because you've got something you enjoy.

Here are our general observations about the current levels of radio prices:

High-priced	Catalins
	Ureas
	Extremely colorful plastics
Moderately high-priced	Deco (wood or plastic)
	Cathedrals
Average	Upright wood table
	Metal table
Low-priced	Horizontal wood table radios
	Consoles
	Portables
	Plain small wood radios
	Plain plastics

1950 Arvin; model 451T; aqua plastic. Once painted plastic starts chipping, it looks just as bad as chipped metal.

1951 Zenith; model H-615 (Ed and Irene Ripley).

122

1950 General Electric clock-radio; model 65.

1951 General Electric; model 423; white plastic; original price $34.95.

1951 Admiral; model 5S22A N; brown Bakelite.

1952 RCA; model 3-RF-91; AM/FM.

1950 Setchell Carlson intercom-radio; model 458R.

Alterations and Fakes

With the surge of interest in Catalin and other early small sets, certain alterations have begun to crop up. Bakelite radios were often painted, but now it's possible to find them in color schemes that the designers of the 1930s never thought of.

Also, the chrome-plating of cheap Arvin and Silvertone metal sets from the late 1940s has begun. The sets originally were painted black or brown or white or ivory. (It's very difficult to imagine Sears, Roebuck chrome-plating sets it was selling through the catalog.) Beware of these plated sets if someone is selling them as original.

Occasionally you will find a modern transistor radio lurking inside an old cabinet. (This kind of substitution may become more common in the future.) It can happen to anyone; it certainly happened to us. We bought a Radiola 60, sight unseen, only to find that someone had switched the insides. Although the switch had probably been made a number of years ago, that didn't make us feel any better. If we had checked the radio out properly, we never would have bought it.

1951 General Electric; model 422; marbleized maroon plastic.

1951 Silvertone; model 132.881; brown Bakelite (Ed and Irene Ripley).

1951 Admiral radio-phonograph; model 6J21N;
3-speed; black Bakelite. Notice case variations.

1951 Sparton; model 141XX; AM/SW.

1952 Sentinel; model IU-343; black Bakelite.

1953 Sentinel; model 344; black plastic.

1953 Philco Transitone; model 53-561; white plastic (Ed and Irene Ripley).

1952 RCA portable; model 6BX63; grey plastic.

1952 Philco Transitone; model 52-542.

1952 Coronado; model 15RA2-43-8230A; burgundy plastic with gold grille.

1953 Westinghouse; model H393T6; maroon plastic.

1954 Packard Bell; model 631; made by Teledyne (Ed and Irene Ripley).

1953 Crosley clock-radio; model D-25MN. A striking design, with gold bezels on burgundy plastic; definitely the 1950s look.

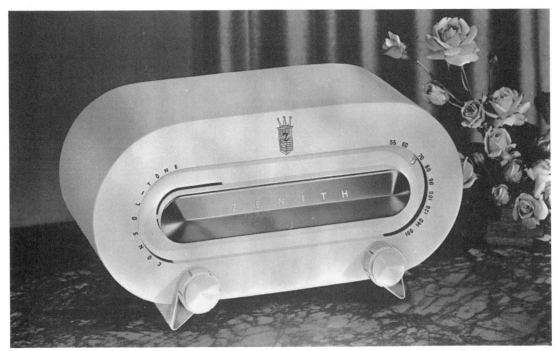

1954 Zenith; model H511W; white plastic, also walnut or ebony (courtesy of Zenith Radio Corp.).

128

1953 CBS Columbia; model 515.

1955 Arvin; model 954P; green plastic portable.

1955 Motorola; model 56R; red plastic.

1957 Motorola; model 66X.

1956 Dumont clock-radio; model RA-346; paint-ed red with gold accents. The label on the bot-tom of the set identifies this number as a clock-radio; however, it shows the tube layout for a similar-looking radio with the same model number.

Capehart portable; model number 213; green metal and plastic case, with interesting tartan grille; mid-1950s.

Trav-Ler; mid-1950s; black plastic (Ed and Irene Ripley).

Dahlberg coin-op radio; model 430-D1; also known as "Pillow Speaker." The speaker, hanging on a book on the left of the radio, goes under a pillow, to keep from disturbing another sleeper. c. 1955.

1957 Silvertone; model 7013; black plastic.

1959 Arvin; model 2585; definitely a 1950s look, in coral and white plastic.

1956 Motorola; model 56H; dramatic gold tuning dial on a brown plastic radio.

1958 Arvin; model 950T2; one of the most striking designs for a cheap radio.

1956 Silvertone radio-phonograph; model 6057A; 3-speed phonograph; blond wood.

1958 Arvin; model 1581; ivory plastic.

131

1959 Zenith; model B-513V.

1960 Motorola; model C9G13; green plastic clock-radio.

132

These are two of the current replicas of the Philco 90B. Philco started it all with its own transistorized, smaller version in 1976. The larger one here is a Windsor, made in Hong Kong. It's AM/FM. The smaller one is a Greenland, made in Taiwan and only 5" high.

Many products have used radio as a selling point. The "microphone" is a glass Avon bottle. The "Radio Bank" is plastic. The jigsaw puzzle is from the 1920s.

1959 Admiral; model 566; transistor table radio; chartreuse and white plastic.

1961 Zenith; model J506C; green plastic.

1964 Admiral; model Y3523; white plastic with black dial.

Part Two

Price Guide

How to Get the Most out of This Price Guide

REMEMBER that this price guide (or any other) is simply that—a guide to prices. A price guide is subject to many variables. Use it for assistance only.

These prices come from many sources. Where possible, they include published prices realized at auctions, want ads in various radio journals, lists of radios sold through the mails, and radios actually seen in shops and at swap meets. Actual pictures of the radios had a lot to do with settling on prices.

Prices gathered from various sources don't tell the whole story. Auction prices don't tell you what sort of auction it was. Were there a lot of radio buyers (forcing prices higher) or were there just a few (making the radios real bargains)? Classified ads include prices, but don't mention whether the seller would dicker or if the prices are firm. Flea markets post prices, but it's almost expected that no one will pay them. How much less will the seller take— 10 percent, 25 percent, a trade of some sort? Antique shops, shows, and malls are more likely to be firm on their prices, but there are still many dealers (certainly not all) who will accept 10 percent less than the marked price.

Realize also that prices are affected by a lot of things. These prices are at least a year old by the time you use them. There is no way to avoid this. Prices are gathered during the last year or so the book is being written. To that year is added another period of six months before the book is actually on the bookstands, plus whatever time goes by before you buy it and use it.

Prices in one part of the country may not be the same as in another. Fads and fancies can cause abrupt changes. Condition of the radio itself (working, sort of working, not working) affects the price. The condition of the cabinet is very important when pricing a radio. But in the end, it always comes down to the fact that a fair price is a price on which both a buyer and a seller agree.

In general, these prices listed in this guide are based on certain assumptions:

- The radio is in reasonable working condition.
- The cabinet looks good enough to put in your living room.
- The prices are those you would pay in a retail antique shop setting.

Warning: Take all prices with a grain of salt.

Model Numbers

There is no standard way to write model numbers. They come in all sorts of alphanumeric combinations, with or without dashes and sometimes even with periods. In this listing, RCA and Zenith have been arbitrarily separated into alphabetical and numerical groups, simply to make their numbers easier to use. As for the models of other companies, their numbers are grouped as the manufacturer listed them, as far as possible; however, the manufacturers were not always consistent. Numbers that come from classified ads are even less consistent. Everyone tends to break up long strings of characters into comfortable groupings, which may not have a lot to do with the way the manufacturer originally listed the models. Be creative when you search. For example, you might look for a particular radio under 7-501 or 75-01 or 750-1 or 7501.

Early manufacturers used the word *type* in much the same way we use *model*. All radios in this guide are listed as models, but don't let the word type throw you.

Where a model name (such as "Bluebird" or "Pup") is used, it will usually follow the model number. If there is no model number, the model name is listed alphabetically.

Numbers are listed before letters.

Price Ranges

Most prices will include a range (20–40 or 200–300, for example). There is no clear-cut formula for determining how wide this range is. Mostly it's determined by selling prices, which sometimes are very far apart. If you buy a radio within the range (even if it seems like a wide spread), you will probably be doing all right. If you get a radio for lower than the bottom price (all things being equal), you are doing very well. If you pay higher than the top price, be aware that you are doing so. You may want the radio very badly. Or the prices may have climbed higher in your area than the prices listed in this guide. Or another fad is starting.

Occasionally a single price is listed when there are too few prices to come up with an average and no picture of the radio is available to help out. A single price is a guide, but no great weight can be placed on it.

Some prices are in the 500 + or 2500 + categories. In these "plus" cases, we have found examples of extremely high prices actually being paid or advertised. There is no way to know if the prices will continue at this level, or if the high price was the result of a single "price-is-no-object" collector. Arbitrarily we lowered these prices (often by 25 to 40 percent) and added the "+" to show that the sky may be the limit.

Not many radios are priced in this guide for 1925 or earlier. We didn't find enough prices for most of them to come up with realistic averages.

Descriptions

Descriptions of radios (cabinet styles, colors, dials, etc.) are to the best of our knowledge. Since these descriptions rely on many types of sources, they are not guaranteed. If something has been left out (for instance, "2 dials"), it does not mean that the radio absolutely won't have that detail. If a detail is listed, though, the radio should have it.

Cabinet. Radio cabinets are usually wood, unless otherwise noted. In a few cases, it was impossible to tell from the picture or description whether or not the cabinet was wood, so cabinets such as these will have no further description. Odds are that a radio without a description of material, however, will be wood.

When a radio is plastic, we have tried to identify the more common plastics, such as Bakelite, Catalin, urea, and so on. If we were not sure, we used the term "plastic" (although the correct scientific term is *molded phenolic resin*).

Color. Radios come in many different colors and finishes. When cabinets are wood, they will be varnished or lacquered. If they are painted or covered with a fabric, we have tried to indicate that. If a cabinet is some sort of plastic, it will most likely be brown or black unless something else is listed. However, there is always a possibility that a manufacturer used several colors without identifying them in its model information.

Bakelite didn't come in white or very light colors. If the description says "Ivory

Bakelite" it means that the Bakelite was painted ivory.

Style. The following descriptions should help to distinguish the various styles. Don't rely on how manufacturers advertised their models. General Electric identified one model as highboy and another as lowboy, but from the illustrations there seems to be no difference in leg heights.

Box	Table radio with the tubes and knobs on the top of the box. It may have a cover.
Breadboard	Early sets with no cabinet; the electronics are right out in the open. Atwater Kent built many of these. Few other companies did. Most early sets were panel sets.
Cathedral	An upright table radio whose style supposedly reminds you of a church window. It ranges from the truly pointed top of a traditional arch to a rounded shape that follows the same general lines. Another group (Jackson-Bell, for instance) were radios defined as "Moderne" when they were manufactured. These had the same proportions, the same single-piece wood front, but the curve was replaced by sharp angles. They are sometimes referred to in ads as "Deco Cathedral."
Chairside	A set built into the top of an end table. It allowed someone sitting in a chair to operate the controls without getting up. Do not confuse it with an end table set.
Chest	Looks like a chest. Sometimes it looks like a pirate chest, with a rounded cover instead of a flat one.
Console	Upright floor model radio higher than it is wide, or one lacking a description. The sides go straight to the floor or the feet are 4 inches or shorter. The upright style is considered normal for floor models. If no better descriptions were given in ads, it can include highboys and lowboys as well.

Deco	A style that originated in the mid-1920s and was popular until 1950. It is characterized by one or more of the following: chrome trim, large geometric shapes, sharp angular forms, streamlined appearance. "Deco," instead of the more purist "Moderne," seems to be what radio collectors have settled on. Not everything we have listed as Deco may be; in some cases we're taking the word of a seller.
End table	Made the radio practically disappear by building it into the end of a conventional end table.
Highboy	A 4- to 6-legged upright floor model. The legs are approximately one-half the height of the set.
Horizontal	Can apply to console, lowboy, or highboy. It means that the radio is wider than it is high.
Lowboy	A 4- to 6-legged upright floor model. The legs are over 4 inches high and less than one-half the height of the radio. ("Highboy" and "lowboy" were used interchangeably by some manufacturers, most likely based on what they expected would sell.)
Panel	No cabinet. There is a front panel, which allowed the set to be built into a wood box, if desired.
Table	Either a horizontal table radio or one lacking a description. The horizontal style (wider than it is high) is considered usual for table radios.
Upright table	Higher than it is wide. It may have a flat or slightly rounded top. A variant of the upright table is the tombstone. The tombstone is generally considered to be a tall table radio with rounded top corners. Because it is a popular term, current advertisers are using this word to describe anything that could even conceivably be called a tombstone. We prefer upright table.

Dates. Dates reflect the model year. All dates may be plus or minus one year because *Rider's Manuals,* which we used as a primary source for dating, often overlap two calendar years. If the circuit diagrams are not dated, there is no easy, accurate way to narrow the range. Radios, like automobiles, were likely to start the next model year somewhere during the fall of the year. A 1940 Philco, for instance, may have first been advertised in 1939.

Bands. What we call AM was known as the "broadcast band" in early radio (shortened to BC). Nowadays we're so used to referring to AM/FM that AM is a more understandable name for general broadcasting. If an ad refers to BC/SW, it's what we call AM/SW (SW: shortwave).

There are a few radios listed with "old" FM, a prewar band that was changed by the end of the war to what we now think of as the FM band. Some radios had both FM bands.

Sources. To help identify radios, we've included page references to photographs or ads found in some of the standard sources for radio information. For instance, FOS-120 means *Flick of the Switch,* page 120. Photographs from this book (*Guide to Old Radios*) are not listed with page numbers. Books listed can be found in "Further Helps" at the end of the book.

AR	*Antique Radios: Restoration and Price Guide,* by Johnson
FOS	*Flick of the Switch,* by McMahon
GOR	*Guide to Old Radios* (this book)
RGA	*Radio: the Golden Age,* by Collins
VR	*Vintage Radio,* by McMahon

A-C DAYTON

It is A-C in their ads, even though it's often written now either as AC or A.C. The company produced AC motors in 1901. They were advertising radios in 1922. Dayton was last heard of in 1930.

Model Name/Number	Price Range ($)	Description
AC-98 "Navigator"	50–70	Table. Walnut wood. Inlay on lid. 1929. (GOR)
AC-9960 "Navigator"	70–90	Lowboy. Walnut. Matte finish. 1929. (GOR)
AC-9970 "Navigator"	80–100	Lowboy. Wood. Sliding doors. 1929. (AR 45; GOR)
AC-9990 "Navigator"	100–125	Highboy with doors. Wood. 1929. (GOR)
XL 5	55–85	Table. Battery. 3 dial. 1925. (VR 135)
XL 5 "Polydyne"	60–80	Table. Battery. 3 dial. 1925.
XL 10	60–80	Table. Battery. 3 dial. 1925.
XL 20	60–80	Table. Battery. 3 dial. 1926.
XL 25	65–85	Table. Battery. 2 dial. 1926. (VR 135)
XL 30	60–80	Table. Battery. 2-dial. 1926.
XL 71 "Navigator"	75–100	Table. Battery. 1929.

A.C. GILBERT

Experimenter's set	200–225	Kit.

ACE (see both Crosley and Precision)

ADDISON

5F	750–1000	Table. Burgundy and butterscotch Catalin. Deco. Columns in front of grille. AM/SW. c.1940. (RGA 56, 57)
	575–600	Yellow Catalin.
	650–700	Green and caramel Catalin.
6E	400–600	Yellow and green Catalin with maroon grille and knobs.
55	25–30	Brown Bakelite.
A2A	675–750	Table. Green and caramel Catalin. c. 1940. (RGA 50, 51)
	1000+	Caramel and red Catalin.
L2	150–200	Table. Brown with cream.
RSA-1	100–125	Deco table.

ADLER

Royal	200–300	Table. Battery. 1924. (GOR; VR 142)

ADMIRAL

Made by Continental Radio & Television Corporation before the war. Later became Admiral.

4B21	20–25	Portable. AC/battery. Black. 1954.
4B22	15–20	Maroon plastic. Same as 4B21.
4B24	10–15	Beige plastic. Same as 4B21.
4B28	15–20	Green plastic. Same as 4B21.
4B29	10–15	Grey plastic. Same as 4B21.
4L20/4L20A	15–20	Table. Plastic. Grey. 1959.
4L21/4L21A	10–15	Black plastic. Same as 4L20.
4L24/4L24A	25–30	Pink plastic. Same as 4L20.
4L25/4L25A	25–30	Red plastic. Same as 4L20.
4L26/4L26A	20–25	Yellow plastic. Same as 4L20.
4L28/4L28A	20–25	Green plastic. Same as 4L20.

4M22	10–15	Clock-radio. Brown plastic. 1959.
4M23	15–20	Ivory plastic. Same as 4M22.
4M25	25–30	Coral plastic. Same as 4M22.
4M28	20–25	Green plastic. Same as 4M22.
4V12	20–25	Portable. Brown plastic. AC/battery. 1952.
4V18	25–30	Green plastic. Same as 4V12.
4V19	40–45	Black plastic with red handle, knobs, and dial face. Same as 4V12.
4Y11	10–12	Portable. Black plastic. Metal grille. AC/battery. 1953.
4Y12	15–20	Maroon plastic. Same as 4Y11.
4Y18	15–20	Green plastic. Same as 4Y11.
4Y19	10–15	Grey plastic. Same as 4Y11.
4Z11	8–10	Portable. AC/battery. Black plastic. 1954.
4Z12	15–20	Maroon plastic. Same as 4Z11.
4Z14	10–15	Beige plastic. Same as 4Z11.
4Z19	10–15	Grey plastic. Same as 4Z11.
5A32	20–25	Clock-radio. Brown plastic. Bright panel. 1952.
5A33	20–25	Ivory plastic. Same as 5A32.
5D31	40–45	Radio-phonograph. Black plastic. Table. 1953.
5D32	45–50	Maroon plastic. Same as 5D31.
5D33	45–50	Ivory plastic. Same as 5D31.
5D38	50–55	Green plastic. Same as 5D31.
5E21	15–20	Table. Large dial. Black plastic. 1951.
5E22	20–25	Ivory plastic. Same as 5E21.
5E23	15–20	Brown plastic. Same as 5E21.
5E31	15–20	Clock-radio. Black plastic. 1953.
5E32	25–30	Maroon plastic. Same as 5E31.
5E33	20–25	Ivory plastic. Same as 5E31.
5E38	25–30	Green plastic. Same as 5E31.
5E39	15–20	Grey plastic. Same as 5E31.
5F1	15–20	Portable. Plastic. Flip-up lid. AC/battery. 1949.
5F31/5F31A/5F31B	25–30	Clock-radio. Black plastic. 1954.
5F32/5F32A/5F32B	30–35	Maroon plastic. Same as 5F31A.
5F33/5F33A/5F33B	20–25	Ivory plastic. Same as 5F31A.
5F34B	20–25	Beige plastic. Same as 5F31A.
5F38/5F38A/5F38B	30–35	Green plastic. Same as 5F31A.
5G31	25–30	Table. Black plastic. 1953.
5G32	25–30	Brown plastic. Same as 5G31.
5G33	25–30	Ivory plastic. Same as 5G31.
5J31	50–60	Desk set (pen, clock, radio in stand). Black plastic. 1953.
5J33	45–50	Ivory plastic. Same as 5J31.
5J38	60–70	Marbelized green plastic. Same as 5J31.
5K13	30–35	Table. Maroon with gold trim. 1948.
5K31	15–20	Portable. Black plastic. AC/battery. 1954.
5K32	15–20	Maroon plastic. Same as 5K31.
5K34	15–20	Beige plastic. Same as 5K31.
5K38	20–25	Green plastic. Same as 5K31.
5K39	15–20	Grey plastic. Same as 5K31.
5R33	10–15	Table. Plastic. 1955.
5RP41	75–100	Radio-phonograph. Bakelite. Table. 1958.
5S21/5S21AN	20–25	Table. Black plastic. 1952.

AR: *Antique Radios: Restoration and Price Guide* / **FOS:** *Flick of the Switch* / **GOR:** *Guide to Old Radios*
RGA: *Radios: The Golden Age* / **VR:** *Vintage Radio*

5S22/5S22AN	15–20	Brown plastic. Same as 5S21.
5S23/5S23AN	15–20	Ivory plastic. Same as 5S21.
5S32	20–25	Clock-radio. Maroon plastic. 1954.
5S33	20–25	Ivory plastic. Same as 5S32.
5S34	15–20	White plastic. Same as 5S32.
5S35	30–35	Red plastic. Same as 5S32.
5S36	25–30	Green plastic. Same as 5S32.
5X21	30–35	Clock-radio. Black plastic. 1952.
5X22D	25–30	Brown plastic. Same as 5X21.
5X23	25–30	Ivory plastic. Same as 5X21.
5Y22/5Y22A	75–100	Radio-phonograph. Brown Bakelite. 1952.
5Z22	15–20	Table. Brown plastic. Large dial. 1952.
5Z23	20–25	Ivory plastic. Same as 5Z22.
6A21	25–30	Table. Black plastic. 1950.
6A22	20–25	Brown plastic. Same as 6A21.
6A23	20–25	Ivory plastic. Same as 6A21.
6C11	10–15	Portable. Flip-up lid. AC/battery. 1949.
6C22/6C22A	30–35	Table. Brown plastic. 1952.
6C23/6C23A	30–35	Ivory plastic. Same as 6C22.
6J21	75–100	Radio-phonograph. Black Bakelite. 1949
6J21N	90–125	Radio-phonograph. Table. 3-speed. Black Bakelite. 1950–51. (GOR)
6J22	75–100	Brown Bakelite. Same as 6J21.
6R11	75–100	Radio-phonograph. Bakelite. AM/FM. 1949.
7C65W	40–50	Radio-phonograph. Horizontal console. 1947.
7C73	40–50	Radio-phonograph. Horizontal console. AM/FM. 1947. (FOS-50)
7C93B/7C93M/7C93W	65–75	Radio-phonograph. Horizontal wood console. AM/FM. 1947.
7G11/7G12/7G14/7G15	40–45	Radio-phonograph. Wood horizontal console. 1948.
7G16	40–45	Blond wood. Same as 7G11.
7T10E-N	30–35	Table. Bakelite. 1948.
14X18	30–35	Portable.
42-KR3	30–50	Table. White painted wood. 1942. (GOR)
251/251A	15–20	Clock-radio. Black. 1954.
566	15–30	Table. Early transistor radio. Chartreuse and white plastic. 1959. (GOR)
935-11S	45–50	Console. AM/SW .
4203-B6	35–40	Table. Wood. 1942.
4204-B6	35–40	Table. Wood. AM/SW. 1941. (GOR)
AM786	30–60	Console. AM/LW/SW. 1936. (FOS-48)
GY19	15–20	Portable.
Y3523	20–30	Table. White plastic with black dial. 1964. (GOR)

AERO

Midget	100–150	Cathedral. 1931.

AETNA

Sold by Walgreen's Drug Stores.

	75–85	Upright table. Black Mt. Aetna dial. 1936.

AIR KING

824	125–150	Wood table. AM/SW. 1937.
604-D.	15–25	Wood. Table. Reverse painting on dial. AM/SW. 1946. (GOR)

4700	40–60	Radio-phonograph–wire recorder. Horizontal console. 1948.
A-403 "Court Jester"	20–25	Radio-phonograph. Table. 1947.
A-410	125–150	Portable. Built-in camera. Battery only. Artificial snake-skin. 1948.

AIR CHIEF *(see Firestone)*

AIRADIO

3100	20–25	Table. Wood. FM only. 1948.

AIRCASTLE

Sold by Spiegel's.

7B	40–50	Radio-phonograph. Horizontal table. FM/AM. 1948.
572	40–45	Radio-phonograph. Horizontal console. 1949.
603.880	35–40	Portable. Leatherette. Radio-phonograph-recorder. 1954.
652.5C1M/652.5T1M	20–25	Table. Maroon plastic. 1954.
652.5C1V/652.5T1V	20–25	Table. Ivory plastic. 1954.
738.5400	10–15	Portable. Plastic. AC/battery. 1954.
5002	20–25	Table. White plastic. 1947.
10002	15–20	Table. Plastic. 1949.
10003-I	15–20	Table. Ivory plastic. Wraparound speaker grille. 1949.
108014	15–20	Table. Plastic. 1949.
127084	35–40	Radio–phonograph. Upright console. 1949.
138104	45–50	Radio-phonograph. Upright console. 1949.
147114	10–15	Portable. Metal. Flip-up lid. AC/battery. 1949.
G-521	25–30	Portable. Leatherette. Tambour top. AC/battery. 1949.
G-724	20–25	Table. Wood. AM/FM. 1948.

AIRLINE

Sold by Montgomery Ward. The store was active in radio very early, advertising radio catalogs in 1922 radio magazines. Tri-City made their early sets.

	140	Table. 1 tube. 1925.
05BR-1525	10–20	Table. Brown Bakelite. 1950.
14BR-522A	20–30	Table. White plastic. 1941. (GOR)
14WG-624A	30–40	Table. 1941.
14WG-806A	40–60	Table. Wood. Push-button. Cabinet curves out over grille. 1941. (GOR)
15GMH-1070A	10–20	Table. 1952.
25BR–1542A	30–35	Table. Plastic. 1953.
54BR-1503B	25–30	Table. 1946.
54BR–1506	30–50	Table. Ivory plastic. Push-button. 1946. (GOR)
62-77	50–75	Cathedral. Battery. 1933.
62-229	50–100	Cathedral. Battery. Movie-dial drive. 1936.
62-267	150–200	Console. Movie-dial drive. 1936.
62-277	75–125	Table. Movie-dial drive. 1936.
62-326W	100–125	Cathedral. Battery. 1936.
62–370	45–65	Table. 1939.
62-376	25–40	Table. Wood. AM/SW. Battery. 1939. (GOR)
62-425	25–35	Table. 1936.

AR: *Antique Radios: Restoration and Price Guide* / **FOS:** *Flick of the Switch* / **GOR:** *Guide to Old Radios*
RGA: *Radios: The Golden Age* / **VR:** *Vintage Radio*

62-437	50–100	Cathedral. Battery. Movie-dial drive. 1936.
62-476	30–50	Table. White or brown Bakelite. Telephone dial. 1941. (GOR)
62-502	100–125	Table. White Bakelite. Push-button. 1939.
64BR–1808	25–40	Table. Wood. AM/2SW. Push-button. 1947. (GOR)
64WG-1804	20–25	Table. Wood. 1946.
74BR-1053A	10–15	Portable. AC/battery. 1948.
74KR-2706B	30–35	Radio-phonograph. Upright console. 1948.
74WG-1057A	20–25	Portable. AC/battery. 1947.
84BR-1815B	30–35	Table. Wood. Unusual plastic dial and grille. 1949.
84GCB-1062A	10–15	Portable. Flip-up lid. Metallic plastic front. Battery. 1948.
84KR-1520A	25–45	Table. Metal. Available in ivory, red, green, yellow, and blue. 1948.
84WG-2015A	20–25	Radio-phonograph. FM/AM. Wood table. 1948.
84WG-2714A	40–50	Radio-phonograph. Console. AM/FM. 1948.
93BR-460A	40–45	Table. Wood. Battery. 1940.
93WG-800B	30–50	Table. AM/SW. Push-button. 1946.
GAA-99A	15–20	Radio-phonograph. Portable. 1956
GSE-1077A	15–20	Portable. Green plastic. AC/battery. Personal style. 1954.
GSE-1078A	15–20	Rust plastic. Same as GSE-1077A.
unknown	25–35	Table. Wood. c. 1940. (GOR)
unknown	35–50	Table. Plastic. Made by Belmont. c. 1940. (GOR)

AIRWAY

F	200–250	Table. Battery. 2-dial. 1923.
G	225–250	Table. Battery. 1923.

ALGENE

AR-406 "Middie"	10–20	Portable. Cosmetic case style. Fake alligator. Battery. 1948.

AMERICAN BOSCH

Originally a sales agency for Robert Bosch (Stuttgart, Germany). In 1912, it became the Bosch Magneto Company with a plant in Massachussetts. However, Robert Bosch returned to Germany at the start of World War I, the plant was seized and its assets sold as enemy property. Bosch, meanwhile, had formed another company in Germany, again with an American sales agency, and there were court fights through much of the 1920s to decide who owned the Bosch name. This dispute was settled in 1929. During 1930 the two companies combined and became United American Bosch Corporation.

5A	60–70	Table. Wood. 1931.
16 "Amberola"	80–120	Table. Battery. 2-dial. 1925.
28	100–125	Table. Wood. 1928.
460	65–75	Upright table. AM/SW. 1934.
505	50–70	Table. Wood. AM/Police. 1936.
515	40–50	Table. AM/SW. 1936.
604	15–25	Table. Wood. 1935. (GOR)
660T	20–40	Table. Wood. AM/SW. 1936. (FOS-53)
unknown	750 +	Table. Wood. Swastikas on knobs. Back-lit German eagle surmounting another swastika on dial. 1936. (GOR)

AMRAD

American Radio and Research Corporation. The idea for the company was one of J. P. Morgan's. By the time the company started, the elder Morgan had died. The company kept busy during World War I. Unfortunately, during the early 1920s, it took vastly more orders than it could ever supply. Lagging behind demand, Amrad couldn't keep up with new ideas. Powel Crosley wanted Amrad's Neutrodyne license and bought the company in 1925. The Amrad name continued, and there was a plan to produce higher-priced sets under this marque. The Depression put an end to this, and Amrad closed in 1930.

2596 & 2634	450–550	Tuner-detector. 2-dial. Near mint. Includes original instructions. One of several Amrad sets referred to as "Double Decker." 1924.
A	250–300	Crystal. 1924.
Neutrodyne	75–100	Table. 3-dial. 1924.
T 5	75–100	Table. 1925.

ANDREWS

II	300–350	Table. Battery. 3-dial. 1925.

ANSLEY

41 "Paneltone"	35–50	In the wall model. 1940s.

APEX

7B5	10–15	Table. Plastic. 1948.
41	150–175	Lowboy. Wood.

ARBORPHONE

27	50–75	Table. Battery. 1927.
45	50–75	Table. 1928.
	90–100	Console. 1928. Same as model 45 except installed in a cabinet supplied by another manufacturer.
Arborphone	225–250	Highboy. Included 18″ Metro cone speaker. Battery. 1925.

ARTONE

R-1046-U	35–40	Table. White Bakelite. Aqua dial. 1946. (GOR)

ARVIN

Made by Noblitt Sparks Industries Inc.

78	20–40	Table. Push-button. AM/SW. 1938. (FOS-60)
151TC	15–20	Radio-phonograph. Table. Wood. 1948.
152T	30–35	Table. Plastic. 1948.
182TFM	20–25	Table. Wood. AM/FM. 1947.
242T	20–25	Table. Ivory metal. 1948. (RGA-100)
	30–35	Yellow metal.
243T	30–35	Green metal. Same as 242T.
	35–40	Red metal. Same as 242T.
250P	5–10	Table. Metal. 1948.
255T	10–15	Table. Plastic. 1949.
358T	15–25	Table. Beige Bakelite. 1948. (GOR)

AR: *Antique Radios: Restoration and Price Guide* / **FOS:** *Flick of the Switch* / **GOR:** *Guide to Old Radios*
RGA: *Radios: The Golden Age* / **VR:** *Vintage Radio*

402	25–30	Table. Metal. 1940.
405	15–25	Table. Aqua plastic. 1950. (GOR)
441T "Hopalong Cassidy"	125–250	Table. Metal with foil front panel. Red or black. Foil must be in good condition. The aerial (called a Lariatenna) was designed to coil up when it wasn't in use and be hooked on the "pommel" of a "saddle" on the back of the set. 1950. (FOS-61; RGA-90,91)
442	25–30	Table. Metal. 1948. (FOS-60)
502	15–25	Table. White metal. 1939. (GOR)
522A	25–30	Table. 1941.
532A	750+	Table. Butterscotch Catalin. 1941.
540T	30–35	Table. Red metal.
544	35–45	Table. Bakelite. 1946. (GOR)
581TFM	25–30	Table. Plastic. Brown, rosewood, or black. AM/FM. 1953.
950T2	25–35	Table. Black plastic. 1958. (GOR)
954P	10–15	Portable. Green plastic. 1955. (GOR)
1237 "Phantom Prince"	75–100	Console. Wood. Telephone dial. 1937. (FOS-59; GOR)
1581	10–15	Table. Ivory plastic. 1958. (GOR)
2585	25–40	Table. Coral with white plastic. 1959. (GOR)
8573-1	15–20	Portable. Battery. 1958.

ATWATER KENT

Atwater Kent had been producing automobile parts for a number of years. A recession after World War I led Kent to look for another product that would use the production techniques he knew. Deciding that radio was the coming thing, the company started making radio components, and soon radios were being wired together at the factory. Eventually Atwater Kent became a household word.

The radios were available in table models, but, until the end of the 1920s, other companies produced the highboys, lowboys, and tables to house them. Later on Atwater Kent made a full line of radio cabinets. Kent closed his business in 1936.

5	1500+	Breadboard. Battery. 1921. (VR-73)
9	500–900	Breadboard. Battery. 2-dial. 1924. (VR-75)
10	300–600	Breadboard. Battery. 3-dial. 1923.
10A	500–700	Breadboard. Battery. 3-dial. 1924. (VR-75)
10B	300–450	Breadboard. Battery. 3-dial. 1924.
10C	250–350	Breadboard. Battery. 3-dial. 1924. (VR-75)
	400–500	Console. Same as model 10C except installed in a cabinet supplied by another manufacturer.
12	600–900	Breadboard. Battery. 3-dial. 1924.
19	200–300	Table. Battery. 2-dial. 1924. (VR-76)
20	50–100	Table. Battery. 3-dial. Often called the "Big Box." 1924. (AR-9)
20C	50–100	Table. Battery. 3-dial. May be known as the "20 Compact." 1925. (VR-76)
20 "DeLuxe"	75–150	Table. 1925.
21	150–250	Table. 3-dial. Dry cell set. 1925.
24 "DeLuxe"	225–275	Table. Battery. 3-dial. 1925.
30	50–100	Table. Battery. 1926. (VR-76; AR-21)
	175–225	Console. Same as model 30 except installed in a cabinet supplied by a different manufacturer. (AR–11 has one example of a console cabinet. There were many others.)

32	40–60	Table. Battery. 1926. (VR-6)
33	40–70	Table. Battery. 1927. (VR-76)
35	30–70	Table. Metal. Battery. 1926. (VR-77; AR-22)
	100–150	Console. Made by other companies.
36	75–100	Table. Metal. 1927. (VR-77)
37	50–100	Table. Metal. 1927.
40	30–60	Table. Metal. 1928. (VR-77)
	100–150	Console. Same as model 40 except installed in a cabinet supplied by a different manufacturer.
42	50–80	Table. Metal. 1928.
43	40–60	Table. Metal. 1928.
44	50–100	Table. Metal. 1928. (VR-77)
45	50–80	Table. Metal. 1929.
46	35–60	Table. Metal. 1929.
47	40–60	Table. Metal. 1929.
48	40–60	Table. Wood. Battery. 1928. (VR-77)
	350	Same as model 48 above except this one was advertised as "Mint in Carton." Note the difference in the asking price.
49	40–60	Table. Metal. Battery. 1928.
50	40–60	Table. Battery. 1928. (VR-77)
52	75–100	Console. Metal. 1928. (AR-40)
55	40–60	Table. Metal. 1929. (VR-77)
	125	Table. Red and black metal.
	125–175	Highboy and lowboys. Same as model 55, but installed in various cabinets supplied by different manufacturers. (AR-40, 42 show examples of different cabinets.)
	200–300	Kiel table. Same as model 55 except installed in a Kiel table, where the chassis is in the drawer and the speaker faces down underneath the table and bounces the sound from the floor.
55C	75–125	Lowboy. Wood. 1929. (AR–40 – picture identified as model 55 is really a 55C; AR–41 – chassis)
60	50–75	Table. Metal. 1929.
	100–125	Lowboy. 1929. (FOS-63)
	200–300	Kiel table. Same as model 60 except installed in Kiel table. See model 55 for description.
70	100–125	Lowboy. 1929.
75	150–200	Radio-phonograph. Lowboy. 1930.
80	300–350	Table. 25-cycle. 1931.
84	250–350	Cathedral. 1931. (VR-263; FOS-64)
89	50–75	Lowboy. 1931.
90	300–400	Cathedral. 1931.
145	60–80	Upright table. AM/SW. 1934. (FOS-68)
165	150–250	Cathedral. AM/SW. 1933. (FOS-66)
185A	125–150	Upright table. Wood. 1934.
206	150–250	Upright table. Round top. AM/SW. 1934. (FOS-66)
217	250–350	Table. Round top. AM/SW. 1933. (FOS-66)
318	125–175	Console. AM/SW. 1934. (AR-59; FOS-68; GOR)
425	50–80	Console. AM/SW. 1934.
545	100–150	Upright table. Wood. 1936.
555	250–350	Chest. Inlaid walnut. 1933.

AR: *Antique Radios: Restoration and Price Guide* / **FOS**: *Flick of the Switch* / **GOR**: *Guide to Old Radios*
RGA: *Radios: The Golden Age* / **VR**: *Vintage Radio*

627	300–400	Cathedral. 1932.
700	1000 +	Console. Oriental style.
708	250–300	Table. Round top. AM/SW. 1933. (FOS-66)
735	150–250	Table. 1935.
856	100–125	Upright table. AM/SW. 1935.
944	250–300	Cathedral. 1934. (FOS–68)
Radiodyne	550–650	Box. Battery. 1923.

AUTOMATIC

TT 600	20–30	Portable. 1955.
Tom Thumb Buddy	15–20	Portable. Metal and plastic. AC/battery. 1949.

AZTEC

Made by the Fred W. Stein Co.

130C	125–150	Cathedral. 1930.

BEARDSKY

Made by the Beardsky Radio Shop.

unknown	200–225	2-tube radio.

BELMONT

Belmont Radio Corporation also made radios for several other companies, including Airline, Truetone, and Wings.

4B 115	10–25	Table. Battery. Plastic. Large dial surrounding speaker. 1948.
6D 111	50–100	Table. Brown or ivory Bakelite. 1946. (RGA-69)
602	30–50	Table. Bakelite. 1937. (GOR)
636	30–45	Table. Brown Bakelite. Push-button. 1939. (GOR)
840	60–80	Console. Wood. AM/2SW. 1937. (GOR)

BENDIX

A division of Bendix Aviation, it began making radios after World War II.

0526A	35–45	Table. Brown Bakelite. 1946.
0526C	400 +	Table. Green and black Catalin. 1946.
0526D	250–400	Table. Tan and brown Catalin. 1946.
65P4	25–30	Table. Plastic. Built-in handle. Metal grille. 1948.
75P6U	20–40	Table. Brown plastic. AM/FM. 1949. (GOR)
114	150–350	Table. Tan and brown polystyrene. Styled like 0526C/0526D. 1947.
115	150–350	Table. Ivory and burgundy polystyrene. Styled like 0526C/0526D. 1947. (RGA-70)
301	15–20	Table. Wood. 1948.
416A5	10–20	Table. Wood. 1948.
613	15–20	Radio-phonograph. Table. 1948.
1524	50–75	Radio-phonograph. Horizontal console. AM/FM. 1948.
PAR-80	30–35	Portable. Leatherette. AC/battery. AM/LW/SW. 1948.

BEVERLY

Made by the Warwick Manufacturing Company. Warwick produced radios under at least 40 trade names, including Clarion and Steinite.

unknown	175–225	Cathedral.

BLAUPUNKT

20003 "Ballet"	40–50	Table. AM/FM/SW. Ivory Bakelite. 1961.

BRANDES

B-15	125–175	Highboy. 1929.

BREMER TULLY

This was a company known for the quality of its workmanship. For more information about the company, see Brunswick.

unknown	50–75	Kit. Nameless parts only. Battery. 1925. (VR-149)
Counterphase 5	50–75	Kit. Battery. 2-dial. 1925.
Counterphase 6	50–75	Kit or Table. Battery. 2-dial. 1926.
Counterphase 8	75–100	Table. Battery. 1926.
81	75–100	Console. 1929.

BRYANT

	300	Table. Wood. Battery. 1922.

BROWNING-DRAKE

After several years of producing a kit radio which not only had innovative circuitry but also worked, Browning-Drake began business in 1927 to make complete receivers under its own name. By 1930 the company was in financial trouble; it folded in 1937.

5R	50–75	Table. Battery. 2-dial. 1926–7. (VR-130)
6A	50–75	Table. Battery. 1927.
7A	50–75	Table. Battery. 1927.
	175–200	Same as 7A above, but installed in a cabinet supplied by a different manufacturer.
B-D	75–125	Kit. Battery. 1925. (VR-149)

BRUNSWICK

The Radiola name is found on Brunswick radios as well as RCA radios. Brunswick bought the Radiola chassis from RCA, then put its own nameplate on it. Brunswick-Balke-Collendar had been making bowling and billiard supplies since 1845 (and still is). After using RCA radios in the 1920s, Brunswick bought Bremer-Tully and the Farrand Loudspeaker Company and made its own complete sets. In 1930, due to poor business, Brunswick sold the radio, phonograph, and recording business to Warner Brothers. Warner kept the record end but closed the radio business in 1932. (There was a 1933 line of Brunswicks brought out by Brunswick Engineers Inc., New York City).

D-1000	100–125	Radio-phonograph. Horizontal console. AM/FM. 1949.

BUCKINGHAM

2	100–125	Console. 1928.

BULOVA

Bulova made radios at two different times in its history—once in the early 1930s and again in the late 1950s.

310	35–40	Table. Bright blue plastic. 1957.
600 series	175–200	Clock-radio. Cathedral. 1933.

AR: *Antique Radios: Restoration and Price Guide* / **FOS:** *Flick of the Switch* / **GOR:** *Guide to Old Radios*
RGA: *Radios: The Golden Age* / **VR:** *Vintage Radio*

CBS-COLUMBIA

515	10–15	Table. Plastic. 1953. (GOR)

CAPEHART

The company was eventually purchased by Farnsworth.

2C56	25–30	Clock-radio. Ivory plastic. 1956.
3T55E	15–25	Table. Brown plastic. 1950. (GOR)
213	25–35	Portable. AC/DC/battery. Metal. Tartan grille. Mid 1950s. (GOR)
406D	750	Radio-phonograph. Flip-over changer. 1935.
P-312	15–20	Portable. Plastic. AC/battery. Available in green, grey, blue, black. 1954.
TC-100	15–20	Clock-radio. Brown or ivory plastic. 1953.
TC-101	20–25	Clock-radio. Grey plastic. 1953.

CASE

The Phillip Case & Company, with its model name of "Cassco," has only one model listed in *Radio Collector's Guide*.

Radio Frequency	50–75	Table. Battery. 1926.

CISCO

1A5	15–20	Table. 1948.

CLAPP-EASTHAM

HR Radak	200–300	Table. 1-tube. 2-dial. Battery. 1922.
R4	150–200	Box. 1-tube. Battery. 1924.
Radak DD	100–125	Table. Battery. 1925.
RZ Radak	500–700	Table. Battery. 2-dial. 1922.

CLARION

Gamble's house brand. Clarion radios were produced by the Transformer Corporation of America. Up until 1930, when it began making radios, TCA had been making radio parts. The company was sold in 1933, although the name stayed around until at least 1946. Current models with this name are being produced in Japan.

80	50–75	Upright table. Wood. 1931.
220	75–100	Upright table. Wood. 1931.
470	125–150	Cathedral. 1933.
510	75–100	Upright table. Wood. 1934.
691	40–60	Table. Wood. Telephone dial. 1937. (GOR)
770	20–40	Table. Wood. AM/SW. 1937. (GOR)
12708	25–30	Radio-phonograph. Small console. 1948.
12801-N	20–25	Table. Plastic. 1948.
12110M	40–50	Radio-phonograph. Horizontal console. AM/FM. 1949.
AC40	100–150	Cathedral. 1931.
Junior	75–125	Cathedral. 1932.

CLEARFIELD

Made by Sherman Radio Corporation, New York City.

TRF 6 RC	2000+	Table. Plate glass case. 1925.

CLEARTONE

110 "Standard"	150–200	Table. Available in both a 1-dial and 2-dial version. Wood. 1926.

COLONIAL

32 "Cavalier AC"	100–150	Highboy with doors. Wood. 1929. (GOR)

COLUMBIA

When radio came in, phonograph and record sales dropped disastrously. Columbia Phonograph Company decided to move into the new broadcasting market and also began producing radios. In 1927 it became the Columbia Phonograph Broadcasting Company and began network broadcasting. The network later was sold and became Columbia Broadcasting System.

530	35–40	Radio-phonograph. Horizontal console. AM/FM. 1957.
C-4	125–175	Highboy. 1928.

CONCORD

1-504	10–15	Table. AM/2 SW. Plastic. 1949.
6C51B	30–40	Table. Deco. Plastic. 1947.
6F26W	30–35	Table. AM/SW. 1947.
CD61P	25–30	Radio-phonograph. Table. 1947.

CONTINENTAL

44	35–40	Table. Plastic. Bullet shape.
1000	30–60	Table. Plastic. Deco. c. World War II. (GOR)

J. K. COOR

	45–55	Crystal.

CORONADO

Sold by Gamble's.

Note: Although Coronado used the entire model number on its radios, it isn't always found when looking at a set. In the Sams circuit diagrams, the first group of numbers is omitted. Therefore, if you don't find your set using the first numbers, check all of the numbers, starting with 43.

05RA1-43-7755A	25–30	Radio-phonograph. Console. AM/FM. 1950.
05RA1-43-7901A	40–50	Radio-phonograph. Horizontal console. AM/FM. 1950.
05RA2-43-8515A	30–40	Table. Plastic. AM/FM. 1950. (GOR)
05RA4-43-9876A	10–15	Portable. Plastic. Metallic grille. AC/battery. 1950.
05RA33-43-8120A	25–30	Table. Plastic. 1950.
05RA33-43-8136A/8137A	15–20	Table. Walnut or ivory plastic. 1950.
05RA37-43-8360A	40–75	Table. Plastic. Aqua front panel. 1950. (GOR)
15RA1-43-7654A	30–35	Radio-phonograph. Console. AM/FM. 1950.
15RA1-43-7902A	40–50	Radio-phonograph. Horizontal console. AM/FM. 1950.
15RA2-43-8230A	15–25	Table. Burgundy plastic. Gold metallic grille. 1952. (GOR)
15RA33-43-8245A	40–50	Table. Red plastic. 1951.
15RA33-43-8246A	20–25	Table. Ivory plastic with green dial. 1951.
15RA33-43-8365A	25–30	Table. Plastic. AM/FM. 1951.
15RA37-43-9230A	20–25	Radio-phonograph. Table. Wood. 1951.
15RA38-43-8235A/8236A	20–25	Clock-radio. Walnut or ivory plastic. 1950.
15RA38-43-8238A/8239A	15–20	Clock-radio. Brown or ivory plastic. 1952.

AR: *Antique Radios: Restoration and Price Guide* / **FOS:** *Flick of the Switch* / **GOR:** *Guide to Old Radios*
RGA: *Radios: The Golden Age* / **VR:** *Vintage Radio*

35RA33-43-8125A "Chatterbox"	10–15	Table. Plastic. 1953.
35RA33-43-8145 "Ranger"	15–20	Table. Black with white plastic. 1953.
	30–35	Red with white plastic.
35RA33-43-8225 "Moderne"	25–30	Table. Plastic. 1953.
35RA33-43-8375	25–30	Table. Brown with tan plastic. 1953.
35RA37-43-8355	15–20	Table. Plastic. 1953.
35RA40-43-8247A	20–25	Clock-radio. Plastic. 1953.
43-37I-1	25–30	Table. Brown plastic. 1948.
43-37I-2	30–35	Same as 43-37I-1. Ivory plastic.
43-6301	20–30	Table. Wood. Battery. 1946.
43-6730	50–60	End table. 1949.
43-6927	30–35	Console. 1948.
43-6951	40–45	Console. AM/FM. 1948.
43-7601/7601A/7601B	30–35	Radio-phonograph. Console. 1946.
43-7602	35–40	Radio-phonograph. Console. 1947.
43-7603	35–40	Radio-phonograph. Console. 1948.
43-7851	40–45	Radio-phonograph. Horizontal console. AM/FM. 1948.
43-8130	15–20	Table. Plastic. 1946.
43-8177	20–25	Table. Plastic. 1947.
43-8180	15–20	Table. Plastic. 1947.
43-8190	45–60	Table. Plastic. Contrasting handle, knobs, dial. 1947. (RGA-77)
43-8201	25–30	Table. Plastic. 1947.
43-8213	15–20	Table. Wood. 1946.
43-8240	10–15	Table. Plastic. 1946.
43-8305	20–25	Table. Plastic. 1947.
43-8312	15–20	Table. Plastic. 1946.
43-8330	25–30	Table. Square shape. 1947.
43-8351/8351A/8351B	15–20	Table. Plastic. Push-button. 1946.
43-8354	20–25	Table. Plastic. Push-button. 1947.
43-8420	20–25	Table. Blond wood. 1947.
43-8437	20–25	Table. Wood. 1946.
43-8470/8471	15–20	Table. Wood. 1946.
43-8576	15–20	Table. Wood. AM/SW. 1946.
43-8685	20–25	Table. Wood. 1947.
43-9196	20–25	Radio-phonograph. Table. 1947.
43-9201	15–20	Radio-phonograph. Table. 1947.
43-9235A	25–30	Radio-phonograph. Console. 1954.
43-9751	10–15	Portable. AC/battery. Leatherette. 1947.
45RA1-43-7666A	25–30	Radio-phonograph. Horizontal console. 1953.
45RA1-43-7910A	40–45	Radio-phonograph. Horizontal console. AM/FM. 1953.
45RA33-43-8147A/8148A	20–25	Table. Black or maroon plastic with contrasting front. 1953.
45RA37-43-9235A	25–30	Radio-phonograph. Table. Wood. 1954.
94RA1-43-6945B	30–35	Console. AM/FM. 1948.
94RA1-43-7605A	35–40	Radio-phonograph. Console. 1948.
94RA1-43-7656A	40–45	Radio-phonograph. Horizontal console. AM/FM. 1949.
94RA1-43-7853A	40–45	Radio-phonograph. Horizontal console. 1949.
94RA1-43-8510A/8511A	30–35	Table. Brown or ivory plastic. AM/FM. 1948.
94RA31-43-8115A/8115B	10–15	Table. Plastic. 1949.
94RA31-43-9841A	10–15	Portable. AC/battery. 1949.
94RA33-43-8130C/8131C	10–15	Table. Brown or ivory plastic. 1949.
94RA4-43-6945A	30–35	Console. AM/FM. 1948.

94RA4-43-8129A/8129B/ 8130A/8130B/8131A/ 8131B	10–15	Table. Plastic. Brown, white or black. 1948.
675	60–85	Upright table. AM/SW. 1934.
686	20–40	Table. Wood. AM/2SW. 1935. (GOR)
813	10–15	Table. 1938.
908	35–45	Upright table. 1939.
990B	100–125	Console.
RA12-8121A	10–15	Table. Plastic. 1957.
RA33-8115A "Pal"	15–20	Table. Plastic. 1955.
RA37-43-9240A	15–20	Radio-phonograph. Table. Wood. 1955.
RA37-43-9855	10–15	Portable. Plastic. AC/battery. 1954.
RA44-8140A/8141A	25–30	Table. Rosewood or coral plastic. 1955.
RA44-8340A/8341A	25–30	Table. Green or ivory plastic. 1955.
RA48-8257	10–15	Table. Plastic. 1958.
RA48-8342A	15–20	Table. Brown plastic. 1956.
RA48-8351A	25–30	Table. Ivory plastic. Striking "V" and crown grille. 1956.
RA48-8357	10–15	Table. Plastic. 1958.
TV2-9245A/9246A/9246B	30–35	Console. 1955

CROSLEY

Powel Crosley came up with a cheap radio design when he found that, in 1921, it would cost $130 to buy a set for his son. A talented engineer, Crosley found ways to produce better, cheaper parts for radios. Station WLW (Cincinnati) was started to promote radio sales. In 1929, Crosley acquired Amrad. Always interested in making good-quality, cheap appliances, Crosley produced refrigerators in the 1930s, including one with a radio built into the front of the cabinet. He also tried to compete in the field of cheap cars, both before and after World War II.

Note: Roman numerals are listed in numerical sequence with arabic numerals.

3R3 "Trirdyn"	50–80	Table. 2-dial. Battery. 1924.
IV	125–175	Table. 2-dial. Battery. 1922.
4-29	100–150	Table. Battery. 1926.
V	150–175	Table. Battery. 1923.
5-38	45–60	Table. Sloped front panel. 3-dial. Battery. 1926. (VR-81)
5-50	50–85	Table. Slope-front. Battery. Wood. 1926.
VI	125–150	Table. 2-dial. Battery. 1923. (VR-78)
	250	Same as above but with rare mahogany case.
6-60	85–125	Table. Battery. Wood. 1927.
7H3	60–65	Table. Wood. 1934.
7V2	90–100	Upright table. Deco. 1934.
VIII	150–200	Table. 2-dial. Battery. 1923.
9-113	10–15	Table. Plastic. Metal grille. 1949.
9-121	15–20	Table. Plastic. 1949.
9-202M	40–50	Radio-phonograph. Horizontal console. AM/FM. 1948.
9-207M	40–50	Radio-phonograph. Horizontal console. AM/FM/SW. 1949.
9-212M	35–40	Radio-phonograph. Horizontal console. 1949.
9-302	15–20	Portable. AC/battery. 1948.
X	100–150	Table. Battery. 2-dials. 1922. (GOR; VR-78, 81)

AR: *Antique Radios: Restoration and Price Guide* / **FOS:** *Flick of the Switch* / **GOR:** *Guide to Old Radios*
RGA: *Radios: The Golden Age* / **VR:** *Vintage Radio*

11-103U	50–60	Table. Orange plastic. Bull's-eye grille. 1949.
11-119	50–60	Table. Blue plastic. Bull's-eye grille. 1950.
11-123U	50–80	Clock-radio. Maroon plastic. Deco.
XV	200–250	Table. Battery. Same as model X with speaker. 2-dial. 1922.
31-S	80–120	Table radio with legs. Metal. Deco. Speaker has design of electric bolts. 1929. (GOR)
33-S	79–90	Lowboy. Wood. 1929. (GOR)
34-S	80–100	Lowboy with doors. Wood. 1929. (GOR)
50	100–125	Table. Battery. 1-tube. 1924. (VR-79)
50P	225–300	Portable. Leatherette. Battery. 1924.
51D	65–100	Table. Battery. 1924.
51P	75–125	Portable. Leatherette. Battery. 1924. (VR-79, 80)
51S	75–100	Table. Sloped front panel. Battery. 1924. (VR-79)
51SD "Special DeLuxe"	75–100	Table. Battery. 1924.
52	75–100	Table. Battery. 1924. (VR-81)
52S "Special"	75–125	Table. Battery. 1924.
52SD "Special DeLuxe"	75–100	Table. Battery. 1924.
52-TG	20–30	Table. Wood. 1941. (GOR)
54G "New Buddy"	175–250	Upright table. Molded wood. 1930. (GOR)
56TN-L	15–25	Table. Wood. AM/SW. 1947.
56TP-L	30–45	Table. 1948.
56TZ	30–40	Radio-phonograph. Table. 1948.
58TK	10–15	Table. Plastic. 1948.
58TL	10–15	Table. Ivory plastic. 1948.
58TW	10–15	Table. Plastic. Handle. 1948.
61	50–75	Table. Metal. DC. 1929. (Note: There was a model Six-ty-One, an upright table radio, made in 1934.)
66TA	40–60	Table. Brown Bakelite. AM/SW. 1946.
66TC	50–70	Table. Wood. AM/SW. 1946.
66TC "Victory"	60–80	Table. Wood. Label missing; probably a 66-TC. Cabinet marked 63TJWC. The word "Victory" is decorated in red, white, and blue. 1946. (GOR)
68TW	20–30	Table. White Bakelite. 1948.
82-S	70–90	Highboy with doors. Wood. 1929. (GOR)
87CQ	70–80	Radio-phonograph. Console. AM/FM/SW. 1948.
88TC	15–20	Table. AM/FM. 1948.
124H	125–200	Cathedral. 1931.
125	125–175	Cathedral. 1932. (GOR)
126-1	150–250	Grandfather clock style. 1932.
148 "Fiver D"	60–75	Table. Wood. 1933.
	100–200	Cathedral.
158	125–175	Cathedral. 1932.
167	75–100	Console. AM/SW. 1936.
	125–175	Cathedral. (GOR)
169	125–175	Cathedral. 1934. (FOS-75)
181	50–100	Upright table. Wood. 1934.
515	40–60	Upright table. AM/SW. 1934.
517 "Fiver"	50–75	Upright table. Wood. 1934.
555	40–60	Upright table. AM/SW. Wood. 1935. (GOR)
566	35–50	Table. Wood. Battery. 1937. (GOR)
567 "Fiver"	25–35	Table. Metal. 1941.
601 "Bandbox"	50–75	Table. Metal. Battery. 1927.
608 "Gembox"	50–75	Table. Metal. 1928. (VR-81; AR-32)
635-C "Buccaneer"	60–75	Table. AM/SW. 1935.
635-M "Buccaneer"	75–100	Console. Same as model 635-C.

704 "Jewelbox"	40–50	Table. Metal. 1929.
706 "Showbox"	75–100	Table. Metal. 1928.
716	50–75	Upright table. 1941.
817	50–75	Table. AM/SW. 1937.
7739	90–110	Console. Push-button. AM/SW. 1939.
AC 7	50–75	Table. Slope-front. 1927.
Ace	100–125	Table. 1-tube. 1922.
Ace 3B	100–150	Table. Battery. 1923.
Ace 5	115–135	Table. Battery. 1923.
Bandbox		Applies to both models 601 and 602.
Bandbox Jr.	40–60	Table. Metal. Battery. 1928.
Bookcase	100–125	Radio designed to look like a stack of books. 1932.
Buddy Boy	175–250	Table. Battery. Molded front. 1930.
Coca Cola bottle	1500 +	Bakelite. 1934?
D10CE	50–75	Table. Pale blue plastic. 1950.
D25MN	60–75	Clock-radio. Plastic. 1953. (GOR)
E10BE/CE/RD/WE	20–25	Table. Plastic. 1953.
E15	50–75	Table. White with chrome. 1951.
E75GN	25–35	Clock-radio. Plastic. 1953.
Fiver	75–100	Table. Applies to various models, all with five tubes. About 1936.
Harko	250–450	Crystal. 1921.
Harko Sr.	200–300	Table. Battery. 1922.
Harko Sr. V	250–350	Table. Battery. 1922.
Oracle	300–400	Clock-radio. Grandfather clock style. 1931.
Pup	150–250	Box. Metal. 1-tube. Battery. 1925. (VR-79)
RFL 60	75–125	Table. Wood. Battery. Picturesque front panel. (AR-22)
RFL 75	100–175	Table. 3-dial. Battery. 1926.
RFL 90	40–60	Table. Wood. Battery. 1926.
Showbox		Applies to both model 705 and 706.
Super 11	50–75	Console. AM/SW. 1937.
Super XJ	175–225	Table. Battery. 2-dial. 1924.
Super Trirdyn	75–100	Table. Battery. 2-dial. 1925.
Super Trirdyn Special	60–100	Table. Battery. 2-dial. 1925.
Trirdyn		See 3R3.
XJ	150–200	Table. 2-dial. Battery. 1923. (GOR; VR-81)
XL	175–225	Table. 2 dials. Battery. 1923.

CRUSADER

unknown	100–125	Cathedral.

CUTTING AND WASHINGTON

11A	225–300	Table. Battery. 2-dial. 1922.

CYART

unknown	2000 +	Table. Lucite.

DAY-FAN

The Dayton Fan and Motor Company began in 1889 and made all sorts of heavy-duty fans for large buildings. In 1922 the company came out with its first radios, which could be mounted on panels or breadboards. In 1926 the company changed its name to the

---

AR: Antique Radios: Restoration and Price Guide / **FOS:** *Flick of the Switch* / **GOR:** *Guide to Old Radios*
RGA: *Radios: The Golden Age* / **VR:** *Vintage Radio*

Day-Fan Electric Company. Continuing to lose money (reported to be $200,000 a year), it was finally sold to General Motors and RCA in 1929. The government brought an antitrust suit, and the company was finally liquidated in 1931.

5 (5114)	50–65	Table. Battery. 1925. (VR-128)
Dayola (5112)	65–90	Table. Battery. 4-dial. 1925.
OEM 7	50–100	Table. Battery. OEM 7 includes both model 5106 (1924) and model 5111 (1925). 3-dial.
OEM 11 (5105)	75–100	Table. Battery. 3-dial. 1924.

DE FOREST

When Lee De Forest invented the Audion tube, one that actually amplified, he created a major breakthrough in radio broadcasting. Unfortunately, his business mind wasn't as sharp as his scientific one. When he sold his patents to AT&T, however, he kept the right to produce amateur equipment. Always interested in broadcasting, he returned to the air in 1916 on a regular schedule, which helped create a market for his equipment. He also broadcast the election returns in 1916. Using a special line from the New York *American*, he announced to his audience that the winner was—Charles Evans Hughes.

15 panel	1500+	Panel. 2-dial. Battery. 1919. (VR-83)
D7	650	Table. Battery. 2-dial. 1922.
D10	400–500	Table. 2-dial. Loop antenna. Battery. 1923. (VR-84)
D12	250–300	Table. Battery. Loop antenna. 2-dial. 1924. (GOR)
D17	200–350	Table. 2-dial. Loop antenna. Battery. 1925.
DT600 "Everyman"	50–300	Crystal. 1922. (VR-84)
DT900 "Radiohome"	300–400	Box. 1-tube. 2-dial. Battery. 1922. (VR-84)
F-5 M	50–80	Table. Wood. 3-dial. Battery. Enclosed speaker. 1925. (AR-10; GOR)
F-5 AW	60–100	Table. Wood. Battery. 3-dial. 1925. (GOR)

DE FOREST CROSLEY

Canadian company.

51	75–100	Table. Battery. 1924.

DE WALD

Originally produced by the Pierce Airo Company.

562	1000+	Catalin. 1941.
802	100–150	Upright table. AM/3SW. 1934.
A501/B501	250–850	Catalin. Harp. Price depends on colors. 1946. (RGA-86, 87)
A502	900–1000	Catalin. 1946. (RGA-74)
B400	10–15	Portable. Leatherette. Battery. 1948.
B401	30–35	Table. Ivory plastic. 1948.
	25–30	Table. Brown plastic. 1948.
B403	400–600	Clock-radio. Catalin. Harp grille. 1948. (RGA-86, 87)
B506	25–25	Table. White plastic. 1948.
B510	10–15	Table. Plastic. 1948.
B512	400–600	Clock-radio. Catalin. 1948.
B614	35–45	Radio-phonograph. Portable. Alligator. 1949.
H528	20–25	Clock-radio. Plastic. 1954.

DEARBORN

100	20–25	Chairside. Radio-phonograph. 1947.

DELCO

We think of Delco as a division of General Motors. However, the division was really the United Motor Service, which produced GM parts. Delco was simply the trade name.

R-1119	40–45	Console. AM/2SW/LW. 1937.
R-1128	65–75	Table. AM/SW. 1937.
R-1229	15–25	Table. 2-tone wood. 1947. (GOR)
R-1235	30–35	Table. Bakelite. 1946.
R-1238	35–40	Table. 2-tone plastic. 1948.
R-1243	25–30	Table. Plastic. 1947.
R-1244	25–30	Radio-phonograph. Wood waterfall front. 1948.

DENCHUM

Made by Wilmak.

unknown	35–50	Table. Wood. Plastic handle. Wood louvers. Small. 1946. (GOR)
WW-446	50–75	Same as above, except stations are preset. Thumb knob is preset using screws on the bottom. 1946. (GOR)

DETROLA

unknown	500+	Similar to Sparton Bluebird, according to the advertisement. Wood. Deco.
100	50–65	Table. 1934.
302	50–75	Clock-radio. Cathedral shape. 1938.
436	10–15	Table.
568-1	25–30	Table. Metal. AM/SW. 1946.
580	100–125	Chairside. Radio-phonograph. 1947.
610-A	20–25	Table. Wood. Battery. 1949.

DOTSON

E 7	50–75	Table. Battery.

DRAY

599	60–75	Table. Battery. 1925.

DUMONT

RA-346	75–125	Clock-radio. Red lacquer with gold trim. Controls on side of cabinet. 1956. (GOR)

DYNAVOX

3-P-801	20–25	Portable. Leatherette. AC/battery. 1948.

EAGLE

Neutrodyne	40–80	Table. Battery. 1923. (VR-133)
Neutrodyne, type B	50–80	Table. Battery. 1926.

ECHOPHONE

Radio Shop (which consisted of three different companies) produced the earlier radios. Echophone was the sales organization. In the 1930s, the radios were produced by the Echophone Radio Manufacturing Company.

AR: *Antique Radios: Restoration and Price Guide* / **FOS:** *Flick of the Switch* / **GOR:** *Guide to Old Radios*
RGA: *Radios: The Golden Age* / **VR:** *Vintage Radio*

3	100–200	Table. 2-dial. Battery. 1923.
80	150–200	Cathedral. 1931.
A	150–200	Table. 2-dial. Battery. 1923. (VR-126)
EC-1A	75–100	Table. Communications receiver. AM/2SW. 1940.
EC 600	40–50	Table. Battery. 1946.
R-3	50–75	Table. Sloped panel. Battery. 1925.
R-5	50–75	Table. Sloped panel. 2-dial. Battery. 1925.
S-3	100–125	Cathedral. 1930.
S-4	100–150	Cathedral. 1931.
S-5	200–250	Console. 1931.

EDISON

Edison, for many years, did not approve of radio. When he heard his Edison phonograph being used to play records over WJZ (Newark), he phoned to ask them to stop using the machine. "If the phonograph sounded like that in any room, nobody would ever buy it." But when he decided to build a radio himself, he built it in typical Edison fashion—as a substantial, solid piece of furniture, well-engineered, and built to last.

C4	600–750	Radio-phonograph. Console. 1929.
R2	100–150	Console. 1929.
R5	125–175	Console. 1929.

EICO

HFT-90	15–25	FM tuner.

EISEMANN *(see also Freed-Eisemann)*

6-D	50–80	Table. Wood. 3-dial. Battery. 1925. (GOR)

EKCO (British)

AD 65	150–250	Table. Bakelite. Deco. 1934.

ELECTROMATIC

512	100–125	Radio-phonograph. Wood. 1946. (GOR)

EMERSON

38	60–75	Table. 1934. (FOS-82, identified as U6D)
107	40–60	Table. Deco. AM/SW. 1936.
238	200–250	Chest. Looks like jewelry box. 1939.
375	750+	Table. Catalin. 5 slats left, 1 slat right. 1941.
400 "Patriot"	450–650	Table. Catalin. Various colors. 1940. (RGA-53)
	1500+	Red, white, and blue. Same as above.
410 "Mickey Mouse"	1000+	Table. Wood with metal trim. Black with chrome or ivory with cream. 1933. (FOS-82; RGA-13)
411 "Mickey Mouse"	1000+	Table. Molded wood. 1933. (RGA-12)
507	30–35	Table. Brown or ivory plastic. 1946.
520	100–200	Table. Swirled brown Catalin, white front. Aqua dial. 1946. (GOR)
522	50–75	Table. Ivory Bakelite. 1946.
530	20–25	Table. AM/SW. 1947.
536	15–25	Portable. AC/battery. Leatherette. 1948.
539	20–25	Table. 1946.
541	25–30	Table. Wood. 1948. (GOR)
543	35–45	Table. Plastic. Metal grille. Deco. 1947.
544	25–35	Table. Plastic. 1947.

547A	25–30	Table. White plastic. 1947. (GOR)
553A	40–50	Portable. New in box. 1947.
559A	15–25	Portable. Swirled maroon plastic front. Molded alligator grain case. 1948. (AR-67)
576A	30–35	Radio-phonograph. Horizontal console. 1948.
578A	25–40	Table. Wood. European styling. 1946. (GOR)
587	15–20	Table. White plastic. 1949.
602C	35–40	Table. Plastic. Side controls. FM only. 1949.
610A	20–25	Table. Plastic. Side controls. 1949.
641B	15–20	Table. Brown plastic. 1953.
645	15–20	Portable. AC/battery. 1949.
652	20–40	Table. White plastic. 1950.
659	20–25	Table. AM/FM. 1949.
671B	20–40	Clock-radio. Plastic. 1950.
688	20–40	Table. Wood. AM/FM. 1951.
729B	15–20	Table. Ivory plastic. Metallic grille. 1953.
	30–35	Red plastic.
	25–30	Blue or green plastic.
745B	20–25	Portable. Battery/AC. Tartan grille. 1954.
747	10–15	Portable. Plastic. Battery. 1954.
754D	10–15	Portable. Leatherette. Black or brown. AC/battery. 1954.
756B	15–20	Table. Black or brown plastic. 1953.
	30–35	Red plastic.
778B	20–25	Table. Black or ivory plastic. 1953.
	30–35	Red or green plastic.
779B	20–25	Table. 1953.
783B	25–30	Radio-phonograph. Table. 1953.
788B	15–20	Clock-radio. Brown, black, or ivory plastic. 1953.
801	10–15	Portable. Battery. Green, maroon, black, or grey plastic. 1954.
805B	10–15	Table. Brown or ivory plastic. 1954.
808B	20–25	Table. Black, ivory, or grey plastic. 1954.
	30–35	Red, green, yellow, or maroon plastic.
809A	40–45	Radio-phonograph. Horizontal console. 1954.
810	15–25	Table. Black plastic. 1954.
810B	10–15	Table. Brown, black, or ivory plastic. 1954.
	15–20	Green or maroon plastic.
811B	10–15	Table. Black, brown, ivory, green, or grey plastic. 1954.
812B	10–15	Table. Black. green, grey, or ivory plastic. 1954.
813B	15–20	Table. Black, brown, ivory, green, or grey plastic. 1954.
814B	20–25	Radio-phonograph. Table. 1954.
823B	15–20	Table. Brown or ivory plastic. 1955.
	20–25	Black plastic.
	25–30	Green plastic.
825B	15–20	Clock-radio. Black, ivory, brown, green, or grey plastic. 1955.
826B	20–25	Clock-radio. Black, ivory, brown, green, or grey plastic. 1955.
	35–40	Red or pink plastic.
830B	10–15	Portable. Plastic. AC/battery. 1955.
832B	15–20	Table. Brown, grey or ivory plastic. Side control. 1955.
	25–30	Green plastic.

AR: *Antique Radios: Restoration and Price Guide* / **FOS:** *Flick of the Switch* / **GOR:** *Guide to Old Radios*
RGA: *Radios: The Golden Age* / **VR:** *Vintage Radio*

835A	30–35	Radio-phonograph. Small console. 1955.
837A	15–20	Portable. Leather. 1955.
AX-235 "Baby"	450–550	Table. Catalin. 1938. (FOS-83; RGA-29)
BA-199	75–100	Table. Brown bakelite. 1938. (FOS-82; GOR; RGA-31)
BD-197	300–325	Table. Wood. AM/SW. Deco. Now known (for self-evident reasons) as the "Dolly Parton" set. 1941–1942.
BM-206	30–50	Table. Bakelite. 1938.
CH-256	75–100	Table. Wood. Violin-shaped case. 1939.
CQ-273	50–75	Table. Wood. AM/SW. 1939.
FP-421	30–35	Table. 1941.
FU–427	15–25	Portable. Cloth covered. 1941. (GOR)
J-106	50–60	Table. 1935.
L-559 "Radio Chest"	125–175	Chest. 1932.
Mickey Mouse	1000+	One of two models. Model 410 is wood with metal trim, model 411 is molded wood. 1933. (FOS-82; RGA-12, 13)
Patriot 400	450–650	Table. Catalin. Various colors. 1940.
	1500+	Red, white, and blue.
Q-236 "Snow White"	750+	Table. Molded wood, with the characters hand-painted by Disney artists.
R-156	50–100	Upright table. Wood. 1936.
U5A	1500+	Upright table. Plastic. 1935. (FOS-82; RGA-18)

EMUD (German)

Rekord 196 Junior	50–75	Table. 1960. (AR-68)

ERLA

unknown	200–250	Cathedral with clock.
DeLuxe 5	50–75	Table. Battery. 3-dial. 1925.
Pearson 5	60–70	Table. Battery. 3-dial. 1925.
Single 6	60–75	Table. Battery. 1927.

EVEREADY

1	125–150	Table. Battery. 1927.
2	50–75	Table. Battery. 1928.
3	60–80	Table. Battery. 1928

FADA

Frank A. d'Andrea to Frank A. D. Andrea to F. A. D. Andrea and finally to Fada. Even though the corporate name might change, the sets were always Fada. As with so many companies, F. A. D. Andrea failed during the Depression. In 1932, the company was sold and its new name was the Fada Radio & Electric Corporation. Andrea had meanwhile formed the Andrea Radio Corporation and was still running it when he died in 1965.

In spite of current usage, Fada was not spelled in uppercase letters.

35-B	100–150	Highboy with doors. Wood. 1929. (GOR)
115	300–600	Table. Catalin. 1941. (RGA 64, 65)
160	100–150	Console. Wood. AM/SW. 1935.
160-T	75–100	Table. Wood. AM/SW. 1935.
170-A	50–100	Console. AM/SW. 1935.
175	60–75	Radio-phonograph. Console. AM/SW. 1941. Note: Fada also made the 175A, a 3-dial set, in 1924.
185	65–75	Radio-phonograph. Console. AM/SW. 1941.

185/90A "Neutrola Grand"	100–150	Lowboy. Slant front panel. Drop front. Base has doors. Enclosed speaker above radio panel. 1925. (GOR)
192-A	80–100	Table. Battery. 1924. This model number was also used with different suffixes in 1935.
195	70–80	Radio-phonograph. Console. 1940.
254	150–200	Table. Black Bakelite. 1937. (RGA/27)
652	350–700	Table. Catalin. 1946. (RGA-67)
unknown	55–75	Table. Wood. Similar to series 652 Bakelite radios. 1947. (GOR)
700	500–700	Table. Catalin. Handle. 1947.
790	75–100	Table. White urea. AM/SW. Deco. 1948. (GOR)
795	20–25	Table. Plastic. FM only. 1948.
845	75–100	Table. White plastic. Red handle and knobs. 1950.
1000	300–600	Table. Catalin. 1946. (GOR; RGA-64)
Bullet		Refers to both model 115 and model 1000.
Streamliner		Refers to both model 115 and model 1000.

FAIRBANKS MORSE

9AC-4	75–125	Console. Wood. Telephone dial. 1937. (GOR)

FARNSWORTH

Farnsworth also made Capehart after World War II.

AT-50	30–60	Upright table. AM/SW. Push-button. 1939.
DT-64	10–15	Table. 1946.
ET-066	40–60	Table. Wood. 1946.
ET-067	25–35	Table. Wood. 1946. (GOR)
GT-050	30–40	Table. Plastic. Deco. 1948.
GT-051	40–50	Table. Plastic. 1948.
GT-064	20–25	Table. Plastic. 1948.
GT-065	20–25	Table. Ivory plastic. 1948.

FEDERAL

57	300–400	Table. Metal. Battery. 1922. (VR-86)
58-DX "Orthosonic"	350–500	Table. Wood or metal. Battery. 1922. (VR-86)
59	350–450	Table. Wood or metal. Battery. 3-dial. 1923. (VR-86)
61	600–800	Table. Wood or metal. Battery. 3-dial. 1924. (VR-86)
102	275–325	Portable. Battery. 2-dial. 1924.
110	300–400	Table. Wood or metal. Battery. 2-dial. 1924.
141	200–250	Table. Battery. 2-dial. 1925.
161	750–1000	Highboy. Battery. 3-dial. 1925.
200	50–100	Panel. 3-dial. 1925.
A10 "Orthosonic"	75–100	Table. Battery. 3-dial. 1925.
Orthosonic		Refers to many models during 1925 and 1926 besides the A10.

FERGUSON

TRF	50–75	Portable. Battery. 1925.

FERRAR

T61-B	10–15	Table. AM/SW. 1948.

AR: *Antique Radios: Restoration and Price Guide* / **FOS**: *Flick of the Switch* / **GOR**: *Guide to Old Radios*
RGA: *Radios: The Golden Age* / **VR**: *Vintage Radio*

FIRESTONE

4-A-1	10–20	Table. Plastic. 1948.
4-A-3	10–20	Table. Plastic. 1948.
4-A-10	10–20	Table. Plastic. 1948.
4-A-15	100–125	Radio-phonograph. Horizontal console. Large. AM/FM/SW. 1948.
4-A-17	25–30	Radio-phonograph. Table. 1948.
4-A-21	60–75	Table. AM/SW. 1946.
4-A-26	15–20	Table. White plastic. 1948.
4-A-27	15–25	Table. Black plastic. 1947. (GOR)
4-A-41	10–15	Table. White plastic. 1948.
4-A-60	60–75	Radio-phonograph. Horizontal console. AM/FM. 1948.
4-A-68	15–20	Table. Plastic. 1949.
4-A-160	10 15	Clock-radio. Plastic. 1957.
4-C-3	20–25	Portable. AC/battery. 1947.
4-C-5	30–35	Portable. AC/battery. 1948.
4-C-24	20–25	Portable. Cloth. AC/battery. 1954.
R-3051	40–60	Table. Wood. AM/SW. 1939. (GOR)
S-7403-4	40–60	Table. Wood. Small. Angled grille. 1939. (GOR)
S-7403-8	75–100	Upright table. Wood. Push-button. AM/2SW. 1939. (GOR)

FREED EISEMANN *(see also Eisemann)*

The company made both Freed and Freed-Eisemann. Later it became the Freed Radio and Television Corporation.

10	75–100	Table. Battery. 1926.
30	80–100	Table. Battery. 1926.
50	85–100	Table. Battery. 1926.
FE15	50–80	Table. Battery. 3-dial. 1925. (VR-88)
FE-28	30–50	Table. Wood. AM/SW. 1937. (GOR)
NR5	55–80	Table. Battery. 3-dial. 1923. (VR-88)
NR6	60–80	Table. Battery. 3-dial. 1924.
NR7	75–100	Table. Battery. 3-dial. 1925. (VR-88)
NR20	100–150	Table. Battery. 3-dial. 1924.
NR45	50–75	Table. Battery. 3-dial. 1925

FRESHMAN

Freshman radios of the 1920s were made by the Charles Freshman Company. It's worth noting, however, that B.R.C. Company made cathedrals with this name in the 1930s.

Masterpiece	70–100	Table. 3-dial. Battery. 1924 or 1925. (AR-8; VR-89)

GAROD

4B-1	10–15	Portable. Plastic. Battery. 1948.
V	20–50	Table. Battery. 3-dial. 1924. (VR-132)
5A-1 "Ensign"	10–20	Table. Plastic. 1947.
5A-4	20–25	Table. Plastic. 1948.
5D-55	25–30	Portable. AC/battery. Metal and plastic. 1948.
6AU-1 "Commander"	750+	Table. Catalin. 1941. (RGA-58)
11FMP	75–90	Radio-phonograph. Blond wood. Horizontal console. 1948.
126	40–50	Table. Plastic.
769	80–100	Table. Wood. Push-button. AM/SW. Mid-1930s. (GOR)
RAF	100–150	Table. Battery. 3-dials. 1924–1926.

GEC

GEC is the British General Electric Company.

8336	40–60	Upright table. European styling. Severe lines. c. 1936. (GOR)

GENERAL ELECTRIC

General Electric was one of the originators of RCA in an effort to keep transoceanic communication out of the hands of the English. Under the original agreements, RCA wasn't allowed to make radios, but it could market them under its own name. Ironically, in 1986 the RCA consumer electronics division was reabsorbed by G.E. And then, as a final step, this combined consumer electronics division was bought by the giant Thompson S.A., a French electronics company.

Note: The earliest General Electric sets were made for and sold under the RCA name. Look for them there.

42 "Musaphonic"	200–250	Radio-phonograph. Horizontal console. AM/2FM/3SW. Large. 1947.
60	30–35	Clock-radio. Plastic. 1948. (FOS-95)
65	10–15	Clock-radio. White plastic. 1950. (GOR)
113	10–15	Table. Plastic. 1948.
119W	30–40	Radio-phonograph. Horizontal console. 1948.
160	10–15	Portable. Plastic. AC/battery. 1949.
202	20–25	Table. White plastic. 1948. (GOR)
203	20–30	Table. Wood. 1946. (FOS-93)
210/211/212	20–25	Table. Plastic. Cloth front. AM/FM. 1948.
254	15–20	Portable. AC/battery. 1947.
304	30–35	Radio-phonograph. Table. 1947.
321	20–30	Table. Wood. Push-button. 1946. (GOR)
354	60–75	Radio-phonograph. Horizontal console. 1948.
356	25–30	Table. Plastic. AM/FM. 1948.
357	15–20	Table. Plastic. 1948.
400	90–125	Console. AM/2SW. Push-button. 1941. (GOR)
408	30–35	Table. Plastic. 1949.
409	15–25	Table. Plastic. 1952.
414	20–25	Table. Dark red swirled plastic. 1950.
	10–15	Brown plastic.
422	50–65	Table. Marbelized maroon plastic. 1951. (GOR)
440	20–25	Table. Plastic. AM/FM. 1954.
502	100–125	Radio-phonograph. Horizontal console. AM/2FM/3SW. Large. 1948.
511	10–15	Clock-radio. 1949.
517	25–30	Clock-radio. Red plastic. 1949.
555	15–20	Clock-radio. Ivory plastic with brown knob and dial. 1954.
555G	15–20	Same as model 555. Grey, with brown knob and dial.
	25–35	Red, with ivory knob and dial.
606	15–20	Portable. Green plastic. AC/battery. 1950.
913	30–35	Clock-radio. Pink plastic.
A-63	40–60	Upright table. AM/SW. 1935. This same model number was available as AM-only in 1936.
A-82	125–150	Console. Deco. AM/3SW. 1936.

AR: *Antique Radios: Restoration and Price Guide* / **FOS:** *Flick of the Switch* / **GOR:** *Guide to Old Radios*
RGA: *Radios: The Golden Age* / **VR:** *Vintage Radio*

B-52	65–100	Car radio. Metal. Crackle brown paint. Dual voltage (6v and 110v). 1934. (FOS-91; GOR)
C-420B	15–30	Clock-radio. Plastic. 1958.
C-453	20–25	Table. Plastic. 1960.
C-517	20–25	Table. Red with white plastic. 1961.
Coca Cola	20–25	Coca Cola logo on usual style transistor AM/FM radio. 1970s.
E-50	60–90	Table. Red with black trim. 1937.
E-52	15–25	Table. Wood. 1936. (GOR)
E-61	125–150	Upright table. AM/SW. 1936.
E-71	75–100	Upright table. AM/SW. 1936.
E-81	90–100	Upright table. AM/SW. 1936.
E-101	90–120	Upright table. Colorama tuning. 1937.
F-63	30–50	Table. AM/SW. Strong curve on one side. Louvered grille. 1937. (GOR)
F-70	40–50	Table. AM/SW. 1937.
G-50	45–60	Table. Wood. Telephone dial. 1937. (GOR)
H-51	250–400	Lowboy. Push-button. Made by RCA. Same as RCA Radiola 82. 1931.
H-77	250–325	Radio-phonograph. Console. Push-button. AM/SW. 1939. (FOS-92)
H-530	35–40	Upright table. 1939.
H-623	35–45	Table. Wood. AM/SW. 1940.
H-634	30–50	Table. Wood. AM/2SW. 1940.
H-7101Y	800	Lowboy. Push-button. Remote control. Made by RCA. Same as RCA Radiola 86. 1931.
HJ-624	20–40	Table. Wood. Push-button. Curved side. 1939. (GOR)
J-805	60 80	Console. Push-button. AM/SW. 1940.
JCP-562	25–40	Table. Wood. 1942. (GOR)
K40-A	35–40	Table. Wood. 1933. (FOS-88)
K-43	40–50	Table. Wood. 1934. (AR-53)
K-48	75–85	Radio-phonograph. Table. AM/SW. 1933.
K-53	75–100	Table. Wood. Deco. 1933.
K-63	150–225	Upright table. AM/SW. 1933. (FOS-89)
L-630	25–30	Table. 2-tone wood. 1940.
L-641	30–40	Table. Wood. AM/SW. 1942. (GOR)
L-740	30–50	Table. Wood. 3-band. 1941. (FOS-93)
L-916	90–110	Console. AM/2SW. Push-button. 1941. (GOR)
LB530X	45–50	Portable. AC/DC/battery. Self-charging, wet battery. 1940.
Lowboy	90–120	Lowboy. Wood. Plain cabinet. Fancy grille. 1930. (FOS-86; GOR)
M-51A	75–100	Upright table. 1935.
M-62	60–80	Upright table. Wood. Made by RCA. Similar to RCA model 125. 1934.
M-63	40–50	Upright table. Deco. 1933.
M-81	125–150	Upright table. AM/SW. 1934.
Mickey Mouse	40–60	Clock-radio. White plastic. 1950s.
X-415	40–60	Table. Wood. AM/2FM/2SW. 1948. (GOR)
YRB-60-12	15–20	Table. White plastic. 1948.

GENERAL IMPLEMENT

9A5	40–50	Table. Plastic. 1948.

GENERAL MOTORS *(see also Day-Fan and Delco)*

252	125–150	Lowboy. Wood. Pull up door covers dial. Speaker faces the floor. 1932. (GOR)
Little General	150–250	Cathedral. 1931.
Plug In Portable	20–35	Portable. Wood. AC/battery. Late 1930s. (GOR)

GENERAL TELEVISION

5B5	1000+	Table. Catalin. Sausage grille. 1946.
9A5	350–500	Table. Bright yellow, thin green plastic. 1948.
9B6P	35–40	Table. Plastic. Metallic face. 1948.
24B6	25–30	Table. Plastic. 1948.
27C5	15–20	Table. Plastic. 1948.

GILFILLAN

Gilfillan started as a smelting and refining company in 1912. By 1915, it was producing parts for auto ignitions. Moving into early radio, it became a member of the Independent Radio Manufacturers, Inc., a group of fourteen companies fighting RCA over its patents. In 1927, Gilfillan got the West Coast rights to the RCA patents.

66B "Overland"	20–40	Portable. Leatherette. Swing-out doors. Copper grille. 1947. (FOS-98; GOR)

GLOBE

51	60–75	Table. Marbelized plastic. 2-tone. 1947.
62C	30–35	Radio-phonograph. Wood table. AM/SW. 1947.
457	20–25	Table. Plastic. 1948.
770	50–60	Portable. Battery. 2-dial. 1923.
830 "Duodyne"	125–150	Table. Battery. 3-dial. 1925.
900 "Duodyne"	175–200	Table. Battery. 3-dial. 1925.
Duodyne		Applies to at least 10 models from 1924 through 1926.

GLORITONE

Made by U.S. Radio and Television Corporation. U.S. Radio made eight different small brands.

26	100–150	Cathedral. 1929.
26P	100–125	Cathedral. 1929.
27	100–150	Cathedral. Deco style. Dial is on right side, not in center. 1930. (GOR)
99P	100–125	Cathedral. 1931.

GRANTLINE

Sold by the W. T. Grant Company.

501-7	25–30	Table. White plastic. 1948.
508-7	15–20	Portable. AC/battery. 1948.
5610	75–90	End table. 1948.

GRAYBAR

Graybar was begun in 1925 and sold to its employees in 1928.

330	35–40	Table. Basically a Radiola 60 with an RCA 106 speaker. 1929.

AR: *Antique Radios: Restoration and Price Guide* / **FOS:** *Flick of the Switch* / **GOR:** *Guide to Old Radios*
RGA: *Radios: The Golden Age* / **VR:** *Vintage Radio*

GREBE

820	100–200	Highboy with doors. Back panel goes to floor. Wood. 1928. (GOR)
CR-5	300–450	Tuner-detector. Battery. 1921. (VR-93)
CR-8	300–450	Table. Battery. 3-dial. SW. 1922. (AR-7; VR-93)
CR-9	250–375	Table. Battery. 2-dial. 1922. (VR-93)
CR-12	300–400	Table. Battery. 2-dial. 1923.
CR-13	500–650	Table. Battery. 3-dial. 1923.
CR-14	400–500	Table. Battery. 2-dial. 1924.
CR-18	400–500	Table. Battery. SW. 2-dial. 1926. (VR-94)
MU-1 "Synchrophase"	150–250	Table. Battery. 1925. (AR-12)
Synchrophase Five	40–60	Table. Mahogany wood with mahogany Bakelite panel. 1928. (GOR; VR-94)
Synchrophase A-C Six	40–70	Table. Mahogany wood with burled walnut panel. 1928. (GOR)
Synchrophase Seven	100–150	Table. Battery. 1927.
"Synchrophase"		Was model identification. Was combined with model numbers on various models during the 1920s.

DAVID GRIMES

5 B "Baby Grand Duplex"	75–125	Table. 3-dial. Battery. 1925. (VR-127)
Baby Grand	75–150	Table. 2-dial. Battery. 1925.

GRUNDIG

87	30–50	Table. Ivory plastic. AM/FM. 1962.

GRUNOW

Grigsby-Grunow made the early Majestic radios. It folded during the Depression, and General Household Utilities got the Grunow name.

470	100–125	Upright table. 1934.
500	90–100	Upright table. Chrome grille. 1933.
502	40–70	Upright table. Battery. Deco. 1934.
620	30–50	Upright table. Battery. 1935.
680	40–60	Upright table. 1935.
750	60–80	Upright table. AM/3SW. 1934. (GOR)
1183	90–150	Console. Wood. Telephone dial. 1937. (GOR)
1291	100–125	Console. Wood. Telephone dial. AM/3SW. Chassis 12B. 12-tube. 1936. (GOR)
1297 "Teledial 12"	200–300	Console. AM/2SW. 1936. (FOS-97)

HALLICRAFTERS

Hallicrafters originally specialized in amateur radio and communications equipment.

5R230	20–25	Table. Maroon plastic. AM/SW. 1954.
5R231	15–20	Same as 5R230. White plastic.
5R232	25–30	Same as 5R230. Blue plastic.
406	50–60	Radio-phonograph. Horizontal console. AM/FM/SW. 1948.
611	25–30	Table. Brown plastic, beige knobs. 1954.
612	30–35	Same as 611. Green plastic.
S-38E	25–50	Table. Metal. AM/3SW. 1953.
S-53	40–60	Table. Metal. AM/4SW. 1948.
S-55	40–50	Table. Metal. AM/FM. No built-in speaker. 1949.
S-58	30–45	Table. Metal. AM/FM. 1949.

Sky Buddy	25–50	Table. Amateur. 1936.
SX-9 "Super Skyrider"	45–50	Table. Amateur. 1936.
SX-42	90–100	Table. Amateur. 1948.
SX-43	65–75	Table. Amateur. 1948.
TW 500	40–50	Portable. 3-band.
TW 2000 "World Wide"	55–75	Portable. 7-band.

HEATHKIT

GC 1-A "Mohican"	55–75	Table. AM/4SW.
GR 1085	20–25	Table. AM/SW.

HI-DELITY

AM 51	10–15	Table. White plastic. Late 1950s.

HOFFMAN

C-502	75–100	Radio-phonograph. Blond wood. Horizontal console. AM/FM. 1948.
C1007	175–200	Radio-phonograph-wire recorder. Horizontal console. AM/FM. 1949.

HOWARD

In 1929, Howard merged with the Everett Piano Company.

10	75–100	Upright table. Wood. 1931.
368	50–65	Table. Wood. 1938. (GOR)
474	20–25	Table. Plastic. AM/FM. 1947.
906	50–75	Table. Wood. 1947. (GOR)

HUDSON ELECTRONICS

RPM71	15–20	Portable. Radio-phonograph. Leatherette. 1952.

INTERNATIONAL

The International Kadette was the first mass-produced plastic radio, back in 1932.

36	25–50	Table. Wood. AM/SW. 1937. (FOS-101)
40 "Jewel"	75–125	Table. Plastic. Contrasting grille. 1936.
77	50–70	Upright table. Wood. AM/SW. 1936.
B-2 "Kadette"	125–175	Table. AM/SW. 1933.
Classic	100–150	Table. Striking horizontal grille. 1936.
K-28 "Clockette"	100–150	Clock-shaped. Easily mistaken for a clock. Urea.

JACKSON

J-200/J-400	20–25	Portable. Radio-phonograph. Leatherette. 1952.

JACKSON-BELL

Mr. Jackson (primarily a silent partner) and Herb Bell started this company in 1926. One of the Los Angeles companies that began making midget sets in 1929, Jackson-Bell was well-situated when the Depression hit. Because of poor management, however, it was forced into receivership in 1933. Selling off its assets, the company paid off virtually all the money it owed.

---

*AR: Antique Radios: Restoration and Price Guide / FOS: Flick of the Switch / GOR: Guide to Old Radios
RGA: Radios: The Golden Age / VR: Vintage Radio*

60	65–75	Table. 1929. (FOS-102)
62	150–200	Cathedral. Deco. 1930. (FOS-102; the top two models on the page are both 62.)
		Note: There were two distinctly different models known as 62. The one is angular and Deco-styled, with a sunburst grille. The other is a conventional rounded-top cathedral with a swan motif on the grille.

JEWEL

300	15–25	Table. 1948.
304	25–30	Portable. Alligator. Battery. 1948.
814	15–20	Portable. Plastic. Strap-over-arm. 1948.
920	15–20	Clock-radio. Brown plastic. 1949. (GOR)
935	30–35	Table. 1949.

JUBILEE

| unknown | 85–100 | Crystal. |

KADETTE (see International)

KAPPLER

| 102T | 35–40 | Panel. Professional rack mount. 1949. |

KELLER FULLER

| 14 "Radiette" | 70–100 | Cathedral. 1930. |

KELLOGG

| Wavemaster 500 | 50–100 | Table. Wood. Battery. 1925. (VR-138) |

KENMAN

| 5 | 40–60 | Table. Battery. 3-dial. 1925. |

KENNEDY

V	200–350	Table. Battery. Sloped front panel. 2-dial. 1923. (GOR; VR-96)
VI	150–200	Table. Battery. Sloped front panel. 2-dial. 1925.
X	250–300	Table. Battery. Sloped panel. 2-dial. 1923.
XV	200–300	Table. Battery. Wood. 2-dial. 1924. (VR-96)
20	150–250	Table. Battery. Wood. 1925.
110	600–900	Table. Battery. 4-dial. Wood. 1922. (VR-96)
220	300–550	Small console. 1929. (AR-4; VR-96)
281	300–500	Table. Battery. 3-dial. 1921. (VR-96)

KING

| 80 | 75–90 | Table. Battery. Wood. 1927. |
| 81A | 60–75 | Table. Battery. Wood. 1927. |

KLITZEN

| 525 | 75–100 | Table. Battery. 1924. |

KNIGHT

Allied Radio's house brand.

| 4D-450 | 10–15 | Portable. 1948. |

5D-250	10–15	Table. Plastic. 1949.
5D-455	10–15	Portable. AC/battery. 1948.
5F-525	15–20	Table. Plastic. 1949.
5F-565	10–15	Portable. Leatherette. AC/battery. 1949.
6D-235	25–30	Table. 1949.
6D-360	35–40	Radio-phonograph. Console. AM/SW. 1948.
7D-405	15–20	Radio-phonograph. Table. 1948.
11D-302	30–40	Radio-phonograph. Horizontal console. AM/FM. 1949.
B10517	25–45	Table. Wood. Push-button. 1941. (GOR)

KODEL

C-13	150–250	Table. Battery. 2-dial. Wood. 1924. (AR-131; GOR)
C-14	40–60	Table. Wood. Battery. 2-dial. 1925. (AR-131; GOR)

KOLSTER

6D	40–60	Table. Wood. Battery. 1926. (AR-10)
6J	40–60	Table. Wood. 1927.

LAFAYETTE

E 77	15–20	Table. Plastic.

LEARRADIO

RM-4026	30–40	Portable. AM/SW/LW. AC/battery.

LEUTZ

Pliodyne 6	275–350	Table. Battery. 1924.

MAGIC TONE

508	125–175	Keg. 1948.
510	25–30	Portable. Fake snakeskin. Strap for overarm use. 1948.
900	250–300	Keg-lamp. 1948.

MAGNAVOX

Magnavox entered the radio field by producing speakers (*Magnavox* means "great voice" in Latin). Magnavox introduced the first one-dial receiver in 1924. Located in California, the company had difficulty in being competitive with more centrally located companies. The Depression forced them into a merger with a division of Amrad. The company continues to make consumer electronics, although since 1981 it's been as a part of North American Phillips.

Imperial	2000 +	Radio-phonograph. Classic breakfront. 1946. (FOS-105)
TRF-5	75–100	Table with doors. Large. Battery. 1924. (VR-128)
TRF 50	150–200	Upright table with doors. Battery. 1924. (GOR; VR-100)

MAJESTIC

Majestic was the name used by Grigsby Grunow until the company failed in 1934. After that, it continued as the Majestic Radio and Television Corporation while the Grunow name became associated with General Household Utilities.

1 "Charlie "McCarthy"	500 +	Table. 3-dimensional seated figure. 1938. (FOS-108; RGA-35)

AR: *Antique Radios: Restoration and Price Guide* / **FOS**: *Flick of the Switch* / **GOR**: *Guide to Old Radios*
RGA: *Radios: The Golden Age* / **VR**: *Vintage Radio*

1A50	25-50	Table. Wood. Deco. 1939.
1A-59	25-40	Table. Wood. 1939. (GOR)
6FM773	35-40	Radio-phonograph. Console. Blond wood. 1949.
7FM888	30-35	Radio-phonograph. Horizontal console. Leatherette door panels. AM/FM. 1949.
8FM889	50-60	Radio-phonograph. Horizontal console. Leatherette inserts on doors. AM/FM. 1949.
15	75-100	Cathedral. Deco. 1932.
	300-400	Grandfather clock. 1932.
20	100-125	Cathedral. 1932.
50	100-150	Vertical table. 1931. (FOS-107)
52	100-125	Table radio with legs attached. 1932.
	40-50	Table. Plastic. 1938.
		Note: Majestic reused this model number for two very different models, one manufactured in 1932 and the other in 1938.
92	100-150	Highboy. 1929.
101	75-100	Radio-phonograph. Lowboy. 1939.
103	100-125	Radio-phonograph. Lowboy. 1930.
130	35-40	Portable. Leatherette. Battery. Shaped like a purse. 1939. (FOS-107)
		Note: Another example of Majestic using the same number for two different years. There was also a model 130 console in 1930.
151	100-125	Upright table. 1931.
381	75-125	Treasure chest. 1933. (FOS-107)
461	60-75	Table. Deco. Chrome grille. 1933.
463	70-100	Table. Chrome grille. Deco. 1933.
511	300-350	Table. White Bakelite, blue Catalin grille. 1938.
906 "Riviera"	150-200	Bookshelf radio. Deco. 1933.
921 "Melody Cruiser"	250-350	Ship with metal sails. 1946. (RGA-73)
Charlie McCarthy	200-250	Table. 1938. (FOS-108; RGA-35)

MALONE LEMON

Neutrodyne	50-75	Table. Battery. 1924-1925.

MANTOLA

Sold by B. F. Goodrich.

R-654-PM	15-30	Table. Brown Bakelite. 1946.
R-75343	15-20	Table. 1948.
R-75152	15-20	Radio-phonograph. Table. 1948.
R-76162	35-40	Radio-phonograph. Console. 1948.
R-76262	100-125	Chairside. Radio-phonograph. Radio in drawer. 1948.

MARWOL

This company appears to have been in business in 1925 only, but it listed thirteen different models for that year.

Console Grand	50-60	Lowboy. Battery. 1925.
Jewel	50-60	Table. Battery. 1925.

MECK

4C7	10-15	Table. Ivory plastic. 1948.
CD-500	15-20	Radio-phonograph. Table. 1948.

CE-500	10–15	Table. Plastic. 1948.
CM-500	10–15	Portable. Leatherette. AC/battery. 1948.
CR-500	25–30	Table. AM/FM. 1948.
CW-500	10–15	Table. Plastic. 1948.

MELODYNE

This Melodyne was made by the Melodyne Radio Company of New York City. The four models listed in *Radio Collector's Guide* were all made during 1926. Another company using the Melodyne name was the Radio Sales and Manufacturing Company. "Mellodyne" (with two ls) is a still different company.

| 11 | 50–60 | Console. 1926. |

METRODYNE

Made by the Metro Electric Company. Metro used its own name for the crystal radios it produced during 1923 and 1924. When the company began building TRF sets, it used this more glamorous name.

Super 5	40–60	Table. Battery. Wood. 1926.
Super 6	90–110	Table. Battery. 1926.
Super 7	125–200	Table. Battery. Elaborate front panel. 1926. (AR-23; VR-141)

MICHIGAN

Michigan appears to have made radios during a four-year period, from 1922 to 1925.

| Junior | 75–125 | Table. 2-dial. 1-tube. Battery. 1924. |
| MRC-3 | 250–300 | Table. Battery. 1923. (VR-129) |

MIDWEST *(see also Miraco)*

Note: Midwest appears to have one of the finest model numbering systems around. The first number shows how many tubes there are, and the second gives the model year.

| 18-37 | 200–300 | 18 tubes. 1937. (FOS-109) |

MINERVA

| W119 | 30–35 | Table. 1946. |

MIRACO *(see also Midwest)*

Made by the Midwest Radio Company.

| MW | 100–175 | Table. Battery. 2-dial. 1924. |
| Ultra 5 | 500 | Table. Battery. 3-dial. 1924. (GOR) |

MIRRORTONE (Monarch)

| 850 | 30–35 | Deco. About 1935. |

MITCHELL

1250	50–75	Bed-lamp radio. 1948.
1251	50–75	Bed-lamp radio. Ivory plastic. 1948.
1254 "Madrigal"	10–20	Table. Plastic. 1951.
1260	50–75	Lamp-radio. Rocket-shaped. 1949. (RGA-55)
1274	20–25	Table. Brown plastic. 1954.

AR: *Antique Radios: Restoration and Price Guide* / FOS: *Flick of the Switch* / GOR: *Guide to Old Radios*
RGA: *Radios: The Golden Age* / VR: *Vintage Radio*

1275	20–25	Same as 1274. White plastic.
1276	10–15	Portable. Plastic. AC/battery. 1954.
1287	25–30	Portable. Cloth. AC/battery. 1955.
Lullaby		Model name used to identify models 1250, 1251, 1260, and 1261.
Lumitone	100–125	Lamp-radio. 1940.

MOHAWK

After a merger with the All-American Radio Corporation in 1927, Mohawk became known as All-American Mohawk.

110 "Consolette"	80–120	Upright table. Interesting curved top piece. Battery. 1925. (GOR)
115 "Console"	80–120	Lowboy. Same radio as 110, with the addition of a base to make it into a floor model. Battery. 1925. (GOR)
unknown	60–90	Table. Slant front panel. Wood. Battery. 1925. (GOR; VR-131)

MOHICAN

GC-1A	40–50	Portable.

MONITOR

unknown	15–25	Table. Wood. About 1946. (GOR)

MOTOROLA

Paul Galvin began building power supplies in 1928. By 1930 he was building automobile radios (hence "Motorola"). From car radios it was an easy step into home radios.

3A5	15–25	Portable. AC/battery. 1941.
5A1	10–15	Portable. 1946.
5A5	15–20	Portable. AC/battery. Flip-up cover. 1946. (FOS-113)
5A7A	20–25	Portable. AC/battery. 1948.
5A9B	10–15	Portable. Metal. 1949.
5H11	15–25	Table. Brown plastic with red knobs. 1950. (GOR)
5J11R	25–30	Table. Red Bakelite. 1950.
5R1	20–25	Table. Ivory Bakelite. 1951.
5T	40–50	Upright table. 1937.
5T22R1	15–25	Table. Orange plastic. 1958.
10Y	50–90	Console. Wood. 1937. (GOR)
41A	40–60	Table. Brown Bakelite. Battery. 1940. (GOR)
47B11	10–15	Table. Wood. Battery. 1947.
51C	10–15	Table. Brown plastic. 1939.
51X11	15–30	Table. Brown Bakelite. 1941.
52B1U	10–15	Portable. Plastic. AC/battery. 1953.
52L1/52L1A	20–25	Portable. Green plastic with green knobs. AC/battery. 1953.
52L2/52L2A	20–25	Same as 52L1. Maroon plastic with maroon knobs.
52L3/52L3A	15–20	Same as 52L1. Grey plastic with green knobs.
53F2	25–30	Radio-phonograph. Bakelite. Table. 1954.
53H1	50–60	Table. Black plastic. 1954.
53H2	35–40	Same as 53H1. Grey plastic.
53H3	40–45	Same as 53H1. Green plastic.
53H4	50–60	Same as 53H1. Red plastic.
53R1/53R1U	10–15	Table. Brown plastic. 1954.
53R2/53R2U	10–15	Same as 53R1. Ivory plastic.

53R3/53R3U	20–25	Same as 53R1. Yellow plastic.
53R4/53R4U	10–15	Same as 53R1. Grey plastic.
53R5/53R5U	15–20	Same as 53R1. Green plastic.
53R6/53R6U	25–30	Same as 53R1. Red plastic.
56H	20–30	Table. Brown plastic. Large domed tuning knob. 1956. (GOR)
56R	40–60	Table. Red plastic. 1955. (GOR)
56X11	25–30	Table. Plastic. 1947.
58A11	10–15	Table. Plastic. 1948.
65T21	60–75	Table. 1946.
66X	10–15	Table. White plastic. 1957. (GOR)
67F12	30–40	Radio-phonograph. Table. Plastic. 1948.
67F14	40–45	Radio-phonograph. Console. 1949.
67L11	30–50	Portable. Simulated alligator. Flip-up lid. 1948. (GOR)
67XM21	25–30	Table. Plastic. AM/FM. 1947.
68T11	15–20	Table. Plastic. 1949.
68X11	25–30	Table. Plastic. 1949.
69L11	40–60	Portable. AC/battery. Dial is a moving tape inside a clear handle. 1949.
75F21	75–100	Radio-phonograph. Console. AM/SW. 1947.
77FM21	75–100	Radio-phonograph. Console. AM/FM. 1948.
77XM21	30–35	Table. 2-tone plastic. AM/FM. 1948.
77XM22	25–30	Table. Wood. Walnut. Wraparound grille. AM/FM. 1948.
77XM22B	25–30	Same as 77XM22. Blond wood.
78X11	40–45	Radio-phonograph. Console. 1949.
78X12	35–40	Radio-phonograph. Horizontal console. 1949.
88FM21	40–45	Radio-phonograph. Horizontal console. AM/FM. 1949.
95F	60–75	Radio-phonograph. Horizontal console. AM/FM/SW. 1947.
107F31	60–75	Radio-phonograph. Horizontal console. AM/FM/SW. 1948.
A15J42	30–50	Table. Aqua plastic. 1960.
C9G13	10–20	Clock-radio. Green plastic. 1960. (GOR)
HS7	15–25	Portable. Cloth covered. 1946. (GOR)

MURDOCK

Bought out by Philco in 1929.

5 Tube Neutrodyne	75–100	Table. Battery. Wood. 1924.
CS-32	100–150	Table. Battery. 3-dial. 1925. (VR-122)

MUSIC MASTER

100	40–80	Table. Slanted front panel. 3-dial. Battery. 1925.
215	75–125	Horizontal highboy. Spinet desk legs. Slanted front panel. Enclosed speaker beneath radio panel. Battery. 2-dial. 1925. (GOR)

MUSICAIRE

Sold by Coast-to-Coast Stores.

576	75–100	Upright table. Wood. Resembles console. 1946. (GOR)
942T	15–25	Table. Wood. 1942. (GOR)
unknown	25–35	Table. Wood. Push-button. AM/SW. 1940–46. (GOR)

AR: *Antique Radios: Restoration and Price Guide* / FOS: *Flick of the Switch* / GOR: *Guide to Old Radios*
RGA: *Radios: The Golden Age* / VR: *Vintage Radio*

NATIONAL AIRPHONE *(see also Somerset)*

Monodyne	250-300	1-tube. 1923. (GOR)

NATIONAL UNION

G-613	20–25	Portable. AC/battery. 1947.
G-619	20–40	Table. Wood. 1947. (GOR)

NEUTROWOUND

Made by Advance Automobile Accessories Corporation.

unknown	175–200	Table. Metal. Battery. 1926.
unknown	300–350	Table. Metal. Blue. Battery. 1927.

NORDEN HAUCK

Admiralty Super 15	450–500	Amateur. 1933.
C-10	1000–1250	Table. Battery. AM/SW. 2-dial. 1925. (VR-144)
Super 10	600–800	Table. Professional. 2-dial. 1926.

NUMECHRON

unknown	30–35	Clock-radio. 1954.

OLYMPIC

7-421W	30–35	Table. Plastic. 1949.
7-435V	25–30	Table. Plastic. AM/FM. 1948.
7-532W	30–35	Table. Plastic. 1947.
7-537	30–35	Table. Plastic. AM/FM. 1948.
7-622	15–20	Radio-phonograph. Table. 1948.
8-61B	20–25	Radio-phonograph. Table. 1948.
8-533W	25–30	Table. Plastic. AM/FM. 1949.
572B	30–35	Radio-phonograph. Console. AM/FM. Front completely covered with grille cloth. 1954.
RP-10	15–20	Radio-phonograph. Portable. Stereo. 1960.

PACKARD-BELL

The Bell in Packard-Bell was the same man (Herb Bell) as the one in Jackson-Bell. After J-B folded in 1933, Bell looked around for a new partner, found one, and began a successful new company that same year. It was sold to Teledyne in 1971.

5DA	10–20	Table. Bakelite. Handle. 1947.
5R1	25–35	Table. Plastic. 1950. (GOR)
100	20–25	Table. Plastic. 1949.
501	10–20	Table. Bakelite.
541	40–50	Radio-phonograph. Console. Blond. 1955.
542	30–35	Console. Blond. 1955.
631	25–35	Table. Plastic. 1954. (GOR)
682	25–30	Table. Wood. 1949.

PAIGE

	150–175	1-tube. 1924.

PARAGON

Originally produced by Adams-Morgan. In 1926, the original company sold out to Paragon Electric Company.

RA 10	400–500	Table. Battery. 1921.

RA 10/DA 2	750–1000	Table. Battery. 1921. (VR-102)
RB 2	200–300	Table. Battery. 1923.

PARAMOUNT

Standard	90–100	Console. Battery. 1924.

PATHÉ

Universal Five	125–200	Table. Sloped front. Battery. 1925.

PFANSTIEHL

Pfanstiehl began producing radios in 1924. The company continued under that name until 1928 when it became known as Balkeit after Grigsby-Grunow-Hinds ("Majestic") bought it out. Later there were Fansteel radios, a phonetic spelling of the original name.

7 "Overtone"	125–175	Table. Battery. 3-dial. 1924. (GOR)
10 "Overtone"	30–60	Table. Battery. Wood. 1924. (GOR)
20	50–100	Table. Battery. Wood. 1926.

PHILCO

Philco has been around for a long time. It started in 1892 as the Helios Electric Company, then became the Philadelphia Storage Battery Company. It entered the home radio market with AC sets in 1927.

Note: Philco used the same model number with various suffixes to designate the style of the radio. For instance, 38-39 could end with a -B, -K, -T, or -X to show whether it was a table, cathedral, or console radio. Certain suffixes seem somewhat consistent: -B is often a cathedral, -CS a chairside, -L a lowboy, -H a highboy, and -T a table. We have tried to include these suffixes, but may not always have succeeded. For more complete identification, refer to Grinder and Fathauer's *The Radio Collector's Directory and Price Guide* (Ironwood Press, 1986).

Philco used a prefix to refer to the model year starting in 1937. Even if a radio was produced at the end of 1936, if it were labelled a model 37-, it is identified as a 1937 model. Sometimes models were produced for more than one year, so it would be possible to find a radio listed as a 37-XXX and a 38-XXX. If you don't have the complete number, check a year or so either way to see if this is the case.

Philco also reused their model numbers from time to time, which can cause confusion. Where we know of a duplication we've mentioned it, but there are probably more of these that we have missed.

Replicas	75–125	Philco-produced miniature cathedral. A two-thirds scale model of the 90B. Plastic cabinet. Transistors. Selling price was $49.95, which was the price of the 1931 original model. AM/FM. 1972. (Another reproduction is a Chinese copy of this 1972 Philco; however, the cabinet is made of wood. AM/FM. Transistors. There are also a couple of more recent transistors illustrated in this book.)
16B	150–250	Upright table. 1933. (FOS-118; GOR)
18B	200–300	Cathedral. AM/SW. 1933.
20B	150–200	Cathedral. First Philco cathedral. 1930. (FOS-117; GOR)
20L	100–125	Lowboy. 1930.
21	350–500	Cathedral. 1930.

AR: *Antique Radios: Restoration and Price Guide* / **FOS:** *Flick of the Switch* / **GOR:** *Guide to Old Radios*
RGA: *Radios: The Golden Age* / **VR:** *Vintage Radio*

37-34	40–50	Table. 6-volt battery. 1937.
37-38	20–30	Upright table. Battery. 1937.
37-60	65–75	Upright table. Wood. 1937.
37-61	70–90	Upright table. AM/SW. 1937.
	35–45	Console. AM/SW. 1937.
37-84	85–100	Cathedral. 1937.
37-89	55–160	Cathedral. 1937.
37-93	100–125	Cathedral. Wood. 1937. (GOR)
37-610B	60–70	Table. Deco. AM/SW. 1937.
37-620	40–50	Table. SM/2SW. 1937.
37-650	50–100	Table. AM/2SW. 1937.
37-650B	100–200	Cathedral. AM/SW. 1937.
37-670B	200–250	Cathedral. AM/SW. 1937.
37-670X	75–150	Console. AM/SW. 1937.
38B	35–70	Cathedral. Battery. 1930.
38-7	125–150	Console. Slant front. Inlaid veneer. 1938. (GOR)
38-7CS	115–150	Chairside. 1938.
38-8	100–125	Console. 1938. (FOS)
38-9	50–75	Table. 1938. (FOS-125)
38-10	100–150	Table. Deco. AM/SW. 1938.
38-10T	50–75	Table. AM/SW. Deco. 1938. (FOS-126)
38-12	30–50	Table. Deco. 1938.
38-14T	25–30	Table. AM/SW. Plastic. 1938.
38-15CS	100–125	Chairside. Oval. 1938.
38-23T	35–50	Table. Deco. 1938.
38-34	30–40	Upright table. Battery. 1938.
38-35B	65–75	Cathedral. 6-volt battery. 1938.
38-38T	50–75	Table. Battery. 1938.
38-62T	35–60	Table. Deco. 1938.
38-93B	40–50	Cathedral. 1938.
38-116	100–150	Console. Large. 1938.
38-620	100–150	Upright table. AM/2SW. Deco. 1938.
38-690X	300–450	Console. Large. 1938.
39-70	30–50	Upright table. Battery. Wood. 1939. (AR-63)
39-116RX	200–350	Console. Push-button. Remote control. 13 tubes. 1939. FOS-127)
40-120	15–25	Table. Plastic. Handle. 1940. (GOR)
40-130	50–100	Upright table. Inlaid veneer. AM/SW. 1940.
40-130F	35–45	Upright table. 1940.
40-150	40-50	Table. Push-button. AM/SW. 1940. (FOS-127)
40-155	60–90	Table. Wood. Push-button. Sloped front. AM/2SW. 1940. (GOR)
40-180	50–100	Console. AM/2SW. Push-button. 1940.
40-215RX	200–350	Console. Remote control. 1940.
40-510	300–400	Radio-phonograph. Console. AM/SW. 1928.
41-221C	25–40	Table. Wood with swirled plastic grille. 1941.
41-226C	35–50	Table. Deco. 1941. (FOS-133)
41-240	30–45	Table. 1941.
41-250	75–125	Table. Wood. Push-button. 1941.
41-285	60–75	Console. 1941.
42-22CL	20–25	Clock-radio. 1942.
42-321	20–30	Table. Wood. 1942. (FOS-134; GOR)
42-350	40–60	Table. Wood. 1942. (FOS-134; GOR)
42-390	100–175	Console. AM/old FM/SW. Push-button. 1942.
42-400	125–200	Console. Push-button. AM/old FM/SW. 1942.

42-1006	40–60	Radio-phonograph. Console. AM/SW. 1942.
42-KR3	30–50	Table. White painted wood. 1942. (GOR)
44B	125–200	Cathedral. 4 bands. 1934. (AR-52)
45C	30–40	Table. 1934.
45F	75–90	Console. 1934.
46-250	25–35	Table. Brown Bakelite. 1946.
46-420	35–50	Table. Plastic. Controls on top. 1946. (FOS-135)
46-427	15–25	Table. Plastic. AM/SW. 1946.
46-480	100–125	Console. AM/FM/SW. 1946.
46-1201	60–80	Radio-phonograph. Slide-in record player. Wood. 1946. (FOS-135; GOR)
46-1209	35–50	Console. 1946.
47-204	15–20	Table. Wood with textured paint. 1947. (AR-66)
48-141	15–25	Table. Bakelite. Battery. 1948.
48-200	15–20	Table. Brown plastic. 1948.
48-200I	20–30	Same as 48-200. Ivory plastic.
48-206	25–30	Table. Wood with textured paint, plastic grille. 1948. (FOS-137)
48-214	20–25	Table. 1948.
48-225	20–25	Table. Maroon Bakelite. 1948.
48-230	25–30	Table. Plastic. 1948.
48-250	25–30	Table. Brown plastic. 1948. (GOR)
48-250I	25–30	Same as 48-250. Ivory plastic.
48-300	20–25	Portable. Wood. AC/battery. 1948.
48-360	40–50	Portable. Wood front, leatherette sides. Tambour door. AC/battery. 1948.
		Note: This style radio was produced for several years before 1948 as the model 350.
48-460	25–30	Table. Brown plastic. Top controls. 1948.
48-460I	35–40	Same as 48-460. Ivory plastic.
48-461	20–25	Table. 1948.
48-475	40–45	Table. Blocky style. AM/FM. 1948.
48-1253	25–30	Radio-phonograph. Table. 1948.
48-1256	25–30	Radio-phonograph. Table. 1948.
48-1262	75–90	Radio-phonograph. Console. 1948.
48-1263	75–90	Radio-phonograph. Console. AM/SW. 1948.
48-1264	60–80	Radio-phonograph. Console. AM/FM. 1948. (FOS-137)
48-1266	70–85	Radio-phonograph. Console. AM/FM/SW. 1948. (FOS-137)
48-1286	50–65	Radio-phonograph. Horizontal console. AM/FM. Open album storage on both sides. 1948. (FOS-138)
48-1401	75–100	Radio-phonograph. Slide-in record player. Black plastic top, wood bottom. 1948. (FOS-140; GOR)
49-501	40–45	Table. Brown plastic. Highly curved. 1949. (FOS-140)
49-501I	35–40	Same as 49-501. Ivory plastic.
49-503	25–30	Table. Plastic. Light grille. 1949.
49-504	15–20	Table. Brown plastic. 1949.
49-504I	20–25	Same as 49-504. Ivory plastic.
49-505	30–35	Table. Plastic. Sculptured style cabinet. 1949. (FOS-140)
49-506 "Transitone"	15–30	Table. Wood. 1949. (GOR)
49-602	15–25	Portable. Handbag style. Brown plastic. 1949. (GOR)

49-901	40–55	Table. Plastic. Single control—tap to change stations. 1949. (FOS-140)
49-902	15–20	Table. Plastic. White front. 1949.
49-905	20–25	Table. Plastic. AM/FM. 1949.
49-906	20–25	Table. Wood. AM/FM. 1949.
49-909	35–40	Table. Wood. Massive. AM/FM. 1949.
49-1405	40–45	Radio-phonograph. Table. 1949.
49-1602	35–40	Radio-phonograph. Console. 1949.
49-1606	30–35	Radio-phonograph. Horizontal console. 1949.
50	125–225	Cathedral. 1931. (AR-49)
51-532 "Transitone"	20–30	Table. Plastic. 1951.
51B	15–300	Cathedral. 1932. (FOS-117)
52-542	15–25	Table. Plastic. 1952. (GOR)
52-1750	75–125	Drop-leaf end table. 1952.
53	30–40	Table. 1932.
53-561	20–25	Table. Green, beige, ivory, or maroon plastic. 1953.
53-562	20–25	Table. Ivory, maroon, or dark-green plastic. 1953.
	25–30	Tangarine plastic.
53-564	20–25	Table. Ivory plastic. 1953.
53-652	15–20	Portable. AC/battery. Beige or green plastic. 1953.
53-956	10–20	Table. Bakelite. 1953.
53-1350	90–125	End table. Radio-phonograph. 1953.
53-1754	35–40	Radio-phonograph. Console. AM/SW. 1953.
54	50–75	Table. Wood. 1932.
60B	100–175	Cathedral. AM/SW. 1933. (FOS-118). Note: Model 60B was also made in both 1933 and 1936.
60MB	100–150	Upright table. Deco. AM/SW. 1934. (FOS-119—the model identified as a 60B is really the 60MB.)
65	175–200	Horizontal lowboy. 1929. (FOS-120)
66B	65–75	Upright table. AM/SW. 1934.
70	300–450	Grandfather clock. 1932. (FOS-122)
70B	200–350	Cathedral. 1932. (FOS-117)
	75–125	Upright table. 1938. (FOS-120). Note: same model number reused.
70L	125–175	Lowboy. 1932. (FOS-121)
71B	150–300	Cathedral. 1932.
80B "Philco Jr."	100–125	Cathedral. 1933. (FOS-118)
81 "Jr."	100–150	Cathedral. 1933. (FOS-118; GOR)
84B	125–200	Cathedral. 1934. (FOS-119; GOR)
	100–175	Cathedral. 1936. (FOS-119) Note: Same model number reused.
86	100–125	Horizontal lowboy. Drop front desk. 1929. (VR-148)
89B	125–200	Cathedral. AM/SW. 1933. (FOS-119) Note: Other models were made in 1934–35 and in 1936.
90B	300–450	Cathedral. This is the epitome of cathedral radios. 1931. (AR-49; FOS-117; VR-263)
91B	225–325	Cathedral. 1932.
96H	150–175	Lowboy. 1930. (FOS-121)
105	40–50	Radio-phonograph. Table. 1939.
116	100–125	Upright table. 1935. (FOS-124)
118B	100–150	Cathedral. AM/SW. 1934.
501	150–200	Radio-phonograph. Console. AM/SW. 1934.
511	100–150	Table. Metal, with painted flowers on the front panel. 1928 (VR-147)

514	125–140	Table. Hand-painted flowers on front panel. 1928. (VR-127)
520B	45–60	Upright table. 3-band. 1936. (FOS-120)
A-801	100–125	Chairside. Deco. 1941.
B-570	25–30	Table. Red plastic. 1954.
	20–25	Sand plastic.
Beach radio	40–50	Portable. Flashlight built into side of radio.
E-670	10–15	Portable. AC/battery. 1957.
E-1370	15–20	Radio-phonograph. Portable. 1957.
PT2	30–50	Table. Wood. Celluloid grille. 1940.
PT25 "Transitone"	25–40	Table. Brown Bakelite. Small. 1940. (FOS-126)
PT33 "Transitone"	30–50	Table. Brown Bakelite with handle. 1940. (GOR)
PT87	40–50	Portable. Suitcase style. Battery. 1942. (FOS-132)
Transitone		Philco used this name to refer to many different models.

PHILHARMONIC

100C	35–40	Radio-phonograph. Horizontal console. 1948.
100T	25–30	Radio-phonograph. Table. 1948.
249C	40–50	Radio-phonograph. Horizontal console. 1949.

PHILIPS

French company.

4A	50–65	Table. 3-band.

PILOT

Pilot was an extremely successful kit manufacturer during the 1920s and didn't produce its first complete, non-kit radio until 1930.

423	100–125	Cathedral. AM/SW. 1937.
G-184	100–150	Radio-phonograph. 1936.
T-511	10–20	Table. Wood. AM/SW. 1946.
T-521	35–40	Table. AM/FM. 1947.
T-601	20–30	FM tuner. Wood. 1947. (GOR)
T-741	25–40	Table. 1948.

PITTSBURG

SP 2	125–150	Battery. 1922-1923.

POLICALARM

Made by Regency Electronics.

PR8	15–25	Table. Plastic. Police band only. 1950. (GOR)

PORTOLA *(see Sentinel and Zenith; made by United Air Cleaner.)*

POWERTONE

Sold by Reliable Radio Company, New York.

unknown	90–120	Cathedral. Wood. 1934. (GOR)

AR: *Antique Radios: Restoration and Price Guide* / **FOS**: *Flick of the Switch* / **GOR**: *Guide to Old Radios*
RGA: *Radios: The Golden Age* / **VR**: *Vintage Radio*

PRECISION *(see also Crosley)*

Ace 3B	125–175	Table. Wood. Battery. 1923.
Ace type V	200	Table. Battery. 1922.

PURITAN

Sold by Gamble's stores.

6A35WG-504W	20–25	Table. AM/SW. 1948.
503	25–40	Radio-phonograph. Table. Wood. 1946. (GOR)

PYE

English company.

PE94MB9-LW	75–90	Table.

RAYTHEON

T-2500	30–35	Table. 1956.

RCA (Radio Corporation of America)

RCA was formed by four other companies (General Electric, American Telephone & Telegraph, Western Electric, and the United Fruit Company) to keep overseas communication in the control of the United States. (Later Westinghouse joined the group.) Although the RCA name was on the radios, RCA was simply the merchandiser for radios produced by General Electric and Westinghouse. In 1929, RCA merged with the Victor Talking Machine Company in order to gain production facilities.

RCA was the founder of what eventually became the National Broadcasting System in 1926. At that time, it was the Red Network and the Blue Network. In 1940, the government realized that NBC really was two networks—a definite breach of the antimonoploy laws. NBC kept the stronger Red Network (what is now NBC). The Blue Network eventually became ABC.

Note: All RCA model numbers have been separated into number and letter groups with dashes between. RCA, in its service information, was not consistent about the way it separated its model numbers. However, we hope our organization will help you find the information you need more easily.

Radio-phonographs use the suffix -C for crystal cartridges (high fidelity) and—M for magnetic cartridges.

RCA radios were also supplied in Victor radio-phonographs. Look under Victor for several others.

I "Radiola"	300–500	Box. Crystal. 1923. (VR-109)
1-AX	10–15	Table. Plastic. 1941.
1-AX-2	10–15	Table. Ivory plastic. 1941.
1-RA-23	20–35	Table. Pink plastic. 1962.
1-X-1-H	15–20	Table. Aqua plastic. 1961.
II "Radiola"	175–225	Portable. 2-dial. Battery. 1923. (GOR; VR-109)
2-S-7	25–30	Radio-phonograph. Horizontal console. 1953.
III "Radiola"	50–100	Box. Battery. 1924. (AR-9; GOR; VR-109)
III-A "Radiola"	100–150	Box. Battery. 1924. (AR-10; VR-110)
3-BX-51	10–15	Portable. Brown plastic. AC/battery. 1954.
3-BX-52	10–15	Portable. AC/battery. Tan plastic. 1954.
3-BX-53	10–15	Portable. Green plastic. AC/battery. 1954
3-BX-54	20–25	Portable. Red plastic. AC/battery. 1954.
3-BX-671 "Stratoworld"	40–50	Portable. 7 bands. 1951.
3-RF-91	20–40	Table. Plastic. AM/SW. 1952. (GOR)

3-US-5	30–35	Radio-phonongraph. Plastic table. 1955.
IV	250–350	Table with doors. Battery. 3-dial. 1922. (VR-110)
4-T	75–125	Cathedral. 1936.
4-X-641	15–30	Table. Black plastic. 1954.
4-Y-511	75–100	Radio-phonograph. 45 rpm only. Table. Plastic. 1954.
V "Radiola"	150–250	Table. Wood and metal. Battery. 2-dial. 1923. (VR-110)
5-A-410-A	300–350	Coca Cola cooler.
5-Q-1	20–25	Upright table. AM/2SW. 1940.
5-Q-2	65–75	Upright table. AM/2SW. 1940.
5-Q-4	15–20	Table. Wood. 1940.
5-Q-5A	10–15	Table. Plastic. AM/2SW. 1940.
5-Q-5-B	15–20	Table. Black plastic. AM/2SW. 1940.
5-Q-5-C	15–20	Table. Ivory plastic. AM/2SW. 1940.
5-Q-5-D	30–40	Table. Maroon plastic. AM/2SW. 1940.
5-Q-5-E	30–35	Table. Black plastic with metal grille. AM/2SW. 1940.
5-Q-6	15–20	Table. Plastic. AM/2SW. 1940.
5-Q-8	15–20	Table. Plastic. AM/2SW. 1940.
5-Q-12	15–20	Table. Plastic. 1940.
5-Q-55	20–25	Table. Plastic. AM/2SW. 1940. (FOS-153)
5-Q-56	10–15	Table. Plastic with ivory paint. AM/2SW. 1940.
5-T	50–60	Upright table. AM/SW. 1936. (FOS-152)
5-T-6	40–60	Table. Wood. AM/SW. 1936.
5-X-5	10–15	Table. Ivory plastic. 1939.
6-BX-63	10–15	Portable. Grey plastic. 1952. (GOR)
6-Q-1	10–15	Table. Plastic. AM/2SW. 1940.
6-Q-4	15–20	Table. Plastic. AM/2SW/LW. 1940.
6-Q-4-X	10–15	Table. Plastic. AM/2SW/LW. 1940.
6-Q-7	30–35	Table. Wood. AM/2SW. 1940.
6-Q-8	15–20	Table. Wood. AM/2SW. 1940.
6-T	40–50	Upright table. AM/SW. 1936.
6-X-2	10–15	Table. Ivory plastic. 1942.
7-Q-4	15–20	Table. Wood. AM/2SW/LW. 1941.
7-Q-4-X	15–20	Table. Plastic. AM/2SW. 1940.
7-QB	15–20	Table. Wood. AM/2SW. 1941.
7-QBK	50–65	Console. AM/2SW. 1941.
7-QK-4	45–50	Radio-phonograph. Console. AM/2SW/LW. 1941.
VIII "Radiola"	125–175	Highboy. 2-dial. Battery. 1924.
8-BX-6	25–40	Portable. Aluminum and plastic. AC/battery. 1948. (FOS-157; GOR)
8-Q-1	50–65	Table. Wood. AM/2SW. 1940.
8-Q-2	25–30	Table. Wood. AM/2SW. 1940.
8-Q-4	50–60	Table. Wood. Curved grille. AM/2SW. 1940.
8-QB	30–50	Upright table. AM/2SW. 1940.
8-QBK	40–60	Console. AM/2SW. 1940.
8-QU-5-M	25–30	Radio-phonograph. Table. Wood. AM/2SW. 1940.
8-R-71	25–30	Table. Plastic. AM/FM. 1949.
8-V-90	35–40	Radio-phonograph. Horizontal console. AM/FM. 1949.
8-X-53	20–25	Table. Wood. 1948.
8-X-71	15–25	Table. Brown Bakelite. 1949. (GOR)
8-X-521	20–25	Table. Plastic. Top tuning dial. 1948.
8-X-681	30–50	Table. Brown Bakelite. 1950.

IX "Radiola"	750+	Battery. Designed to be built into a phonograph. 1923.
9-Q-1	35–40	Table. Wood. AM/6SW. 1940.
9-Q-4	30–35	Table. Wood. AM/3SW. 1940.
9-QK	75–85	Console. AM/6SW. 1940.
9-SX-1 "Little Nipper"	30–35	Table. Brown plastic with ivory knobs. AM/SW. 1939.
9-SX-2 "Little Nipper"	35–40	Same as 9-SX-1. Brown plastic with ivory front and brown knobs.
9-SX-3 "Little Nipper"	30–35	Same as 9-SX-1. Ivory plastic with red knobs.
9-SX-4 "Little Nipper"	75–100	Same as 9-SX-1. Red plastic with ivory front and red knobs.
9-SX-5 "Little Nipper"	45–50	Same as 9-SX-1. Black plastic with marble-colored front and black knobs.
9-SX-7 "Little Nipper"	45–55	Same as 9-SX-1. Onyx plastic with maroon knobs.
9-SX-65 "Little Nipper"	70–80	Same as 9-SX-1. Blue plastic with onyx front and blue knobs.
9-SX-8 "Little Nipper"	65–75	Same as 9-SX-1. Marble-colored plastic with black knobs.
9-T	50–60	Upright table. AM/3SW. 1935.
9-TX-1	40–50	Table. Brown plastic with mottled tan dial and knobs. 1939.
9-TX-2	15–20	Table. Ivory plastic. 1939.
9-TX-3	20–25	Table. Wood. 1939.
9-TX-4	40–50	Table. Onyx plastic with maroon dial and knobs. 1939.
9-TX-5	60–75	Same as 9-TX-4. Green onyx plastic with ivory dial and knobs.
9-TX-21	20–25	Table. Brown plastic with tan knobs. 1939.
9-TX-22	10–15	Table. Ivory plastic. 1939.
9-TX-23	40–50	Table. Wood. 1939.
9-TX-31	20–25	Table. Brown plastic with tan knobs. 1939. (FOS-153)
9-TX-32	10–15	Table. Ivory plastic. 1939.
9-TX-33	40–50	Table. Wood. 1939.
9-TX-50	20–25	Table. Wood. Handle. 1939.
9-X	20–25	Table. Wood. 1939.
9-X-1	750+	Table. Brazilian onyx and green Catalin. 1939.
9-X-2	750+	Table. Black Catalin. 1939.
9-X-3	750+	Table. Arizona onyx and cream Catalin. 1939.
9-X-4	500–1000	Table. Burl onyx and brown Catalin. 1939.
9-X-6	20–25	Table. Wood. 1939.
9-X-11	750+	Table. Brazilian onyx and green Catalin. 1939.
9-X-12	750+	Table. Black Catalin. 1939.
9-X-13	750+	Table. Arizona onyx and cream Catalin. 1939.
9-X-14	500–1000	Table. Burl onyx and brown Catalin. 1939.
9-X-561	25–40	Table. Beige or brown Bakelite. 1950. Same as 9-X-571.
9-X-571	25–40	Table. Brown plastic. Large brass horn grille. 1950. (FOS-161; GOR)
9-X-572	40–60	Table. Blond plastic. 1949. (GOR)
9-Y-7	85–125	Radio-phonograph. Bakelite. 45-rpm (only) changer . 1949.
9-Y-510	50–80	Radio-phonograph. Table. Bakelite. 45-rpm (only) changer . 1950.
X "Radiola"	200–250	Upright table. Battery 2-dial. Enclosed speaker. 1924. (VR-111)
10-Q-1	40–50	Upright table. AM/2SW. 1940.
10-T	100–150	Upright table. AM/SW/LW. 1937.

10-X	15–20	Table. Plastic. 1941.
11-Q-4	40–50	Upright table. AM/2SW/LW. 1940.
11-QK	85–100	Console. AM/2SW/LW. 1940.
11-QU	125–150	Radio-phonograph. Horizontal console. AM/2SW/LW. 1940.
11-X-1	10–15	Table. Plastic. 1941.
12-Q-4	60–75	Upright table. Wood. AM/2SW/LW. 1940.
12-QK	100–125	Console. AM/2SW/LW. 1940.
12-QU	125–150	Radio-phonograph. Horizontal console. AM/2SW/LW. 1940.
12-AX	15–20	Table. Plastic. Handle. 1942.
12-X	15–20	Same as 12-AX.
13K	125–175	Console. AM/3SW. Tuning eye. 1936. (GOR)
14-AX	10–15	Table. Plastic. 1941.
14-AX-2	10–15	Table. Plastic. 1941.
14-X	25–30	Table. Plastic. 1941.
15-BP-4	15–20	Table. Wood. AC/battery. 1941.
	10–15	Portable. Cloth.
15-BP-615E	15–20	Table. Wood. AC/battery. 1941.
15-BT	10–15	Table. AM/SW. AC/battery. 1941.
15-X	15–25	Table. Bakelite. 1940.
16 "Radiola"	40–75	Table. Battery. 1927. (VR-113)
16-K	30–40	Console. AM/SW. 1940.
16-T-2	25–30	Table. AM/SW. 1940.
16-T-3	30–35	Table. Push-button. AM/SW. 1940.
16-T-4	30–35	Table. Push-button. AM/2SW. 1940.
16-X-1	10–15	Table. Push-button. 1941.
16-X-2	15–20	Table. Ivory plastic. 1941.
16-X-3	15–20	Table. 1941.
16-X-4	15–20	Table. Push-button. 1941.
16-X-11	15–20	Table. Plastic. AM/SW. 1941.
16-X-13	15–20	Table. Wood. AM/SW. 1941. (AR-64)
16-X-14	20–25	Table. Push-button. AM/SW. 1941.
17 "Radiola"	45–75	Table. Wood. 1927. (VR-113)
17-K	45–55	Console. Push-button. AM/2SW. 1940.
18 "Radiola"	45–85	Table. Wood. 1927. (AR-22)
	125	Installed in a spool-legged cabinet with hinged door.
18-T	30–35	Table. Push-button. AM/2SW. 1940.
19-K	100–125	Console. Push-button. AM/2SW. 1940.
20 "Radiola"	100–150	Table. Slant front. 2-dial. Battery. 1925. (VR- 113)
	125–175	Highboy or lowboy. Installed in a cabinet made by another manufacturer.
21 "Radiola"	100–125	Table. Battery. 1929.
22 "Radiola"	50–70	Console. Battery. 1929.
24 "Radiola"	250–300	Portable. Loop antenna. 2-dial. Battery. Superhet. 1925. (VR-112)
25 "Radiola"	100–150	Table. Loop antenna. 2-dial. 1925. (VR-112)
25-BP	10–15	Portable. Leatherette. AC/battery. 1942. (FOS-156)
25-X	10–15	Table. Wood. 1942.
26 "Radiola"	200–275	Portable. 2-dial. Battery. Loop in lid. Superhet. Gold-colored dials. Wood. 1925. (GOR; VR-112)

AR: *Antique Radios: Restoration and Price Guide* / **FOS**: *Flick of the Switch* / **GOR**: *Guide to Old Radios*
RGA: *Radios: The Golden Age* / **VR**: *Vintage Radio*

26-BP	35–45	Portable. White and leatherette. AC/battery. Tambour door. 1942.
26-X-1	15–20	Table. Plastic. AM/SW. 1942. (FOS-156)
26-X-3	15–20	Table. AM/SW. 1942. (FOS-156)
26-X-4	30–35	Table. Push-button. AM/SW. 1942. (FOS-156)
27-K	40–50	Console. Push-button. AM/SW. 1942.
28 "Radiola"	175–225	Table radio with legs. Designed to go together. 2-dial. Loop antenna. 1925.
28-D	100–150	Table. Wood. Tambour door. 1933. (AR-51; FOS-147)
28-T	40–45	Table. Push-button. AM/2SW. 1942. (FOS-156)
28-X	30–35	Table. AM/SW. 1942. (FOS-156)
28-X-5	35–40	Table. Push-button. AM/SW. 1942. (FOS-156)
29-K	60–100	Console. AM/2SW. Push-button. 1942.
29-K-2	75–125	Console. Stepback top with horizontal knobs. AM/2SW. Push-button. 1942.
30 "Radiola"	150–175	Console. Battery. 1926.
32 "Radiola"	150–200	Console. Wood. 1927.
33 "Radiola"	50–75	Table. Metal. 1929.
34-X	15–20	Table. Wood. 1942.
35-X	15–20	Table. Wood. 1942.
36-X	20–25	Table. Wood. 1942.
40-X-30	10–15	Table. Plastic. 1940.
40-X-31	15–20	Table. Ivory plastic. 1940.
40-X-50	30–35	Table. Wood. Handle. 1940.
44 "Radiola"	50–75	Table. Wood. 1929. (AR-42)
45-E	60–75	Bookcase with radio on top. Maple. 1940.
45-X	25–30	Table. Wood. 1940.
45-X-1	10–15	Table. Plastic. 1940. (FOS-155)
45-X-2	15–20	Table. Ivory plastic. 1940.
45-X-3	25–30	Table. Wood. 1940.
45-X-4	30–35	Table. Wood. 1940.
45-X-5	15–20	Table. Plastic. 1940.
45-X-6	20–25	Table. Ivory plastic. 1940.
45-X-11	20–30	Table. Plastic. 1940. (FOS-155; GOR)
45-X-12	15–20	Table. Ivory plastic. 1940.
45-X-13	30–35	Table. Wood. 1941. (FOS-155)
45-X-16	30–35	Table. Wood. 1940.
45-X-17	40–45	Table. Wood. 1940.
45-X-18	25–30	Table. Wood. 1941.
45-X-111	15–20	Table. Plastic. 1940.
45-X-112	20–25	Table. Ivory plastic. 1940.
45-X-113	25–30	Table. Wood. 1940.
46-X-1	10–15	Table. Plastic. 1940.
46-X-2	15–20	Table. Ivory plastic. 1940.
46-X-3	20–25	Table. Wood. 1940.
46-X-11	15–20	Table. Plastic. AM/SW. 1940. (FOS-155)
46-X-12	20–25	Table. Ivory plastic. AM/SW. 1940.
46-X-13	30–35	Table. Wood. AM/SW. 1940. (FOS-155)
46-X-21	15–20	Table. Plastic. AM/SW. 1940.
46-X-23	25–30	Table. Wood. AM/SW. 1940.
46-X-24	25–30	Table. Push-button. AM/SW. 1940.
48 "Radiola"	100–200	Lowboy. 1930. (FOS-146)
55-X	20–25	Table. Plastic. 2 speakers. 1942. (AR-65; FOS-157)
56-X-2	15–20	Table. Bakelite. 1946.
60 "Radiola"	75–100	Table. 1928. (AR-31; VR-113)

61-1 "Radiola"	50–80	Radio-phonograph. Table. Bakelite. 1946.
64 "Radiola"	400–500	Lowboy with doors. 1928.
65-AU	40–60	Radio-phonograph. Table. Wood. 1946. (FOS-157)
65-X-1	25–35	Table. Brown Bakelite. 1946. (FOS-158; GOR)
66 "Radiola"	175–200	Lowboy. Tapestry front. 1929.
66-X-1	50–65	Table. Brown Bakelite. Deco. AM/SW. 1946.
66-X-2	35–45	Table. Bakelite. AM/SW. 1948. (FOS-158)
66-X-12	10–15	Table. Ivory plastic. Deco. 1947.
68-R-1	15–25	Table. Bakelite. AM/FM. 1947. (FOS-158)
75-X-1*	75–100	Table. Brass front. Oriental style. (*Last digit not known.) 1948. (FOS-158)
75-X-11	50–75	Table. Walnut plastic. Brass front. 1948.
75-X-12	50–75	Same as 75-X-11. Ivory plastic.
75-X-16	50–75	Same as 75-X-11. Golden-brown "fine woods" plastic. (GOR)
75-ZU "Radiola"	30–35	Radio-phonograph. Table. Wood. 1948.
76-ZX-11 "Radiola"	20–25	Table. Plastic. 1948.
77-U	35–40	Radio-phonograph. Table. Wood. 1948. (FOS-158)
77-X-1	35–40	Radio-phonograph. Horizontal console. 1948.
85-T-1	10–15	Table. Wood. 1936. (FOS-152)
85-T-2	40–60	Table. Wood. Red finish. 1936. (FOS-152)
86 "Radiola"	250–350	Radio-phonograph-recorder. 1930.
86-T	60–75	Table. Wood. Left side curves into top. AM/SW. Deco. 1938. (GOR)
86-T-6	50–60	Table. Wood. Curved top. AM/2SW. 1938.
87-T	20–40	Table. Wood. AM/SW. 1937. (GOR)
91-BT-61	25–30	Upright table. Wood. 6-volt battery. 1938.
94-BK	20–25	Console. Battery. 1938.
94-BP-1	10–15	Portable. Leatherette. Battery. 1941. (FOS-157)
94-BT	10–15	Table. Wood. Battery. 1938.
94-X	30–40	Table. Wood. 1938.
94-X-1	40–45	Table. Wood. Push-button only. No tuning dial. 1938.
94-X-2	40–45	Same as 94-X-1. Blond wood.
95-T	25–30	Table. Wood. 1938.
95-T-5	35–40	Table. Wood. Push-button. 1938. (FOS-153)
95-T-5-LW	25–30	Table. Wood. Push-button. 1940.
95-X-1	25–30	Table. Wood. Push-button. 1938.
95-X-11	20–25	Table. Wood. Push-button. 1938.
95-XLW	15–20	Table. Wood. AM/SW. 1940.
96-E	75–100	Chairside. Push-button. 1938.
96-E-2	125–150	Chairside. Push-button. AM/2SW. 1939.
96-K	45–55	Console. Push-button. AM/SW. 1938.
96-K-5	50–60	Console. Push-button. AM/2SW. 1939.
96-K-6	65–80	Console. Push-button. AM/2SW. 1939.
96-T	30–35	Table. Wood. Push-button. 1938.
96-T-1	35–40	Table. Wood. Push-button. 1938. (FOS-153)
96-T-2	25–30	Table. Wood. AM/SW. Push-button. 1938.
96-T-3	25–30	Table. Wood. Push-button. AM/2SW. 1938.
96-T-4	20–40	Table. Wood. AM/SW. Push-button. 1937.
96-T-7	25–30	Table. Wood. Push-button. AM/2SW. 1939.
96-X	20–25	Table. Wood. Push-button. 1938.
96-X-1	25–30	Table. Brown plastic. Wraparound grille. AM/SW. 1939.

AR: *Antique Radios: Restoration and Price Guide* / **FOS**: *Flick of the Switch* / **GOR**: *Guide to Old Radios*
RGA: *Radios: The Golden Age* / **VR**: *Vintage Radio*

96-X-2	30–35	Table. Black plastic. Wraparound grille. AM/SW. 1939.
96-X-3	35–40	Same as 96-X-2. Brown and ivory plastic.
96-X-4	30–35	Same as 96-X-2. Ivory plastic.
96-X-11	25–30	Table. Brown plastic. Wraparound grille. Push-button. AM/SW. 1939.
96-X-12	30–35	Same as 96-X-11. Black plastic.
96-X-13	35–40	Same as 96-X-11. Brown and ivory plastic.
96-X-14	30–35	Same as 96-X-11. Ivory plastic.
97-E	100–175	Chairside. Push-button. AM/2SW. 1938.
97-K	60–75	Console. Push-button. AM/SW. 1939.
97-K-2	85–100	Console. Pushbutton. AM/2SW. 1939.
97-KG	75–90	Console. Push-button. AM/2SW. 1938.
97-KT	60–80	Console. Push-button. AM/2SW. 1938.
97-T	30–35	Table. Wood. Push-button. AM/2SW. 1938.
97-T-2	45–50	Table. Wood. Push-button. AM/2SW. 1939.
97-T-4	25–30	Table. Wood. Push-button. AM/SW. 1939.
97-T-5	25–30	Table. Wood. Push-button. AM/SW. 1939.
97-T-6	30–35	Table. Wood. Push-button. AM/SW. 1939.
97-X	20–40	Table. Wood. Push-button. 1938.
97-Y	60–75	Console. Push-button. AM/2SW. 1938.
98-EY	125–150	Chairside. Push-button. AM/2SW. 1938.
98-K	75–100	Console. Push-button. Curved dial. AM/2SW. 1938.
98-K-2	40–50	Console. Push-button. AM/2SW. 1939.
98-T	40–50	Table. Wood. Push-button. AM/2SW. 1939.
98-T-2	35–40	Table. Wood. Push-button. AM/2SW. 1940.
98-X	40–45	Table. Wood. Push-button. AM/2SW. 1938.
98-YG	75–85	Console. Push-button. AM/2SW. 1938.
99-K	85–100	Console. Push-button. Curved dial. AM/2SW. 1938.
99-T	40–50	Table. Wood. Push-button. AM/2SW. 1938.
100	30–50	Table. Wood. AM/SW. 1932.
103	40–60	Upright table. Wood. AM/SW. 1934.
110	150–250	Cathedral. AM/SW. 1933.
110-K	80–110	Console. Push-button. AM/3SW. 1941. (FOS-155)
110-K-2	40–55	Console. Push-button. AM/3SW. 1941.
111-K	75–90	Console. Push-button. AM/3SW. 1941.
118	50–75	Upright table. AM/SW. 1934.
120	150–250	Cathedral. AM/SW. 1933.
128	150–200	Upright table. AM/2SW. 1934.
143	75–100	Upright table. AM/3SW. 1934. (AR-53; FOS-148)
211-K	100–125	Console. AM/3SW. 1942.
224	125–175	Console. 6-legged. AM/SW. 1934.
380	75–90	Radio-phonograph. Console. 1934.
500 "Radiola"	20–25	Table. Plastic. 1941.
501 "Radiola"	20–25	Table. Ivory plastic. 1941.
510 "Radiola"	10–15	Table. Plastic. 1940.
	20–25	Ivory plastic.
511 "Radiola"	10–15	Table. Plastic. 1941.
	20–25	Ivory plastic.
512 "Radiola"	25–35	Table. Wood. 1941. (GOR)
513 "Radiola"	25–30	Table. Wood. 1941.
515 "Radiola"	20–25	Table. Wood. AM/SW. 1941.
516 "Radiola"	10–15	Table. Plastic. Handle. 1942.
517 "Radiola"	15–20	Table. Wood. Nipper on dial. 1942.
520 "Radiola"	15–25	Table. Wood. 1942. (GOR)
522 "Radiola"	15–20	Table. Wood. 1942.

526 "Radiola"	10–15	Table. Plastic. Handle. 1942.
527 "Radiola"	15–20	Table. Wood. 1942.
710-V-25	40–50	Radio-phonograph. Horizontal console. AM/FM. 1948.
810-K-1	100–150	Console. Deco. 1938. (FOS-153)
811-K	80–120	Console. Wood. Push-button. 1937. (GOR)
910-KG	50–60	Console. AM/2SW. 1938.
911-K	100–115	Console. AM/4SW. 1938.
AA-1400	100–150	Detector, amplifier, battery. 1922.
Aeriola Jr.	150–250	Box. Crystal. 1922. (VR-106)
Aeriola Sr.	100–150	Box. 1-tube. 1922. (VR-107)
BP-10	20–30	Portable. Small. 1941. (FOS-156, 157)
BT-6-5	70–90	Upright table. AM/SW. Battery. 1935.
BT-40	10–15	Table. Wood. Battery. 1939.
C-13-2	125–200	Radio-phonograph. Console. AM/LW/3SW. 1935. (FOS-151)
C-15-3	100–150	Console. AM/3SW/LW. 1935.
Coca Cola 5-A-410-A	300–350	Cooler.
D-22-1	400+	Radio-phonograph-recorder. Console. Large. AM/LW/3SW. Microphone. 1935.
HF-1	100–125	Console. Modern 6-leg style. 1938.
HF-2	70–80	Horizontal console. 1938.
HF-4	80–100	Horizontal console. AM/4SW. 1938.
HF-6	100–120	Console. AM/6SW. 1938.
HF-8	120–150	Console. AM/6SW. 1938.
K-50	50–60	Console. Push-button. 1940.
K-60	60–90	Console. Push-button. AM/2SW. 1940.
K-61	60–90	Console. Push-button. AM/SW. 1940.
K-62	50-70	Console. Push-button. AM/2SW. 1940.
K-80	70–100	Console. Push-button. AM/2SW. 1940.
K-81	50–55	Console. Push-button. AM/2SW. 1940.
K-82	55–60	Console. Push-button. AM/2SW. 1940.
K-105	50–65	Console. AM/2SW. 1940.
K-130	90–120	Console. AM/2SW. Push-button. 1939.
P-5 "Radiola"	10–15	Portable. AC/battery. 1941.
Q-11	10–15	Table. Wood. AM/2SW. 1942.
Q-12	10–15	Table. Plastic. AM/2SW. 1942.
Q-14	15–20	Table. Wood. AM/2SW. 1942.
Q-14-E	15–20	Same as Q-14.
Q-15	15–20	Table. Wood. AM/2SW. 1942.
Q-15-E	15–20	Same as Q-15.
Q-16	30–35	Table. Wood. AM/4SW. 1942.
Q-17	30–35	Table. Wood. AM/4SW. 1942.
Q-18	15–20	Table. Wood. AM/2SW. 1942.
Q-20	10–15	Table. Plastic. AM/SW. 1940.
Q-21	15–20	Table. Wood. AM/SW. 1940.
Q-23	35–40	Table. Wood. AM/4SW. 1942.
Q-24	45–50	Table. Wood. AM/4SW. 1941.
Q-25	25–30	Table. Wood. AM/4SW. 1941.
Q-26	15–20	Table. Wood. AM/4SW. 1942.
Q-27	20–25	Table. Wood. AM/4SW. 1942.
Q-30	35–40	Table. Wood. AM/5SW. 1942.
Q-31	25–30	Table. Wood. AM/5SW. 1942.

Q-33	25–30	Table. Wood. AM/4SW. 1942.
Q-44	40–50	Table. Wood. AM/7SW. 1941.
QB-2	10–15	Table. Plastic. Battery. 1941.
QK-23	50–60	Console. AM/4SW. 1941.
QU-2-M	50–60	Radio-phonograph. Console. AM/4SW. 1941.
QU-3-M	15–20	Radio-phonograph. Table. Wood. AM/4SW. 1941.
QU-5	80–100	Radio-phonograph. Horizontal console. AM/4SW. 1941.
QU-7	200–225	Radio-phonograph-recorder. AM/7SW. Horizontal console. 1942.
QU-8	300–350	Radio-phonograph-recorder. AM/7SW. Horizontal console. Top of the line. 1941.
QU-51-C/QU-51-M	70–85	Radio-phonograph. Horizontal console. Push-button. AM/4SW. 1942.
QU-52-C/QU-52-M	50–60	Radio-phonograph. Horizontal console. AM/4SW. 1942.
QU-55	60–75	Radio-phonograph. Horizontal console. AM/4SW. 1942.
QU-56-C/QU-56-M	30–35	Radio-phonograph. Table. AM/2SW. 1942.
QU-72	40–45	Radio-phonograph. AM/SW. 1947.
R-5 "Radiolette"	150–200	Cathedral. 1931. (GOR)
R-7 "Radiola"	40–45	Table. 1931.
R-8	85–100	Table. Wood. 1932.
R-28-P	40–45	Table. Wood. 1932.
R-73	350	Table. Mint in carton. 1933.
R-560-P "Radiola"	20–25	Radio-phonograph. Table. Wood. 1942.
R-566-P "Radiola"	20–25	Radio-phonograph. Table. Wood. 1942.
RA/DA	125–150	Regenerating receiver/amplifier combination. First commercial receiver sold by RCA. 2 boxes. 1921.
Radiola		This was a model name often used by RCA. Where possible, radios in this list are located under their model numbers and also are identified as "Radiola."
Radiola Grand	300–450	Box with lid. Battery. 1923. (VR-113)
Radiolette		See model R-5.
RAE-26	125–150	Radio-phonograph. Console. 1931.
RC-1023-C (chassis number)	30–60	Metal hotel/motel radio.
RGD-30-E	10–15	Table. Grey plastic. 1966.
RS "Radiola"	200–275	Box. Battery. Combined the RA/DA in one box. 1923. (VR-109)
Super VIII	175–300	Console. Battery. 1924.
T-4-8	40–60	Upright table. Wood. 1934.
T-6-1	60–75	Upright table. AM/2SW. 1935.
T-6-7	75–125	Upright table. AM/2SW. 1935.
T-8-14	80–120	Upright table. AM/2SW. 1935.
T-55	35–40	Table. Wood. Push-button. 1940.
T-56	30–35	Table. Wood. Push-button. 1940.
T-60	25–30	Table. Wood. Push-button. AM/SW. 1940.
T-62	30–35	Table. Wood. AM/SW. 1940. (FOS-155)
T-63	25–30	Table. Wood. Push-button. AM/SW. 1940.
T-64	30–40	Table. Wood. Push-button. AM/2SW. 1940.
T-65	35–40	Table. Wood. AM/2SW. 1940.
T-80	35–40	Table. Wood. AM/2SW. 1940.
U-8	20–25	Radio-phonograph. Table. 1939.
U-9	10–15	Radio-phonograph. Table. 1940.
U-10	10–15	Radio-phonograph. Table. 1940.
U-20	50–60	Radio-phonograph. Horizontal console. AM/SW. 1940.

U-25	45–50	Radio-phonograph. Horizontal console. AM/2SW. 1940.
U-26	45–50	Radio-phonograph. Horizontal console. AM/2SW. 1940.
U-30	60–75	Radio-phonograph. Horizontal console. AM/2SW. 1939.
U-40	50–65	Radio-phonograph. Horizontal console. 1940.
U-42	60–75	Radio-phonograph. Console with doors. Tuning eye. 1940.
U-43	50–65	Radio-phonograph. Horizontal console. Tuning eye. 1940.
U-44	40–45	Radio-phonograph. Horizontal console. AM/2SW. 1940.
U-45	50–60	Radio-phonograph. Horizontal console. AM/2SW. 1940.
U-46	100–125	Radio-phonograph. Horizontal console. AM/2SW. 1940.
U-50	20–25	Radio-phonograph. Table. AM/2SW. Leatherette. 1939.
U-104	25–30	Radio-phonograph. Push-button. Table. 1939.
U-111	20–25	Radio-phonograph. Table. 1938.
U-112	20–25	Radio-phonograph. Table. 1938.
U-115	20–25	Radio-phonograph. Table. Wood. Push-button. 1939.
U-119	35–40	Radio-phonograph. Table. Wood. Push-button. AM/2SW. 1938.
U-121	65–75	Radio-phonograph. Horizontal console. Push-button. 1939.
U-122-E	100–150	Chairside. Radio-phonograph. AM/2SW. Push-button. 1938.
U-123	75–90	Radio-phonograph. Horizontal console. Push-button. 1939.
U-124	50–65	Radio-phonograph. Console. AM/2SW. Push-button. 1938.
U-125	85–100	Radio-phonograph. Console. AM/2SW. Push-button. 1939.
U-126	50–60	Radio-phonograph. Horizontal console. AM/2SW. 1938.
U-127-E	125–150	Chairside. Radio-phonograph. Push-button. 1939.
U-128	50–65	Radio–phonograph. Horizontal console. AM/2SW. 1938.
U-129	60–70	Radio-phonograph. Horizontal console. AM/2SW. 1939.
U-130	60–70	Radio-phonograph. Horizontal console. 1938.
U-132	100–125	Radio-phonograph. Horizontal console. AM/6SW. 1938.
U-134	125–150	Radio-phonograph. Horizontal console. AM/6SW. 1938.
UY-122-E	125–150	Chairside. Radio-phonograph. Push-button. AM/2SW. 1942.
UY-124	70–80	Radio-phonograph. Push-button. Console. AM/2SW. 1942.
V-100	30–40	Radio-phonograph. Table. 1940.
V-101	35–40	Radio-phonograph. Table. 1940.
V-104	40–45	Radio-phonograph. Push-button. Table. 1941.
V-105	25–30	Radio-phonograph. Table. 1942.
V-135	20–25	Radio-phonograph. Table. 1942.
V-140	25–30	Radio-phonograph. Table. 1942.
V-170	60–75	Radio-phonograph. Horizontal console. Push-button. AM/SW. 1941.
V-175	60–75	Radio-phonograph. Horizontal console. Push-button. AM/SW. 1942.
V-200	50–60	Radio-phonograph. Horizontal console. Push-button. AM/SW. 1941.
V-201	50–60	Radio-phonograph. Horizontal console. Push-button. AM/SW. 1941.

AR: *Antique Radios: Restoration and Price Guide* / **FOS:** *Flick of the Switch* / **GOR:** *Guide to Old Radios*
RGA: *Radios: The Golden Age* / **VR:** *Vintage Radio*

V-205	75–100	Radio-phonograph. Horizontal console. AM/2SW. 1941.
V-209	70–85	Radio-phonograph. Horizontal console. AM/SW. 1942.
V-210	70–85	Radio-phonograph. Horizontal console. AM/SW. 1942.
V-215	85–100	Radio-phonograph. Horizontal console. AM/2SW. 1942.
V-219	100–125	Radio-phonograph. Horizontal console. AM/2SW. 1942.
V-221	85–100	Radio-phonograph. Horizontal console. AM/2SW. 1942.
V-225	75–100	Radio-phonograph. Horizontal console. AM/2SW. 1942.
V-300	100–125	Radio-phonograph. Horizontal console. AM/2SW. Push-button. 1941.
V-301	85–100	Radio-phonograph. Horizontal console. AM/2SW. Push-button. 1941.
V-302	100–125	Radio-phonograph. Horizontal console. AM/2SW. Push-button. 1941.
V-405	100–125	Radio-phonograph. Horizontal console. AM/2SW. 1941.
VHR-202	85–100	Radio-phonograph-recorder. AM/2SW. Horizontal console. 1941.
VHR-207	100–125	Radio-phonograph-recorder. AM/2SW. Horizontal console. 1941.
VHR-212	125–150	Radio-phonograph-recorder. AM/2SW. Horizontal console. 1942.
VHR-307	125–150	Radio-phonograph-recorder. AM/2SW. Horizontal console. 1941.
VHR-407	100–125	Radio-phonograph-recorder. AM/2SW. Horizontal console. 1941.
Wings	750 +	Wings cigarette pack. 8″ × 12″ × 10″
X-55	35–40	Table. Wood. Push-button. 1942.
X-60	25–30	Table. Wood. Push-button. 1942.
X-551	15–20	Table. Plastic. 1947. (GOR)

RECORDIO

Made by Wilcox-Gay.

7D44	60–85	Radio-phonograph-recorder. AM/FM. Horizontal console. Blond wood. 1948.

REGAL

747	15–25	Portable. Metal case with plastic lid and back. Flip-up lid. 1947. (GOR)
777	15–20	Portable. Metal. Plastic flip-up lid. 1949.
7251	10–15	Table. Plastic. 1948.

REINARTZ

Made by Elgin Radio Company.

2L0	400–500	Table. Battery. Wood. 1925.

RELIABLE

Sold by Reliable Radio Company, New York.

Treasure Chest	40–60	Chest. 1934. (GOR)

REMLER

9 Tube Super	150–200	Kit. Battery. 1925. (VR-145)
5310	25–30	Radio-phonograph. Table. Wood. 1948.
5500 "Scottie Pup"	50–75	Table. 1949.

REX

Masterdyne	75–100	Table. Battery. 3-dial. 1924.

RIPPNER

	100–125	Crystal.

ROLAND

5T5	15–20	Table. Plastic. 1954.
5X3	15–20	Radio-phonograph. Table. 1954.
8XF1	15–20	Radio-phonograph. Table. 1953.

ROTH DOWNS

Orpheus	75–90	Small console.

SAINT JAMES

Twin 4	300	Kit. Battery. 1927.

ST. REGIS

unknown	100–125	Cathedral. Miniature. Mid-1930s. (GOR)

E. H. SCOTT

This is not the same company as H. H. Scott. H. H. Scott was primarily a producer of high-fidelity equipment and components. When people refer to a "Scott," however, E. H. Scott is the company they mean. This was the company that chrome-plated not only its chassis, but also its tube shields. Because of this, many Scotts were not enclosed in cabinets, but stayed out in the open for everyone to admire.

As in the 1930s, today Scott radios are sold as chassis and speaker only or as a chassis in a particular model cabinet. The names of the cabinets are impressive, such as the "Sheraton" or the "Chippendale Grande." An excellent pamphlet for identifying Scott chassis and cabinets, with lots of pictures, is J. W. F. Puett's *Silver Ghosts* (Puett Electronics, P.O. Box 28572, Dallas, TX 75228).

E. H. Scott's slogan was "The Stradivarius of Radio Receivers."

16	300–500	Lowboy. (FOS-167)
16A	300–500	Chassis and speaker. 28 tubes. AM/FM. 1948.
800-B	200–400	Chassis and speaker. 1946. (FOS-169)
	500+	Chippendale cabinet. Console.
Allwave 2 volt	200-350	Chassis and speaker. Battery. 1934.
Allwave 12 "DeLuxe"	200-350	Chassis and speaker. 1- or 2-dial tuning. 1931. (FOS-168)
Allwave 15	250–400	Chassis and speaker. 1934.
Allwave Imperial	250–400	Chassis and speaker. 1935. Also known as the "Full Range High Fidelity Receiver." (FOS-168)
FM Tuner	125–200	FM. Old FM (pre-1943) band only.
Phantom	250–400	Chassis and speaker. 1940. (FOS-168)
Philharmonic	300–500	Chassis and speaker. 30 tubes. 1937. (FOS-168)
	600+	Chippendale cabinet. Console.
	750+	Chippendale Grande. Horizontal console.
	600+	Warrington cabinet. Console.

AR: *Antique Radios: Restoration and Price Guide* / **FOS**: *Flick of the Switch* / **GOR**: *Guide to Old Radios*
RGA: *Radios: The Golden Age* / **VR**: *Vintage Radio*

SENTINEL

Made by the United Air Cleaner Company.

11	100–150	Lowboy. Wood. Deco. 1930. (GOR)
15	125–200	Lowboy. Wood. Gothic panels. 1930. (GOR)
195ULT	1000+	Table. Butterscotch and maroon Catalin. (What we call "butterscotch," Sentinel called "onyx." The color has changed with time.) Push-button. 1939. (GOR)
238V	75–125	Large book. 1941.
284GA	25–30	Radio-phonograph. Table. Wood. Phonograph automatically plays record when the top is closed. 1947.
286PR	25–30	Portable. Metal top. AC/battery. 1947.
302I	15–20	Table. Plastic. AM/FM. 1948.
305I	15–20	Table. Plastic. AM/3SW. 1948.
309I/309W	25–35	Table. Plastic. 1947. (GOR)
313W	10–15	Table. Plastic. 1948.
314I/314W	20–25	Table. Plastic. 1948.
315I/315W	20–25	Table. Plastic. 1948.
332	10–15	Table. Plastic. 1949. (GOR)
343	20–30	Table. Brown Bakelite. 1952.
344	30–40	Table. Black plastic. 1953. (GOR)
IU-343	15–25	Table. Black Bakelite. 1952. (GOR)
L284	1000+	Table. Caramel Catalin. 1947. (RGA-79)
	1500+	Red and caramel Catalin.
Portola	120–140	Chairside. 1930.

SETCHELL-CARLSON

55	20–40	Portable. AC/battery. Cloth-covered. 1938. (GOR)
416	15–30	Table. Plastic. Top knobs. 1946.
447	25–30	Portable. Leatherette with plastic grille. AC/battery. 1948. (GOR)
458R	20–30	Intercom-radio. Ivory or black plastic. 1950. (GOR)
588	20–30	Table. Wood. 1939. (GOR)

SHOWERS

Consola	100–150	Table. Wood. Gold decoration. Battery. 1926. (GOR)

SIGNAL

These radios, from the late 1940s, were made by Signal Electronics Company (New York). This trade name was used by the Signal Radio and Electric Corporation in 1923 and the Signal Electric Manufacturing Company in 1926.

341-A	10–15	Portable. Imitation snakeskin. AC/battery. 1948.
AF252	35–40	Plastic. Table. AM/FM. 1948.

SILVER MARSHALL

620 "Cockaday"	80–100	Table. Battery. 1928.
720	100–125	Table. Wood. Battery. 1929.
F4	150–250	Cathedral.
Q	100–150	Console with doors. 6 legs. 1931.

SILVERTONE

Sold by Sears Roebuck.

1	30–35	Table. Metal. Brown, with white knob and dial. 1949. (RGA-100)

90	30–35	Table. Metal. Battery. 1935.
107	15–20	Table. Metal. 1934.
132.857	30–40	Table. Brown Bakelite. 1949. (FOS-173; GOR)
132.878	30–40	Table. Brown or white metal. 1950.
132.881	10–15	Table. Brown Bakelite. 1951. (GOR)
1561	40–60	Table. AM/SW. 1940.
1809	30–35	Upright table. Deco. AM/SW. 1934.
2001	20–30	Table. Brown metal. 1950. (GOR)
2028	15–20	Table. Wood. Battery. 1953.
3040A	35–40	Radio-phonograph. Table. Plastic. 1955.
3068	40–45	Radio-phonograph. Horizontal console. AM/FM. 1955.
3215	10–15	Portable. Maroon plastic. AC/battery. 1954.
3216	10–15	Same as 3215. Green plastic.
3217	10–15	Same as 3215. Grey plastic.
4016	15–20	Radio-phonograph. Table. Plastic. 1955.
4032	15–20	Radio-phonograph. Table. Plastic. 1955.
4046A	20–25	Radio-phonograph. Table. 1955.
4408	15–20	Table. Battery. Airplane dial. 1935.
4500	50–75	Table. Black Bakelite, silver grille cloth. First plastic radio offered by Sears. 1936. (GOR)
6050	20–25	Table. Wood. 1947. (FOS-172)
6057	30–50	Radio-phonograph. Horizontal console. 3-speed phonograph. Blond wood. 1956. (GOR)
6220A	30–40	Table. Battery. 1946.
7006	10–15	Table. Brown plastic. 1941.
7013	10–20	Table. Black plastic. 1957. (GOR)
7022	40–50	Table. White metal, red knobs. 1942.
07025	30–50	Table. Brown Bakelite. Deco. 1946. (GOR)
7038	40–45	Upright table. Push-button. 1941.
7048	125–150	Cathedral. 1933.
		Note: A console was made with this number in 1941.
7054	20–30	Table. Blond wood. Push-button. 1949. (GOR)
7200	20–25	Table. Wood. AM/FM. 1957.
8003	25–30	Table. Metal. 1949.
8005	20–25	Table. Plastic. 1948. (FOS-172)
8010	25–30	Clock-radio. Plastic. 1948.
8050	15–20	Table. Wood. 1948.
8055A	30–35	Radio-phonograph. Horizontal console. AM/FM. 1958.
8072	10–15	Radio-phonograph. Table. Wood. 1948.
8080	35–40	Radio-phonograph. Table. Bakelite. 1948.
8100	25–30	Radio-phonograph. Small console. 1948.
8103	35–40	Radio-phonograph-wire recorder. Horizontal console. 1949.
8105A	45–55	Radio-phonograph. Horizontal console. AM/SW. 1948.
8270.A	20–25	Portable. Plastic and aluminum. AC/battery. 1949.
9000	150–20	Table. White plastic. 1950.
9005	10–15	Table. Brown plastic. 1949.
9260	10–15	Portable. Plastic with metallic front. AC/battery. 1948.
G	35–45	Table. Metal. Battery. 1932.
R1181	60–80	Table. AM/3SW. 1940.

AR: *Antique Radios: Restoration and Price Guide* / **FOS**: *Flick of the Switch* / **GOR**: *Guide to Old Radios*
RGA: *Radios: The Golden Age* / **VR**: *Vintage Radio*

SIMPLEX

N	45–125	Cathedral. 1932.

SIMPLI-DYNE

Jr.	35	Table. Battery. 1920.

SLEEPER

54	225–300	Table. Sloped front panel. Battery. 1925.
3300	75–100	Table. Battery. 1920. (VR-119)
Imperial 68	125–150	Console. Battery. 1927.
Serenader	75–100	Table. Battery. 1926. (VR-138)

SOMERSET

Produced by National Airphone in 1924. The company failed in 1925 (although their ads continued in radio magazines). Another attempt was made to produce radios in 1926 under the Somerset brand. After three months, the new owner dropped the brand.

5	50–75	Table. Slant-front panel. Battery. 3-dial. 1926. (GOR)

SONORA

102	10–15	Portable. Plastic. AC/battery. 1949.
335	10–15	Portable. Plastic. AC/battery. 1954.
A30	85–100	Radio-phonograph. Table. 1928.
C	35–40	Table. Battery. 3-dial. 1924.
RBU-176	20–30	Table. Ivory Bakelite. 1946.
RDU-209	20–25	Table. 1946.
RMR-219	75–85	Radio-phonograph. Horizontal console. AM/SW. 1947.
WBRU-239	25–30	Radio-phonograph. Table. Wood. 1947.
WCU-246	50–75	Bed-lamp radio. 1948.
WDU-249	35–40	Portable. Plastic covered. AC/battery. 1948.
WEU-262	35–40	Table. Plastic. AM/FM. 1948.
WJU-252	45–50	Table. Plastic. 1948.
WKRU-254A	45–50	Radio-phonograph. Horizontal console. AM/FM. 1948.
WLRU-219A	50–65	Radio-phonograph. Horizontal console. AM/FM. 1948.

SPARTON

6-66A	10–15	Table. Leatherette. AM/SW. 1948.
6AM06	20–25	Portable. AC/battery. Leatherette. 1948.
7-46	60–90	Console. Wood. 1946. (GOR)
65	85–100	Upright table. AM/SW. 1934. (This came in the original box.)
	50–60	Same radio, without box.
79	60–80	Console. 1928.
100	15–20	Table. Ivory plastic. 1948.
109	80–100	Console. 1928.
141XX	20–40	Table. Wood. AM/FM. 1951. (GOR)
235	250–300	Radio-phonograph. Console. 1930.
301 "Equasonne"	500 +	Highboy with doors. Elaborate decoration. 1929. (GOR)
301	10–15	Portable. Brown plastic over metal. AC/battery. 1953.
305	15–20	Same as 301. Green plastic.
309	10–15	Same as 301. Ivory plastic.
500 "Cloisonne"	750 +	Table. 1939.
506 "Bluebird"	2000 +	Table. Mirror. Chrome trim. AM/SW. 1935.

557	1500+	Blue mirror. 3 knobs. AM/SW. 1936.
	1750+	Peach mirror.
558	2500+	Blue mirror. 4 knobs. AM/SW. 1937.
	3500+	Peach mirror. 4 knobs. 1937.
930	70–100	Console. 1929.
1010	50–60	Radio-phonograph. Horizontal console. 1948.
1030A	45–50	Radio-phonograph. Console. 1948.
1059	20–25	Radio-phonograph. Horizontal console. 1949.
1068	80–100	Console. Wood. Push-button. 1937. (GOR)
1186 "Nocturne"	7500+	Floor model. Large round mirror. 46″ high. Deco. Chrome trim. AM/SW. At this writing, only 9 are known. Available with blue or rose mirror or crystal glass. 1936.
5218	80–90	Table. Push-button. AM/SW. 1938.

SPLENDID

unknown	300	1-tube

SPLITDORF

R-560	40–60	Table. Battery. 3-dial. 1926.

STANDARDYNE

B5	60–100	Table. Wood. Battery. 3-dial. 1925. (GOR)
BH	100–125	Lowboy. Drop-front. Enclosed speaker above radio panel. Cabinet below. 1925. (GOR)

STEELMAN

3AR5U	15–20	Radio-phonograph. Portable. 1956.
4AR11	30–35	Radio-phonograph. Horizontal console. AM/FM. 1959.
595	15–20	Radio-phonograph. Portable. Leatherette. 1952.

STEINITE

unknown	150–250	Crystal. 1925.
26-1	125–175	1-tube. 2-dial. 1925.

STERLING

DeLuxe	125–150	Table. Marbellized plastic with chrome top.

STEWART WARNER

Until 1925, Stewart Warner manufactured auto parts. The company discontinued production of radios and televisions in 1954.

03-5C1-WT	15–30	Table. Wood. 1939. (GOR)
07-5B	50–150	Table. Plastic. 1939.
07-5B3Q "Dionne Quintuplets"	700+	Table. Decals on model 07-5B3. 1939. (FOS-176)
07-513 "Gulliver's Travels"	500–700	Table. Decals on model 07-513. 1939.
07-513Q "Dionne Quintuplets"	700+	Table. Decals on model 07-513. 1939. (FOS-176)

AR: *Antique Radios: Restoration and Price Guide* / **FOS**: *Flick of the Switch* / **GOR**: *Guide to Old Radios*
RGA: *Radios: The Golden Age* / **VR**: *Vintage Radio*

07-713Q (?) "Dionne Quintuplets"	700+	Table. Ivory plastic. Decals on model 07-713. Top controls. 1939. (This is the most likely model number for this set.)
51T56	15–20	Table. Wood. 1948.
300	50–70	Table. Battery. 3-dial. 1925. (VR-138)
325	50–85	Table. Battery. 3-dial. 1925.
525	30–50	Table. Battery. 1927.
0751H	20–40	Table. Plastic. Left side curved from top to bottom. 1940. (GOR)
900	100–150	Lowboy. Wood. 1929. (GOR)
9002A	20–25	Table. Plastic. 1948.
9160AU	15–20	Table. Brown plastic with tan knob and dial. 1952.
9160BU	40–45	Same as 9160AU. Yellow plastic with green knob and dial.
9160CU	25–30	Same as 9160AU. Blue plastic with blue knob and dial.
9160DU	20–25	Same as 9160AU. Rust plastic with tan knob and dial.
9160EU	20–25	Same as 9160AU. Tan plastic with rust knob and dial.
9170-B	10–15	Portable. Green plastic. AC/battery. 1954.
9170-C	10–15	Same as 9170-B. Grey plastic.
9170-D	10–15	Same as 9170-B. Maroon plastic.
9178-C	25–30	Radio-phonograph. Table. 1955.
9187-B	20–25	Clock-radio. Green plastic with ivory knobs. 1954.
9187-E	40–45	Same as 9187-B. Chartreuse plastic with black knobs.
9187-J	30–35	Same as 9187-B. Red plastic with tan knobs.
A51T2	50–65	Table. Brown Bakelite. Top controls. 1947.
A61CR3	35–40	Radio-phonograph. Console. 1948.
A61P1	25–35	Portable. AC/battery (rechargable). 1947.
A72T3	35–40	Table. Wood. AM/FM. 1947.
C51T1	20 30	Table. Ivory Bakelite. 1948. (GOR)
R-180A	30–50	Table. Wood. Speakers on sides of cabinet. 1937. (GOR)
St. James	200–300	Highboy. Solid walnut front. 1930. (GOR)

STROMBERG-CARLSON

Originally a manufacturer of telephone equipment.

1A	66–150	Table. Battery. 3-dial. 1924. (VR-133)
68	125–200	Console. Deco. AM/SW. 1935.
130J	50–100	Table. Deco. 1937.
231R	200–350	Chairside. Semicircular. Mirror top. AM/SW. 1937. (FOS-180)
240R	300–500	Console with doors. Semicircular. Deco. Push-button. AM/4SW. 1937. (FOS-180; GOR)
320H	25–30	Table. AM/FM. 1938. (FOS-180)
400H	30–35	Table. 1939.
410H	40–60	Table. Wood. AM/SW. 1939.
420L	75–100	Console. Push-button. AM/SW. 1939.
520H	45–60	Table. Wood. AM/SW. 1940.
1105	15–25	Portable. AC/battery. 1947.
1121	80–100	Console. 1946.
1202	25–30	Radio-phonograph. Table. 1949.
1204	30–35	Table. Plastic. AM/FM. 1948.
1210PLM	50–60	Radio-phonograph. Horizontal console. AM/FM. 1948.
1400	30–35	Table. Ivory plastic. Full wraparound grille. 1949.
1500	40–50	Table. Red plastic. 1950. (GOR)

SYLVANIA

454BR	10–15	Portable. Brown plastic. Battery. 1954.
454GR	10–15	Same as 454BR. Green plastic.
454H	10–15	Same as 454BR. Ivory plastic.
454RE	15–20	Same as 454BR. Red plastic.
2101TU	10–15	Table. Turquoise plastic. 1957.

TATRO

CR-557	40–60	Lowboy. 6 legs. Wood. c. 1930. (GOR)

TELE-TONE

111	15–20	Table. Wood. 1948.
150	20–25	Table. Ivory plastic. 1948.
159	10–15	Table. Plastic. 1948.
160	40–45	Table. 2-tone plastic. 1948.

TELEFUNKEN

535IW "Jubilate"	25–35	Table. Multi-band. 1950s.
5346W "Contessa"	60–70	Console. Small. AM/2SW.
Andante 8	35–40	Table. AM/FM/SW. 1950s.
Jubilee	40–60	Table. 2-band. 1956.

TELEKING

RK-41	10–15	Table. Plastic. 1953.
RKP-53-A	15–20	Portable. Plastic. AC/battery. Tapered shape. 1954.

TEMPLE

Began in 1928.

E-514	40–45	Table. Wood. 1946.
F-616	10–20	Table. Wood. 1946. (GOR)
G-724	10–15	Table. Wood. AM/FM. 1948.
G-725	40–50	Radio-phonograph. Horizontal console. 1948.

THERMIODYNE

TF-5	45–50	Table. Battery. 1925.
TF-6	65–80	Table. Battery. 1925.

THOMPSON

Thompson began producing radios and speakers in 1923. It went into receivership in 1926.

Neutrodyne 5	75–150	Table. Battery. Wood. 1924.
S70 "Concert Grand"	45–50	Table. Battery. Sloped front panel. 3-dial. 1925.
V-50	100–125	Table. Battery. Sloped front panel. 3-dial. 1925.

TRAV-LER

Made by the Trav-Ler Karenola Radio & Television Corporation, Chicago.

5015	20–25	Table. Plastic. 1948.
5022	10–15	Portable. 1946.
5028	10–15	Portable. Leatherette. AC/battery. 1948.
5030	25–30	Radio-phonograph. Leatherette. Table. 1947.

AR: *Antique Radios: Restoration and Price Guide* / **FOS**: *Flick of the Switch* / **GOR**: *Guide to Old Radios*
RGA: *Radios: The Golden Age* / **VR**: *Vintage Radio*

5036	15–20	Radio-phonograph. Table. Cloth. 1949.
5051	25–30	Table. Plastic. 1947.
5054	15–20	Table. Plastic. 1948.
5066	20–35	Table. Brown plastic. 1946. (GOR)
5372	15–20	Radio-phonograph. Portable. Leatherette. 1954.
8103	15–20	Radio-phonograph. Table. Wood. 1949.
unknown	20–25	Table. Black plastic. Modernistic shape and dial. About mid-1950s. (GOR)
unknown	35–45	Table. Wood. AM/SW. 1937. (GOR)

TRESCO *(See also Tri-City)*

W	200	Receiver and amplifier. (GOR)

TRI-CITY *(See also Tresco)*

Tri-City produced radios for Montgomery Ward in 1923. The company also sold radios under its own brand, "Tresco."

W2	75–150	Box. Battery. Made for Montgomery Ward. 1923.
W6	75–150	Box. Battery. Made for Montgomery Ward. 1923.

TROY

100	40–60	Table. Wood. Telephone dial. 1937. (GOR)

TRUETONE

Western Auto's house brand.

D-1747	65–75	Radio-phonograph. Horizontal console. AM/4SW. 1947.
D-1752	50–60	Radio-phonograph. Console. AM/FM. 1948.
D-1846A	40–45	Radio-phonograph. Console. AM/FM. 1948.
D-1850	45–50	Radio-phonograph. Horizontal console. AM/FM. 1948.
D-2210	40–65	Table. Metal. Deco. 1941.
D-2270	15–20	Radio-phonograph. Portable. Leatherette. 1953.
D-2386	10–15	Table. Black plastic. 1954.
D-2387	10–15	Same as D-2386. White plastic.
D-2388	20–25	Same as D-2386. Red plastic.
D-2418A	20–25	Clock-radio. Black plastic with bright grille. 1954.
D-2419A	40–45	Same as D-2418. Red plastic.
D-2420A	15–20	Same as D-2418. White plastic.
D-2613	10–15	Table. Plastic. 1947.
D-2620	20–25	Table. Wood. 1946.
D-2622	10–20	Table. Wood. 1947.
D-2626	25–30	Table. Wood. AM/SW. 1948.
D-2692	15–20	Table. Wood. Plastic grille. 1948.
D-2810	15–20	Table. Plastic. 1948.
D-2815	40–60	Violin shape. Brown Bakelite. 1948.
	50–75	White Bakelite.
D-2819	25–30	Table. Plastic. AM/FM. 1948.
D-2851	15–20	Radio-phonograph. Table. 1948.
D-3120A	10–15	Portable. Plastic. AC/battery. 1953.
D-3130/3130B	10–15	Portable. Plastic. AC/battery. 1953.
D-3210A	10–15	Portable. Plastic. AC/battery. 1953.
D-3490	10–15	Portable. Plastic. Battery. 1955.
D-3630	25–30	Portable. AC/battery. 1947.
D-3721	15–20	Portable. 1947.

D-3722	10–15	Portable. Leatherette with plastic grille. AC/battery. 1948.
D-3810	10–15	Portable. Leatherette. AC/battery. 1948.

TUSKA

One of the early companies, Tuska incorporated in May 1920, and had its first radios advertised and for sale in August of the same year.

224	200–300	Table. Battery. 2-dial. 1922. (VR-121)
225	200–300	Table. Battery. 2-dial. 1923. (VR-121)
301 "Junior"	150–200	Table. Battery. 1925.
305 "Superdyne"	150–200	Table. Battery. 2-dial. 1925.

U. S. APEX

8A	150	Cathedral. 1931.

ULTRADYNE

Made by the Lacault Company.

L2	60–70	Table. Battery. 1924.

VALLEYTONE

unknown	50–100	Table. 6-tube. 1925.

VICTOR *(see also RCA)*

The Victor Talking Machine Company believed in phonographs, not radio. After the company was sold in 1926, management recognized that radio was hurting the sales of phonographs and records and brought out a radio-phonograph in 1926, using an RCA Radiola 28 for the radio. It appears that Victor was ready to start designing its own radios when the company instead merged with RCA in 1929.

Note: The VV- designation stands for a spring-wound motor. VE- means an electric motor.

RE-45	200–300	Radio-phonograph. Console. 1929. (AR-41)
RE-57	100–150	Radio-phonograph. Console. 1930.
VE-9-55	1000 +	Radio-phonograph. Horizontal console. Uses a Radiola 28. An automatic changer turned the record over. 1927.
VV-7-1	175–225	Radio-phonograph. Highboy. Uses a Radiola 18. Acoustic phonograph. 1928.
VV-9-1 "Florenza"	500	Radio-phonograph. Horizontal lowboy with doors. Uses a Radiola 25. Acoustic phonograph. 1926.

VICTOREEN

Victoreen was a pioneer in kit radios. The company got involved in the nasty, drawn-out patent fights of the 1920s but managed to sell out before the fights came to court.

unknown	150	Kit. 5-tube.
unknown	125–150	9-tube.
unknown	150–175	Superhet.

AR: *Antique Radios: Restoration and Price Guide* / **FOS:** *Flick of the Switch* / **GOR:** *Guide to Old Radios*
RGA: *Radios: The Golden Age* / **VR:** *Vintage Radio*

WARE

Ware produced radios until 1925. At that time, a major disagreement with Music Master (concerning 15,000 radio sets that were, or were not, delivered) forced them to quit. It is reported that most of the Ware radios were then unloaded in New York City department stores.

T	175–250	Table. Battery. 3-dial. 1924. (VR-124)

WELLS-GARDNER

108A1-704	30–50	Table. Telephone dial. Wood. 1937. (GOR)
WG-30A8-A-496	65–75	Radio-phonograph. Horizontal console. AM/FM. 1954.

WESTERN COIL

Lewis	1250	1922.
WC-15-JR "Radiodyne"	125-175	Table. Battery. 1926.
WC17	100–125	Table. Battery. 2-dial. 1924.

WESTERN ELECTRIC

4B	200–350	Table. Battery. 2-dial. 1923.

WESTINGALE

unknown	100–125	Table. Scenic front. 1926–1927. (GOR)

WESTINGHOUSE

There were Westinghouse radios in 1921 and again in 1930. In between, the company continued to make radios, but the sets were sold under the RCA name. As a member of the patent-pool that included RCA, Westinghouse produced 40 percent of the radios sold under the RCA name during that period, namely the Aeriola Jr. and the Aeriola Sr. (General Electric manufactured the other 60 percent). Westinghouse was not only a developer of radios, it was also a strong supporter of broadcasting. Station KDKA (the first licensed broadcasting station in the United States) was started in October 1920. The station's first broadcasting studio was a tent on top of one of a Westinghouse building.

52R11	15–20	Table. Brown plastic with black dial and knob. 1952.
52R12	10–15	Same as 52R11. Ivory plastic with ivory dial and knobs.
52R13	20–25	Same as 52R11. Maroon plastic with black dial and knobs.
52R14	15–20	Same as 52R11. Grey plastic with black dial and knobs
52R15	20–25	Same as 52R11. Green plastic with black dial and knobs.
52R16	30–35	Same as 52R11. Red plastic with black dial and knobs.
H-122	40–50	Radio-phonograph. Radio can be removed from cabinet for use elsewhere. 1946.
H-122A	40–45	Table. Brown plastic. 1946.
H-130	25–40	Table. Wood. 1946. (GOR)
H-146	50–75	Refrigerator radio.
H-147	20–30	Table. Brown Bakelite. 1947.
H-157	20–25	Table. Wood. 1948.
H-161	25–30	Table. Wood. AM/FM. 1948.
H-165	10–15	Portable. AC/battery. 1947.
H-166	80–100	Radio-phonograph. Horizontal console. Curved front. 1948.
H-168	40–45	Radio-phonograph. Horizontal console. AM/FM. 1948.

H-169	150–200	Radio-phonograph. Horizontal console. 2-way speaker. Large. AM/FM/2SW. 1948.
H-171	50–65	Radio-phonograph. Console. Blond wood. Radio is plastic and can be removed from wood cabinet base. 1948. (AR-66)
H-182	35–40	Table. Plastic. Metallic trim. 1949.
H-185	15–20	Portable. Maroon plastic. AC/battery. 1949. (FOS-182)
H-188	25–30	Table. Plastic. "Pagoda" top and grille. 1948.
H-195	10–15	Portable. Leatherette. AC/battery. 1949.
H-204	40–50	Table. Plastic. Deco. 1948.
H-331P4U	15–20	Portable. Green plastic. AC/battery. 1952.
H-333P4U	15–20	Portable. Brown plastic. AC/battery. 1952.
H-382T5	10–20	Table. Brown plastic. 1954.
H-384T5	20–25	Table. Maroon Bakelite. 1953.
H-393T6	10–15	Table. Maroon plastic. 1953. (GOR)
H-494P4	15–30	Portable. 1955.
H-598P4	15–20	Portable. Beige and red plastic. AC/portable. 1957.
H-648T4	10–20	Table. White plastic. 1955.
Refrigerator radio		See model H-146
WR-8-R	325	Grandfather clock. 1929.
WR-15	100–200	Grandfather clock. 1931.
WR-22	75–100	Upright table. AM/SW. 1934.
WR-28	80–100	Upright table. AM/SW. 1934.
WR-274	15–20	Table. AM/SW. Push-button. 1939.

WESTONE

| 30 | 10–15 | Table. |

WILMAK *(see Denchum)*

WOLPER

| RS5 | 75–100 | Table. Slant front. Stepped-back enclosed horn. Mid-1920s. (GOR) |

WOOLAROC

Sold by Phillips Petroleum.

3-15A	25–30	Table. Metal. 1948.
3-17A	20–25	Table. Plastic. 1948.
3-71A	50–60	Radio-phonograph. Horizontal console. 1948.

WORK RITE

Air Master	50–75	Table. Wood. Slant front. Battery. 3-dial. 1924. (GOR)
Aristocrat	125–200	Horizontal highboy. Slant front panel. Two end compartments with doors, one with enclosed speaker. 3-dial. Battery. 1924. (GOR)
Chum	50–75	Table. Slant front panel. 2-dial. Battery. 1925. (GOR)

ZENITH

Chicago Radio Laboratories began in 1918 to supply amateur equipment. CRL's call letters were 9ZN. So, in 1919, CRL installed a new receiver at the station and called it a Z-

AR: *Antique Radios: Restoration and Price Guide* / **FOS:** *Flick of the Switch* / **GOR:** *Guide to Old Radios*
RGA: *Radios: The Golden Age* / **VR:** *Vintage Radio*

Nith, and from there it became Zenith. The company has been innovative: Zenith produced the first portable (1924), the first major production of AC sets (1926), and the first push-button tuning (1927).

Note: Because of the long, complicated sequences in Zenith model numbers, they are separated by hyphens into letter and number groups. The groups are not necessarily broken up like this by Zenith.

1R/2R	650	Table. Battery. 3-dial. 1922.
3R	250–350	Table. Battery. 1923. (VR-115)
4-B-231	30–60	Table. Battery. 1936.
4-G-800	35–40	Portable. Plastic. Flip-up cover. AC/battery. 1948.
4-G-800-Z	25–30	Portable. Plastic. Flip-up cover. Metallic front. AC/battery. 1948.
4-K-422	40–60	Table. Battery. Bakelite. 1939.
4R	300–400	Table. Battery. 1923. (VR-116)
5-D-611	40–45	Table. Wood.
	10–15	Table. Plastic.
5-D-810	15–20	Table. Plastic. Metal grille. 1949.
5-F-134	80–120	Upright table. Battery. AM/3SW. 1941. (GOR) (Cabinet same as 7-D-127 in FOS-193)
5-G-41	25–35	Portable. AC/battery. 1940. (FOS-196)
5-G-617	25–50	Table. Bakelite. Push-button. 1941.
5-R-135	75–100	Upright table. 1937.
5-R-236	60–80	Chairside. Magazine storage. 1937. (GOR)
5-R-312	60–90	Table. Bakelite. Push-button. (AR-61; RGA-71)
5-S-29	125–150	Upright table. AM/2SW. 1936. (FOS-192)
5-S-127	35–40	Upright table. AM/SW. 1936.
5-S-228	125–175	Upright table. AM/2SW. 1938.
5-S-338	125–150	Chairside. 1937.
6-B-129	100–125	Upright table. 6-volt battery. 1936. (FOS-191; GOR)
6-D-015	50–75	Table. Brown plastic. 1946. (RGA-71)
6-D-015-Z	50–75	Table. Green plastic. 1946.
6-D-029	40–60	Table. Wood. 1946. (FOS-195; GOR)
6-D-030	25–30	Table. Wood. Deco. 1946.
6-D-414	40–60	Table. Brown Bakelite. Inverted Bakelite chassis. 1939. (GOR)
6-D-510	20–25	Table. Bakelite. 1941.
6-D-525	45–60	Table. Wood. Black dial. 1941.
6-D-610	35–40	Table. Brown Bakelite. 1941.
6-D-614	40–50	Table. 1940.
6-D-815	30–35	Table. Plastic. Handle. 1949.
6-G-001 "Universal"	20–30	Portable. Black leatherette. 1946.
6-G-038	35–40	Table. Wood. AC/battery. Whip antenna. 1947.
6-G-501-F/-L/-M	30–50	Portable. AC/battery. 1940.
6-G-581-M	30–35	Table. Ship on grille.
6-G-601	25–30	Table. 1941.
6-G-601-M	40–50	Portable. AC/battery. Cloth-covered. 1941. (GOR)
6-G-801	20–25	Portable. Plastic. Front doors open. AC/battery. 1949.
6-J-230	75–100	Upright table. AC/battery. 1941.
6-R-631	25–50	Table. Wood. Push-button. 1941. (GOR)
6-R-886	25–35	Radio-phonograph. Table. Blond wood. 1947. (GOR)
	70–80	Same radio-phonograph with matching table. (GOR)
6-S-128	100–175	Upright table. AC/SW. 1936. (FOS-191)
6-S-229	85–100	Upright table. AM/SW. 1937. (GOR)
6-S-321	75–125	Table. AM/LW/SW. Push-button. 1937.

6-S-254	200	Console. AM/2SW. 1936.
6-V-27	85–100	Upright table. AM/SW. 6-volt battery. 1935. (AR-59; FOS-192)
7-F-04	15–25	Table. Brown plastic. AM/FM. 1949.
7-G-605 "Trans-oceanic"	150–225	Portable. First Trans-oceanic. Multi-band. 1941. (FOS-194; GOR)
7-H-822	20–25	Table. Plastic. AM/FM. 1949.
7-J-03	100–125	Table. Black and white plastic. 1953.
7-R-070	30–35	Radio-phonograph. Wood with textured paint. Plastic grille. 1948.
7-R-887	40–45	Radio-phonograph. Console. 1949.
7-S-240	100–175	Chairside. Walnut wood. Large black dial. AM/2SW. 1938. (GOR)
8-H-034	40–60	Table. Plastic. AM/2FM. 1946.
8-H-061	70–100	Console. AM/2FM. 1946.
8-H-861	30–35	Table. Wood. AM/2FM. 1948.
8-S-226	175	Chairside. 1939. (FOS-193)
8-S-463	200–250	Console. Push-button. 1939. (GOR)
9-S-262	200–300	Console. AM/SW. 1939.
10-H-571	100–125	Looks like a spinet piano. Push-button. AM/FM/SW. 1941.
10-H-573	75–125	Console. AM/SW/old FM. 1940.
10-S-160	180	Console. AM/3SW. 1936. (FOS-191)
10-S-567	150–175	Console. 1940.
11	75–100	Table. Battery. 1927. (GOR).
		Note: Also available as a lowboy in 1931.
11-E	100–125	Table. 1927.
11-S-474	200–225	Console. AM/2SW. 1939.
12-S-265	425	Console. AM/2SW. 1937.
12-S-568	425	Console. AM/2SW. 1940.
15-U-271	1000+	Console. Big. 15-tube. 1937.
33-X	150	Table. 1928.
40A	500+	Horizontal console. Elaborate. Wood. Push-button. 1930. (GOR)
60	100–125	Console. Wood. Small. 1929. (GOR)
64	300–500	Lowboy with doors. Wood. Push-button. 1931. (GOR)
230	100–125	Upright table. 1930. (FOS-190)
250	225–275	Cathedral. 1932.
1000-Z "Stratosphere"	3000+	Console. Big. 23-tube. Multi-band. Multi- speaker. 1934.
1005 (chassis)	300	Console. Push-button. 1939.
5416 (chassis)	20–30	Portable. Cloth-covered. Battery. 1939. (GOR)
B-509	15–25	Table. Red and white plastic. 1968.
B-513-V	10–15	Table. Plastic. 1959. (GOR)
C-730	15–25	Table. AM/FM. 1955.
G-510	15–25	Table. Black plastic. 1949.
G-725	20–25	Table. Bakelite. AM/FM. 1950.
H-511W	35–60	Table. White, walnut, or ebony plastic. 1954. (GOR)
H-615	30–35	Table. Burgundy plastic. Large dial. 1951. (GOR)
H-725	30–40	Table. Black plastic. AM/FM. 1950. (GOR)
HFM-1184-E	50–55	Radio-phonograph. Horizontal console. AM/FM. 1955.
J-402-G	10–20	Portable. Plastic. 1952.

AR: *Antique Radios: Restoration and Price Guide* / **FOS**: *Flick of the Switch* / **GOR**: *Guide to Old Radios*
RGA: *Radios: The Golden Age* / **VR**: *Vintage Radio*

J-509-C	10–15	Table. Green plastic. 1961. (GOR)
K-410	25–30	Portable. Plastic. Heavily chromed. Assorted colors. Battery. 1954.
K-412-W	15–20	Table. White plastic. 1953.
K-622/-F/-G/-W	40–45	Clock-radio. Plastic. Assorted colors. 1953.
K-666-R	60–75	Radio-phonograph. Table. Bakelite. 1953.
K-477-E	40–45	Radio-phonograph. Horizontal console. 1953.
L-410	25–30	Portable. Plastic. Heavily chromed. Assorted colors. Battery. 1954.
L-622/-F/-G/-W	40–45	Clock-radio. Plastic. Assorted colors. Contrasting grille. 1953.
M-403	20–25	Table. Red and black plastic with chrome. 1953.
Portola	125–150	Chairside. Wood. Manufactured by United Air Cleaners for Zenith. 1936. (GOR)
Super VII	125–175	Table. Battery. 2-dial. 1924. (GOR; VR-116)
Super VIII	125–175	Horizontal highboy. Spinet desk style. 2-dial. Battery. Super VII with legs. 1924. (GOR; VR-114, 148)
Super-Zenith X	150-250	Horizontal highboy. Slant-front panel. Two end compartments with doors. Enclosed speaker above radio panel. Two drawers in base. 1925. (GOR)
T-723	20–30	Table. Brown Bakelite. AM/FM. 1956.
Trans-oceanic	50–80	Portable. Early models were cloth; grille cloth had embroidered picture of airplane or sailboat. See 7-G-605 for first model. Later models were black leatherette. All had flip-up lid. Whip antenna for shortwave. AM/5 or 6 SW. These prices are for the more common black leatherette sets. Within these, model differences do not seem to affect the prices noticeably. (AR-68)
Y-723	10–25	Table. White plastic. AM/FM. 1956.
Y-725	20–25	Table. Brown Bakelite. AM/FM. 1956.

Radio-Related Items

Many of the items in this section do not have a range of prices listed, because they mainly came from classified ads. Often there was only one ad for a particular item. This section is intended to give you a general idea of what prices may be. Someone was trying to sell each item at the listed price — whether or not it was the actual paid price, we don't know. Nevertheless, this list may give you an idea of what is happening in radio-related fields.

Advertising Items

Description	Price Range ($)
ADMIRAL	
Neon clock, restored.	300
ATWATER KENT	
Lamp, no shade.	125–150
Lamp, with shade.	350–400
Playing cards, per deck.	75–100
Sign.	100
Wheel cover.	175–225
BENDIX	
Sign.	25–40
CLARION	
Lit sign.	150
CROSLEY	
Coloradio lit sign. (RGA-97)	500
"Magic Chef" timer. Deco style.	25–30
CUNNINGHAM TUBES	
Postcard.	2–3
FADA	
Advertising sign.	20–25
FARNSWORTH	
Advertising banner.	50–75
KENNEDY	
Crate for models 100 and 525.	80–100
MAJESTIC	
Calendar. 1931 calendar pages are complete.	40–70
Streetcar headliner.	50

AR: *Antique Radios: Restoration and Price Guide* / **FOS:** *Flick of the Switch* / **GOR:** *Guide to Old Radios*
RGA: *Radios: The Golden Age* / **VR:** *Vintage Radio*

MOTOROLA

Sign. Tin. 3-color. 14″ x 6'.	110

PHILCO

Clock advertising Philco tubes.	75
Crate top.	10–15
Outdoor advertising sign.	65–75

RCA

Cardboard display. Mickey Mouse and Pluto.	20
Clock. Reverse painting. "RCA Radio Batteries for Extra Listening Hours." 1950s.	150
Clock—RCA Tubes. Plastic. 1950s.	120
Clock—Radiotron.	90
Counter display—RCA Tubes. Metal.	50
Counter clock display—RCA Electron Tubes.	45
Crate—Radiola V.	40–50
Curtain for showroom. Overall pattern of Nipper. 8' X 15'.	200–275
Display case—Radiotron. Lit.	300
Fan—Radiola.	30–40
Lighter. Made by Zippo.	10
Map of world. Prewar. 4' x 8'.	125
Sign. Plastic. 24″ diameter.	35–50
Tapestry.	250

STROMBERG-CARLSON

Desk sign. Brass. "Stromberg-Carlson Authorized Radio Apparatus."	145
Display sign. Brass.	62

WESTINGHOUSE

Advertising clock.	75–100

ZENITH

Trans-oceanic display.	30–50

Novelty Radios

Description	Price Range ($)
ANIMALS	
Horse radio with saddle and blanket. Abbotwares model Z 477.	150–225
Mouse on cheese. Transistor.	20
BAR-RADIO	
Made for Penthouse.	175–200
White French provincial floor model. Philco.	400

AR: *Antique Radios: Restoration and Price Guide* / FOS: *Flick of the Switch* / GOR: *Guide to Old Radios*
RGA: *Radios: The Golden Age* / VR: *Vintage Radio*

Porto Baradio. Model PB520. Bakelite, with glasses. Used
    Stewart-Warner chassis no. 9008-B. (FOS-177).   250–400
Same, without glasses.   85

BEDLAMP

Made by Mitchell. Model Lullaby 1250.   50–75
Made by Mitchell. Model Lullaby 1251.   50–75
Sonora. Model WCU-249.   50–75

BEER

Lager beer keg.   75–100
Beer keg. Magic Tone model 508.   125–175
Beer keg. Made by Radiokeg. 1934.   125–200
Beer keg radio-lamp. Magic Tone model 900.   250–300
Bottle radio. Made by Mackt-Tone.   90–100
Beer bottle. Large. Tubes. (RGA-17).   175–225
Beer bottle. Made by Magic Tone.   350
Budweiser radio. AM/FM.   40–50
Grain Belt signboard radio.   60–100

BOOKS

Crosley. Bookcase model. 1932.   100–125
Sentinel. Model 238V. 1941.   100–150

CAMERA

Camera radio. Made by Cameradio.   100–150

CHARLIE McCARTHY

Majestic model 1. (FOS-108; RGA-35)   500+

CHEST

Atwater Kent model 555. 1933.   250–350
Made by Majestic   75–125
Emerson. Model L-559.   125–175

CHILDREN'S

Batman. Transistor. Original box.   40
Cabbage Patch. Transistor.   15
Gulliver's Travels. Stewart-Warner model 07-513.   500–700
Mork from Ork egg ship. Transistor.   50
Raggedy Ann. Transistor.   40–75
Sesame Street with two Muppets.   30
Snoopy. Transistor.   40
Strawberry Shortcake. Transistor.   15

CHRIS-CRAFT

Transistor. 1960s.   75

CLOCK

Really a radio: looks like a clock. Definitely not a clock-ra-
    dio. International Kadette model K-28, "Clockette."   100–150

COCA COLA

Bottle. Made by Crosley.	1500 +
Bottle. Transistor. AM.	7
Bottle. Transistor. AM/FM.	25–30
Can. 1978.	10
Cooler. RCA model 5-A-410-A. (FOS-185)	300–450
Cooler. Transistor.	32
Logo on usual transistor AM/FM radio. 1970s. General Electric model CL-500.	20–25
Vending machine. AM/FM. Transistor.	50–80

COIN-OPERATED

Coradio	40–50
Tradio. With matching stand.	75

DICK TRACY.

Wrist radio.	50–75

DIONNE QUINTUPLETS.

Made by Stewart-Warner. There are at least three different models With decals of the quintuplets. (Identified in this guide under Stewart-Warner.)	700 +

ELVIS.

No other information.	125

GASOLINE AND CAR

Amalie oil can. Transistor.	30
Champion spark plug.	75
Hubcap. Wall-mounted. Transistor. Made by Toshiba.	45
Sinclair gas pump. Transistor.	15–20

GLOBE

Made by Marc.	40–50
Globe with plane on top of radio.	90

GRANDFATHER CLOCK

Crosley, model 126-1.	200–300
Crosley, Oracle model. Clock-radio.	300–400
Philco model 70.	300–450
Made by Silvertone.	250–350
Made by Simplex.	300–400
Made by Westinghouse.	200–325

HOPALONG CASSIDY

Plastic table radio with foil front. Foil must be in good condition. 1950. Arvin model 441T. (FOS-61; RGA-91)	125–250

JEWELRY BOX.

Emerson model 238.	200–250

AR: *Antique Radios: Restoration and Price Guide* / **FOS:** *Flick of the Switch* / **GOR:** *Guide to Old Radios*
RGA: *Radios: The Golden Age* / **VR:** *Vintage Radio*

LAMP RADIO

Rocket-ship-shaped. Mitchell model 1260.	50–75
Knight shape.	40–50
Lumitone. Mitchell model 1260. (RGA-55).	75–125
Made by Radio Lamp Co. of America (RGA-55)	150–200
Made by Knight.	40–50

LANTERN.

Town Crier. Made by Guild.	75

MELODY CRUISER.

Ship with metal sails. Made by Majestic. (RGA-73)	300–400

MICKEY MOUSE

Molded wood (model 411) or wood with metal trim (model 410). Made by Emerson. (RGA-12, 13)	1000+
Clock-radio. White plastic. 3-dimensional Mickey head. Made by General Electric.	40 60
Mickey head. 2-dimensional. Transistor.	30–40

MICROPHONE.

On the Air mike. Plastic.	90–100

PEPSI COLA

Bottle. 28". With original labels. Bakelite. 1940s?	300–400
Bottle. Plastic. Transistor. Recent.	10–15
Can. 1960s.	15 20
Can. 1970s.	10–15
Cooler. Plastic. 1950s.	200–300
Fountain dispenser. Plastic. 1960s.	150–250
Vending machine (horizontal). Dispenser. Plastic. 1960s.	150–300
Vending machine (upright). "Say Pepsi please." Plastic. 1960s.	50–75
Vending machine (upright). "Vending Machine radio." Plastic. Transis tor. AM/FM. Recent.	15–25
Vending machine (upright). Plastic. AM/FM. Transistor.	15–25

PHONOGRAPH

Grafanola. Made by Guild. Radio-phonograph. AM/FM.	200

PIANO

Made by Continental. (RGA-49)	125–150
Made by General Radio.	125–150

PILLOW RADIO.

Coin-op. Hung from headboard. Pillow speaker. Pink or white. Dahlberg model 430-D1. c. 1955. (RGA-101)	75–150

RADIO NURSE

	750+

REFRIGERATOR.

Westinghouse, model H-146.	50–75

SMOKING

Smokerette. Pipe stand with three tobacco compartments.
AM. Made by Porto. 1947.   125–175
Wings cigarettes. Made by RCA. Pack. 8″ x 12″ x 10″.   750+

SNOW WHITE.

Molded wood cabinet, hand-painted by Disney artists. Emerson model Q-236.   750+

STAINED GLASS

Green and white. Made by RadioGlo.   1000

STATUE OF LIBERTY

Scene on radio made by Radiovision.   200–300

SUNGLASSES

Transistor. Original box. Made by Ross.   25–30

TEAPOT

The porcelain/wood cabinet sits on a pot metal "hot tray"
(the power supply). Made by Guild.   100–125

TELEPHONE

Country Belle wall telephone radio. Made by Guild.   50–60
Same, but restored to original condition.   75–100
French telephone. Transistor.   30

THIN MAN

Made by Wilcox-Gay. 1939.   750+

VIOLIN

Violin shape. Truetone, model D-2815.   50–75

Amplifiers

Model Name/Number	Price Range ($)
Altec 60 (preamp)	60
Amrad DT (1922)	200–225
Bristol (1-tube)	100–125
Clapp-Eastham	
HZV (early version)	175–200
HZV (later version)	90–100
ZRA	250
Crosley	
IV	150–200
VI	150–175
50A	100–125
51A	100–150

AR: *Antique Radios: Restoration and Price Guide* / **FOS**: *Flick of the Switch* / **GOR**: *Guide to Old Radios*
RGA: *Radios: The Golden Age* / **VR**: *Vintage Radio*

Harko Sr.	225–275
DeJur	60–65
Fisher KX 100	40–50
Grebe RORK — 1922	300–400
Heathkit AA-13	10–20
Kennedy	
521	400–550
525	300–350
Magnavox	
AC-2	350–400
C	150–175
McIntosh	
C-8 (preamp)	20–35
MC-30 (Mackit)	95
Michigan Midget M11	200–250
Paramount Radio Shop	250–275
RCA	
AA1400 (detector-amplifier), made by General Electric	100–150
Aeriola (amplifier only)	175–200
DA, made by Westinghouse	100
Radiola Balanced Amp	200
H.H. Scott 200B	30–40
Western Electric	
7-A	125–225
14-A	110–250
Zenith 33M	880

Antennas

Model Name/Number	Price Range ($)
Bodine	50
Clapp-Eastham antenna switch	90
Philco, new in box	20
RCA Radiola AG-814	55

Crystal Sets

Model Name/Number	Price Range ($)
Airchamp	15–25
Amrad, model A	250–300
Aurora, kit	20–25
Beaver Baby Grand	175–200
Blair	100–125
Crosley Harko	250–450
DeForest DT600 Everyman	250–300
Echophone	200–250
Ericson	130
Fada	150–200

Fellows		250–300
Flyver		150
Gecophone (England)		
Model 1		250
Model BC 1501		400
General Electric, model ER-753		175–225
Henry Hyman		70
Howe		75–125
Ken-Rad		150–200
Lemco 340 (VR-68)		85–90
Martian		
Big 4		100–150
Special		200–250
Mengele		200
Meteor		150
Midget		
Blue		45
Black		55
Monarch		160
O-So-EZ		150
Pandora		65
Philmore		
Model 336		50–75
Blackbird		100–125
Polytran		15–20
Rapid Radio		45–65
RCA Radiola I (VR-109)		300–500
Spenser		45
Steinite		150–250
Telefunken		250
Uncle Al Miracle		150
Volta		150–175
Weco		
Used		40–50
Unused		90
World		135

Speakers

Model Name/Name	Type	Price Range ($)
Acme	Cone	40–50
Acme K 1	Cone	30–40
Ambertone Jr.	Cone	25–30
Amplion	Horn	150–175
Amplion AR-19	Horn	100
Amplion AU-5	Horn	125
Arborphone Zeta	—	70
Atwater Kent E	Cone	25–50
Atwater Kent E2	Cone	40–55
Atwater Kent F2	Cone	50–60
Atwater Kent F4A	Cone	25–35
Atwater Kent H	Horn	75

Atwater Kent L	Horn	50–70
Atwater Kent M	Horn	30–60
Atwater Kent N	Horn	40
Baldwin A	Cone	45
Baldwin Concert Grand	Horn	80
Brandes H	Horn	30–55
Brandes Table Talker	Cone	10–20
Bristol Baby Audiophone	Horn	95
Bristol Super C	Horn	30–40
Bristol Super S	Horn	100
Burns	Horn	100–150
Crosley type D	Cone	40–50
Crosley Dynacone F	Cone	30–40
Crosley Musicone	Cone	15–25
Crystal Baby	Horn	35–45
Davis	Horn	45–55
DeForest LS 300	—	125
Dictogrand	Horn	80–100
Dictograph	Horn	100–125
Echo	Horn	60
Farrand Junior 20	Cone	60–80
GGH	Horn	90–100
Granolite	Horn	80–100
Herald B	Horn	40
Jewett Super Speaker	Horn	30–40
King Am-pli-tone	Horn	250–300
Kodel	Horn	225
Kolster K-6	Cone	30–35
Magnavox A2R	Horn	125–150
Magnavox "Beverly"	Cone	30–40
Magnavox M1	Horn	75 125
Magnavox M4	Horn	60–75
Magnavox M20	Horn (cabinet)	40–50
Magnavox R2	Horn	130
Magnavox R2C	Horn	175
Magnavox R3	Horn	50–75
Magnavox R3 (type B)	Horn	75–100
Magnavox "Stanford"	Cone	35–50
Manhatten "Concert Modulator"	—	40–50
Meistersinger	Horn	70–80
Melody Tone	—	90
Midget Cone	Cone	70–80
Music Master	Horn	60–120
Na-Ald Midget	Cone	125
Newcombe-Hawley 83	Cone	50–65
Newcombe-Hawley NH9	Cone	50–65
O'Neil	Cone	60–75
Operadio	—	50–65
Pathé	Cone (cabinet)	20–30
Pathé Westminster	Cone	85
Peerless	Cone (cathedral)	30–60
Plimpton Newell Shurrur	Cone (floor model-3.5')	90–100
RCA Radiola 100	Cone	20–40
RCA Radiola 100A	Cone	25–50

RCA Radiola 103	Cone	40–75
RCA Radiola 106	Cone (floor model)	45–65
RCA 6165	Cone (wall-hung)	55
RCA FH	Horn	65–75
RCA Radiola UZ-1325	Horn	40–85
Radialamp	Cone	400–500
Rola	Cone	160
Rola	Horn	50–75
Saal	Horn	45–60
Snyder	Horn	50–70
Sonora	Horn	25
Speco	—	40
Stewart-Warner 435	Cone	45
Thompson Magnaphone	Horn	15–20
Thorola Junior	Horn	70–125
Timmons Ship	Cone	60–75
Tower Meistersinger	Cone	85–125
Trimm L38	Cone	40–50
Truetone	Horn	30
Utah Acorn	Horn	50–65
Victor Lumiere	Cone	100–150
Voice of the Sky	Horn	250–425
WLS Silvertone	Horn	35
Warren Jr.	Horn	85
Western Electric 10-D	Horn	60
Western Electric 10-F	Horn	50
Western Electric 521-W	Horn	100
Western Electric 540-AW	Cone	85–100
Westinghouse 518W	Horn	25–40
Wirt	Cone	15–25

Test Equipment

Model Name/Number	Price Range ($)
B&K tube tester, model 600	30–40
Beta kilovolt meter	20–25
Calrad 500 watt variac, new in box	20–25
Century condenser tester, model CT1	10–20
Conair 5″ oscilloscope	40–50
Dayrad type F tube tester, Bakelite, with engraved panel	30–40
EICO audio generator, model 377	15–20
EICO dip meter	10–15
EICO oscilloscope, model 460	30–50
EICO 5″ oscilloscope, model 425PP	30–50
EICO signal generator, model 324	20–25
EICO signal tracer, model 147A	25–30
EMC tube tester, model 208	25–30

EICO tube tester, model 625	20–25
EICO mutual conductance tube tester, model 666	30–35
EICO tube tester, model 667	65
EICO VTVM, model 1050	15–25
Espy dynamic tube tester, model 105	35–40
General Radio type 224 Wavemeter	140–160
Heathkit condenser tester, model C3	15–25
Heathkit oscilloscope, model 0-8	25–30
Heathkit professional signal generator, model LG-1	50–60
Heathkit signal generator, model SG-6	25–30
Heathkit signal generator, model SG-7	25–30
Heathkit signal tracer, model T-1	20–25
Heathkit signal tracer, model T-3	30–35
Heathkit tube tester, model TC-1	20–35
Heathkit VTVM, model 1M18	15–20
Heathkit VTVM, model 1M38	10–15
Heathkit VTVM, model WV77B	30–35
Hickock oscilloscope, model 677	20–25
Hickock tube tester, model 51X	40–50
Hickock tube tester, model 531	40–50
Hickock tube tester, model 533A	100–125
Hickock VTVM, model 209A	75–90
Jackson tube tester, model 49	25–40
Jackson dynamic tube tester, model 636	40–45
Jackson tube tester, model 648 A	40–45
Knight tube tester, model KG-600B	30–35
Lafayette tube tester, model 99-5063	25–35
Mercury tube tester, model 990	15–25
Mercury tube tester, model 1200 (with manual)	15–20
Paco electrolytic capacitor tester, model C-25	10–15
Philco tube tester, model 7050	10–15
Precision multimeter/tube tester, model 912	35–50
Precision signal generator, model 200C	30–45
Precision signal generator, model E200C	30–45
Precision tube tester, model 920	25–40
RCA audio generator, model WA44B	30–40
RCA 3″ oscilloscope, model WO57B	25–40
RCA signal generator, model WR49A	30–35
RCA sweep generator, model WR679A	40–50
RCA VTVM, model WV98C	40–65
Realistic tube tester, model 105	15–20
Sencore oscilloscope, model PS127	20–30
Sencore tube tester, model TC109	35–45
Superior tube tester, model TD55	25–40
Superior VOM, model 670A	20–30
Triplett tube tester 3413	30–40
Triumph 3″ oscilloscope, model CTU-60018	25–35
Waterman 3″ oscilloscope S11-A	25–35
Waterman oscilloscope S14-B	25–30
Weston ohm meter, model 689	15–20
Weston tube tester, model 777	20–30

Books

Title/Author	Price Range ($)
Atwater Kent World Wide Radio Station Directory.	8
Audel's Radioman's Guide. 1940.	12
Electricity One-Four, by H.C. Mileaf.	9
Elements of Radio, by Marcus.	8
Experimental Radio, by Ramsey.	10
Fundamentals of Radio, by Jordan.	8
Fundamentals of Radio, by Terman.	8
Hawkins Electrical Guide. (each)	10
How to Conduct a Radio Club, by Bucher.	60
Leutz' Modern Radio Reception. 1924.	50
Leutz' Modern Radio Reception. 1928.	40
Modern Radio Servicing, by Ghirardi.	10–15
Operator's Wireless Telephone and Telegraph Handbook, by V. H. Laughter. 1st ed. Old library copy. 1909.	45
Pictorial Album of Wireless and Radio, by Greenwood. 1961.	12
Pictorial History of Radio, by Settel. 1960.	28
Principles of Radio Communication, by Morecraft. 1927.	15
Radio Boys books. (each)	6–10
Radio Encyclopedia, by Gernsback. 1927.	20–30
Radio Field Service Data, by Ghirardi. 1935.	5
Radio Girls books. (each)	9
Radio Manual. 1928.	16
Radio Master's Encyclopedia. 1941.	25
Radio Physics Course, by Ghirardi.	15
Radio Service Man's Handy Book, vol. 1. 1931.	20–25
Radio Simplified, by Kendall and Koehler. 1923. (Fair condition.)	10
Radio Telephone for Amateurs, by Ballantine. 1922.	13
Radio Telephony, by Goldsmith. 1918.	16
Radio Telephony, by Goldsmith. 1918. (Mint in wrapper.)	25
Radiotron Designer's Handbook. 4th ed.	50
Saga of the Vacuum Tube, by Tyne. Hardcover. 1977.	25–30
Servicing Superheterodynes. 1934.	5
Short Wave, by Leutz and Gable. 1930.	70
Vision of Radio, by Jenkins.	200
Wireless Experimenter, by Bucher. 1919.	25

Catalogs and Instruction Manuals

Title/Date	Price Range ($)
Allied catalog. 1934.	6–8
Beckley-Ralston catalog. Early 1920.	75
J. H. Bunnell catalog #29. 1924.	35
J. H. Bunnell catalog #29. Hardbound, near mint. 1924.	60
Bunnell Wireless catalog #44. 1922.	15
Clapp Eastham Radio Telegraph Apparatus catalog. 1914–1915.	40
Wm. B. Duck catalog #16	50
E. I. catalog #19	50
Grebe Radio Receivers. Fair condition. 1923.	10
Grebe Synchrophase. 1912.	35
Hawkins Electrical Guide #9. 1915.	10

MESCO catalog. 1922.	25
Philco Yearbook. 1942.	5
Pilot catalog. 1927.	15
Radio Enters the Home. Original ed.	30–50
RCA Radio Apparatus. 1st ed. Fair condition. 1921.	35
RCA Radio Apparatus. 5th ed. Good condition. 1921.	32
RCA Radiola. 1st ed. 1927.	15–20
Remler Operating Instructions for the 330/331/333.	15

Courses

Name	Price Range ($)
ICS Radio Handbook.	10
NRI course. Pre-1940. Pamphlet form. (each)	.50
NRI course (no. 1).	35

Magazines

(Price is per issue, unless otherwise noted.)

Issue	Price Range ($)
Popular Radio. 1925–1926.	5
QST. 1917.	22
QST. 1928–1930.	3
QST. 1931–1936.	2
QST. 1927–1931. Complete sets, by year.	175
Radio. 1922–1926. Issue 1–60.	290
Radio Broadcast. 1927. Complete set.	175
Radio Broadcast. 1928. Complete set.	165
Radio Broadcast. 1929. Complete set.	175
Radio Broadcast. 1927–1930.	2.50
Radio Craft. 1939–1947.	2.50–3.00
Radio News. 1927–1929.	4
Radio News. 1930–1935.	2–3
Radio News. 1936–1940.	2.50
Radio News. 1945–1958.	2
Wireless Age. 1916.	22
Wireless News. 1912.	15

Service Instructions

Manual	Price Range ($)
Atwater Kent.	70
General Electric Service Data. 1946–1961.	6
Gernsback's Official Radio Service Manual. 1930.	25
Mallory Radio Service Encyclopedia, 1937.	8
Philco Service Notes, 1928–1937.	10
RCA HB-3 Tube Manual (5 vol.).	35
RCA Receiving Tube Manual. 1937.	4
RCA Service Data (v. 1, 2). 1923–1942. (each)	30

RCA Service Manual (v. 1).	75–85
RCA Service Notes. 1931–2.	25
RCA Service Notes. 1933.	15–25
Radio Circuit Manual. 1941, 1942. (each)	15
Rider's Record Changer Service, 1941.	5
Rider's Record Changer Service, 1949–1950 (v. 3).	12
Rider's Manual, v. 1-5, abridged.	35–50
Rider's Manual (v. 1).	40–60
Rider's Manual (v. 2, 3).	35–40
Rider's Manual (v. 4).	15–20
Rider's Manual (v. 5-22).	10–15
Rider's Manual (v. 23).	75
Sam's Photofacts (sets 100-1210). (each)	.10–.25
Sam's Record Changer Manual, 1951–2 (v. 2).	15
Sam's Record Changer Manual, 1954-55 (v. 7).	15
Supreme (Most-often-needed radio diagrams). 1939 on. (each)	10–12
Sylvania Radio Tubes Technical Manual. 1951.	15
Zenith Schematic Service Manual, 1929–1939.	19
Zenith Service Manual (#2).	15

Odds and Ends

Description	Price Range ($)
Kiel table (without radio)	95–150
Lifetime microphone, model 80	75–90
Marconi stock certificate	27
Radiovision stock certificate	110
RCA Slimline microphone	35
Shure microphone, model 5B	75
Stromberg-Carlson remote control box with cable and plug	200
Universal double-button microphone	55
Western Electric phonograph attachment, model 522-W	40–50
Wizard microphone	20

Further Reading

Restoring old radios

Hallmark, Clayton J. *How to Repair Old-Time Radios.* Blue Ridge Summit, Pa.: Tab Books, Inc., 1979.

Johnson, David, and Betty. *Antique Radios: Restoration and Price Guide.* Des Moines, Iowa: Wallace-Homestead Books, 1982.

General Information

Collins, Philip. *Radios: The Golden Age.* San Francisco: Chronicle Books, 1987.
  Magnificent photographs of primarily Catalin and Bakelite sets of the 1930s and 1940s.

McMahon, Morgan E. *A Flick of the Switch, 1930–1950.*

McMahon, Morgan E. *Radio Collector's Guide.*

McMahon, Morgan E. *Vintage Radio, 1887–1929.*
  These three books are still the most useful ones on identifying old radios. They are being re-published by Antique Electronic Supply, 688 W. First St., Tempe, Ariz. 85281.

Paul, Floyd A. *Radio Horn Speaker Encyclopedia.* Glendale, Ca.: privately printed, 1986.
  Order from Floyd Paul, 1545 Raymond Ave., Glendale, Ca. 91201.

Broadcast Information

Barnouw, Erick. *A Tower in Babel: A History of Broadcasting in the United States to 1933.* Vol. 1. New York: Oxford University Press. 1966.

Barnouw, Erick. *The Golden Web: A History of Broadcasting in the United States, 1933–1953.* Vol. 2. New York: Oxford University Press, 1968.

Birkby, Robert. *KMA Radio: The First Sixty Years.* Shenandoah, Iowa: May Broadcasting Co., 1985.
  More and more histories of specific radio stations are being written. Station histories can be very enjoyable, combining history with stories by and about the early broadcasters.

Index

Ultradyne, 37

Vitalitone speaker, 61
"Voice of the Sky" speaker, 60

WEAF (New York), 45, 52
WHA (Madison, Wis.), 34
WJZ (Newark, N. J.), 38, 39, 41, 52
WOR (Newark, N. J.), 39
WWJ (Detroit), 34
Washington Radio Conference (1922), 42
Wavelength, 10
Wells-Gardner, 75
Western Union College (Le Mars, Iowa), 49

Westingale, 48
Westinghouse, 28, 41, 52, 98, 127. *See also*
    KDKA; WJZ
Williams, J. C., crystal set, 4
Wilmak. *See* Den Chum
Wolper, 44
Work Rite, 35, 37, 46

XWA (Montreal), 33

Zenith, 36, 39, 43, 50, 65, 73–75, 79, 80, 86–
    88, 91, 93, 95, 106, 118, 122, 128, 132,
    134